# Against Marriage

*Against Marriage* is a radical argument for the abolition of state-recognised marriage. Clare Chambers argues that state-recognised marriage violates both equality and liberty, even when expanded to include same-sex couples. Instead Chambers proposes the marriage-free state: an egalitarian state in which religious or secular marriages are permitted but have no legal status.

Part I makes the case against marriage. Chambers investigates the critique of marriage that has developed within feminist and liberal theory. Feminists have long argued that marriage is a violation of equality since it is both sexist and heterosexist. Chambers endorses the feminist view and argues, in contrast to recent egalitarian pro-marriage movements, that same-sex marriage is not enough to make marriage equal. Chambers argues that state-recognised marriage is also problematic for liberalism, particularly political liberalism, since it imposes a controversial, hierarchical conception of the family that excludes many adults and children.

Part II sets out the case for the marriage-free state. Chambers critically assesses recent theories that attempt to make marriage egalitarian, either by replacing it with relationship contracts or by replacing it with alternative statuses such as civil union. She then sets out a new model for the legal regulation of personal relationships. In the marriage-free state regulation is based on relationship practices not relationship status, and these practices are regulated separately rather than as a bundle. The marriage-free state thus employs piecemeal, practice-based regulation. Finally, Chambers considers how the marriage-free state should respond to unequal religious marriage. The result is an inspiring egalitarian approach that fits the diversity of real relationships.

**Clare Chambers** is Reader in Political Philosophy at the University of Cambridge and Fellow of Jesus College. She works on contemporary political philosophy, with particular focus on feminism, liberalism, and theories of social construction. She is the author of numerous chapters and articles on topics such as autonomy, choice, and consent; the body, appearance norms, and cosmetic surgery; multiculturalism, religion, and social practices; and equality and theories of justice. She is also the author of two previous books: *Sex, Culture, and Justice: The Limits of Choice* (Penn State University Press, 2008) and, with Phil Parvin, *Teach Yourself Political Philosophy: A Complete Introduction* (Hodder, 2012).

# OXFORD POLITICAL THEORY

Oxford Political Theory presents the best new work in contemporary political theory. It is intended to be broad in scope, including original contributions to political philosophy, and also work in applied political theory. The series contains works of outstanding quality with no restriction as to approach or subject matter.

## OTHER TITLES IN THIS SERIES

# Against Marriage

## An Egalitarian Defence of the Marriage-Free State

Clare Chambers

OXFORD
UNIVERSITY PRESS

# OXFORD
### UNIVERSITY PRESS

Great Clarendon Street, Oxford, OX2 6DP,
United Kingdom

Oxford University Press is a department of the University of Oxford.
It furthers the University's objective of excellence in research, scholarship,
and education by publishing worldwide. Oxford is a registered trade mark of
Oxford University Press in the UK and in certain other countries

Published in the United States of America by Oxford University Press
198 Madison Avenue, New York, NY 10016, United States of America

British Library Cataloguing in Publication Data
Data available

Library of Congress Cataloging in Publication Data
Data available

ISBN 978–0–19–874400–9 (Hbk.)
ISBN 978–0–19–884568–3 (Pbk.)

*For my family.*

# Contents

# Acknowledgements

Whilst writing *Against Marriage* I have been extremely fortunate to be based at the University of Cambridge, with its great intellectual and cultural riches. I continue to benefit immensely from the support of my colleagues, both academic and administrative, in the Faculty of Philosophy. They provide an extremely congenial philosophical environment and also work hard to ensure that the Faculty is family-friendly, both of which are vital to a successful and happy academic life. I give particular thanks to Tim Crane and Heather Sanderson for supporting my application to the excellent University Career Break Scheme for carers. I am very grateful to Jesus College for providing endless fascinating discussion with wonderful Fellows, a beautiful environment, and a supportive and progressive atmosphere. I am also extremely pleased that Cambridge has such a rich inter-departmental group of political philosophers and theorists, many of whom attend the fortnightly Seminar in Political Thought that I run with Duncan Bell and the fortnightly Workshop in Political Philosophy that I convene. And I am fortunate to teach inspiring, dedicated students.

I worked on parts of *Against Marriage* during two periods as a Visiting Scholar at the Center for the Study of Law and Society (CSLS) in the Boalt School of Law at the University of California, Berkeley, and while an Early Career Fellow at the Centre for Research in the Arts, Social Sciences, and Humanities (CRASSH) of the University of Cambridge. I benefited hugely from the support of both CSLS and CRASSH and am deeply grateful to both. I am particularly grateful to Sarah Song and Rosann Greenspan for supporting my applications to Berkeley.

Parts of *Against Marriage* have been published elsewhere, and I thank the publishers for their permission to reproduce some material here. An overview of the argument as a whole was published as 'The Marriage-Free State' in *Proceedings of the Aristotelian Society* Vol. CXIII No. 2 (2013). A version of Chapter 4 was published as 'The Limitations of Contract: Regulating Personal Relationships in a Marriage-Free State' in Elizabeth Brake (ed.) *After Marriage: Rethinking Marital Relationships* (Oxford University Press, 2016).

I presented work leading to *Against Marriage* at a number of universities and conferences. In approximate chronological order these were: the American Political Science Association Annual Meeting in Washington, DC; the Nuffield Political Theory Workshop at the University of Oxford; the Philosophy Faculty Colloquium at the University of Cambridge; the Centre for Gender Studies

Seminar at the University of Cambridge; the Philosophy Graduate Workshop at Birkbeck College; the Political Theory Project Research Seminar at Brown University; the University of Warwick Philosophy Seminar; the CSLS Speaker Series at the University of California, Berkeley; the CRASSH Work in Progress Seminar; the Institute for Historical Research Seminar at the University of London; the University of York Morrell Conference on Children, Schools and Families; the University of Cambridge Workshop in Political Philosophy; the UK Analytic Legal and Political Philosophy Conference at the University of Leicester; the Political Thought Conference held at St Catherine's College, Oxford; the University of Essex Political Theory Seminar; the University of Hertfordshire Philosophy Research Seminar; the conference in New Directions in Public Reason at the University of Birmingham; the University of Leeds Centre for Ethics and Metaethics and Center for Aesthetics Seminar; the UCL Political Theory Seminar; the Durham University Philosophy Society; the University of Cambridge Forum for Legal and Political Philosophy; the Political Theory Seminar at the University of Manchester; the conference on Beyond the Nuclear Family at Umeå University; the Alan Milne Memorial Address at Durham University; the Religion and Public Justification Workshop at University College London; the Centre for Ethics, Law, and Public Affairs Seminar at the University of Warwick; and the Conference on Topics in Global Justice: Agency, Power, and Policy at the University of Birmingham. I am very grateful to all the participants for their comments, questions, and stimulating discussion. I am particularly grateful to the participants in a workshop on the penultimate draft of the manuscript that I held at Jesus College, Cambridge: Gabriele Badano, Dan Butt, Phil Cook, Jacob Eisler, John Filling, Sam James, Katharine Jenkins, Jess Kaplan, Rae Langton, Maxime Lepoutre, David Miller, Phil Parvin, Paul Sagar, Findlay Stark, and Jens Van't Klooster.

I received pertinent and helpful comments and suggestions, and some-times copies of their own work, from Duncan Bell, Elizabeth Brake, Chris Brooke, Cheshire Calhoun, José Chambers, Esther Dermott, Ira Ellman, Cécile Fabre, Sarah Fine, Daniel First, William Gallagher, Peter Glazebrook, Jack Halberstam, Christie Hartley, Matthew Kramer, Duncan Kelly, Patti Lenard, Andrew Lister, Cécile Laborde, Annabelle Lever, Stephen Macedo, Andrew March, Mara Marin, Andy Mason, Jo Miles, Melissa Murray, Alasia Nuti, Serena Olsaretti, Avia Pasternak, Jesper Pedersen, Anne Phillips, Jon Quong, Miriam Ronzoni, Brook Sadler, Marj Schultz, Liam Shields, Zofia Stemplowska, Adam Swift, Nick Widdows, Jeremy Williams, Alice Wilson, Lori Watson, and several anonymous referees. Emily Dyson was an excellent research assistant over the summer of 2015, researching the recent literature on the same-sex marriage debate as well as the role of marriage in the major world religions. I should also like to thank Peter Momtchiloff at OUP for supporting the book.

*Against Marriage* has taken a particularly long time to write, mainly because its writing was interrupted by the birth of my sons: Harley in 2009 and Caspar in 2012. I am constantly delighted by them. Most importantly, my partner Phil has endured the arguments of this book in more ways than one over the years. I am profoundly grateful for his commitment.

# Introduction

This book is for everyone, regardless of marital status.

It is for the happily married: those whose good fortune is not, and should not be, dependent on injustice.

It is for the happily unmarried: those who do not wish to structure their lives and their social status around a monogamous permanent sexual relationship, or those who do live in that sort of relationship but do not want to have to marry in order to gain legal protection and equal social status.

It is for the unhappily unmarried: those who would like to be married but who are denied entry into that institution because of their sex or sexuality or race or religion or previous marital status. It is also for those made vulnerable by their partners' refusal to marry: the many women and fewer men who devote themselves to caring for their families, leaving themselves economically dependent.

It is for the unhappily married: those who entered into marriage because it seemed like the next thing to do, or because they had always dreamed of the party and the dress and the happy-ever-after fairytale, or because it was the only way to gain acceptance within their community, or because they genuinely believed in vows that have become impossible to keep. It is for anyone who married in hope but now finds themselves in a relationship characterized by fear or abuse or violence or inequality or mistrust or simple unhappiness, who is now weighing their own wellbeing against the sadness, stigma, and costs of divorce.

And it is for children, whose social wellbeing should not depend on their parents' marital status.

This book is *not* for everyone regardless of political conviction.

It is not for the socially conservative who wish to retain a particular patriarchal, heterosexist model of family life at the heart of the state. It is not for religious fundamentalists who wish not only to practise their own religion but to impose it coercively on others. These people are likely to vehemently disapprove of this book.

There are others whose views are not the target of this book, but who might nevertheless find things to endorse. Non-egalitarian libertarians are likely to be unperturbed by my argument that state-recognized marriage is unequal, but they may be more concerned that marriage violates state neutrality and individual liberty. Many of my proposals could be accepted by libertarians.

My real target audience, though, is those who have some sort of egalitarian commitment.

The fundamental premise of this book and all my work is feminism: society is deeply gendered, in a way that harms women, and this is wrong. I have deep respect for both radical and liberal feminism. Radical feminists are absolutely right to identify sexual hierarchy and gendered violence as fundamental to patriarchy; they are right to insist that inequality is not exonerated merely by being chosen; they are right to insist on the importance of capturing the truth and the politics in the everyday and the intimate; and they write the most powerful and challenging philosophy that I know. Liberal feminists are absolutely right to insist that autonomy and rights are goals for women on an equal basis with men; they are right to look for concrete legal reforms and workable solutions; they are right to care about justice; and they are right to take on mainstream political philosophy on its own terms.

Mainstream Anglophone political philosophy may not be feminist, but it is egalitarian. And so this book is also aimed at non-feminist egalitarians, and particularly liberal egalitarians. I argue that the abolition of state-recognized marriage is something that liberalism not only supports but demands, and along the way I hope to show that marriage tells us various more general things about contemporary philosophical liberalism. That is, this book is not just for those who care about marriage, it is also for those who are willing to countenance the idea that marriage might tell us something about the liberal project.

\* \* \* \* \*

As the title indicates, *Against Marriage: An Egalitarian Defence of the Marriage-Free State* presents both a negative and a positive thesis. The negative thesis is a critique of the institution of marriage as it is traditionally understood, and a rejection of the state recognition of marriage in any form. I sometimes refer to a society which has state-recognized marriage as a 'marriage regime'. The positive thesis is an outline of a state in which personal relationships are regulated, the vulnerable are protected, and justice is furthered, all without the state recognition of marriage or any similar alternative. I call this ideal of a state which does not recognize marriage 'the marriage-free state'.

In the marriage-free state the term 'marriage' would have no legal significance. The state would not regulate the term, nor would it provide laws that dealt specifically with the creation and dissolution of marriages. 'Marriage' would be a term like 'friendship'. It would have meaning, and typically be used to denote a certain sort of relationship, but that meaning would not be a matter of legal ruling. Like friendship, marriage would mean different things to different people. Sometimes a friend is a person with whom we share our lives, meeting regularly and sharing social situations, attending events together, holidaying together, discussing all areas of life. But it is also perfectly acceptable and meaningful to use the term to denote someone with whom one has only a virtual connection, such as through social media. Similarly, for some people marriage would be much as it is now: a formal, solemnified ceremony bringing with it weighty social meaning and norms. For others, marriage might be used casually, to denote a fleeting commitment or even a commitment to an object or a cause. As with friendship, not all uses of the word marriage would succeed in achieving uptake. They would not all make sense to others. But their use would not conflict with any legal definition.

Weddings, then, would still take place in the marriage-free state. No state ceremony or registration would be involved, but weddings could persist nonetheless. The marriage-free state would place no regulations on where weddings could take place, since they would not be legal ceremonies: weddings could take place at home, on a mountaintop, in a swimming pool. But weddings could also take place exactly as they do now, in a marriage regime: in churches, temples, synagogues, and mosques; in stately homes and hotels; with receptions and dresses and bridesmaids and speeches.

So the marriage-free state would still contain weddings. It would also contain monogamous, committed sexual partnerships, some of which would be called marriages by their participants and some of which would not. People would introduce each other as husband, wife, spouse, partner, lover, friend, just as they pleased. People could wear rings or not, change their names or not, call themselves Mrs or Miss or Ms. Official documentation would not distinguish between these titles other than as needed to respect people's important interests, such as when a doctor might ask how a patient preferred to be addressed while receiving treatment. But there would be nothing illegitimate in a person using marital or non-marital titles.

The marriage-free state would not recognize or endorse marriages, but nor would it leave relationships and family unregulated. In existing marriage regimes there is and must be regulation: to protect vulnerable parties, to settle matters and disputes that must be determinate in law, and to ensure justice. The conception of justice used in the marriage-free state is liberal in the sense that it prioritizes both freedom and equality, with particular emphasis on equality. But the most basic idea of the marriage-free state and the simplest way to understand it is this: the marriage-free state starts by working out what would be the just way to regulate relationships between unmarried people, and then applies that regulation to everyone.

Of course, I have my own views about the best form of regulation in many areas of family life and personal relationships. By and large, though, I do not defend them here. The aim of this book is not to settle the question of the ideal *content* of regulation, a task that would merit several volumes in and of itself, but rather to propose a *form* or *structure* of regulation. If the reader wishes to evaluate the marriage-free state for herself, without being distracted by dilemmas of regulatory content, she might ask herself the following questions:

> What do I think is the ideal, just way of regulating unmarried people now, in a marriage regime? What laws should apply to unmarried parents, or unmarried cohabitants, or unmarried migrants, or unmarried property-owners? What would it be like if those ideal regulations were applied to everyone, regardless of marital status?

The society she envisages will be her ideal form of the marriage-free state. The most fundamental aim of this book is to convince the reader that she should prefer her ideal version of the marriage-free state to a marriage regime. Along the way, the arguments of the book suggest better and worse ways of filling in the content but do not even attempt to specify it completely.

\* \* \* \* \*

Part I, 'Against Marriage', sets out objections to marriage regimes. Chapter 1, 'Marriage as a Violation of Equality', makes the foundational egalitarian case against marriage. It starts with a historical overview of feminist objections to marriage and notes that feminists tend to criticize marriage for being both sexist and heterosexist. This two-pronged attack looks puzzling. How can it be both bad for women to be married and bad for lesbians and gays to be unmarried? The discussion continues with an analysis of whether same-sex marriage is egalitarian. It concludes that, in a marriage regime, same-sex marriage is both required by and insufficient for equality. Finally, the chapter argues that reformed versions of marriage such as civil union still enact inequality between those who have and those who lack the relevant status. It follows that the abolition of state-recognized marriage best meets the myriad egalitarian objections to the institution.

Chapter 2, 'Marriage as a Violation of Liberty', considers liberal objections to marriage. Perfectionist or comprehensive liberals should reject state-recognized marriage as limiting autonomy in the service of an unappealing and restrictive model of human perfection. But political liberals should go further, and reject state-recognized marriage as *prima facie* incompatible with neutrality. The chapter clarifies the nature of political liberal neutrality, and establishes that there are many reasonable conceptions of the good that are not compatible with the state recognition of marriage. This fact means that marriage is not a neutral, political institution, and that promotion of it is an act of perfectionism.

The chapter then discusses the idea that political liberalism might be compatible with policies that are *prima facie* non-neutral if those policies can be supported by public reason. Political liberalism is ambiguous between two forms of neutrality: *strict* and *lax*. *Strict* neutrality allows state action only if sufficiently weighty public reasons can be adduced in favour of a policy; *lax* neutrality permits the state to act just as long as some public reason can be given. If political liberalism is to be an interesting philosophical approach it will defend strict neutrality, so any public reasons offered in support of state-recognized marriage must be weighty enough to overcome the non-neutrality of that institution.

This line of argument continues in Chapter 3, 'A Liberal Defence of Marriage?' This chapter considers and rejects five potential liberal arguments in favour of marriage: arguments that, if successful, might work as public reasons for political liberals or might make marriage into an attractive account of human flourishing for perfectionist or comprehensive liberals. These arguments are based on communication, gender equality, care, the interests of society, and children's interests. The chapter argues that, while these arguments do highlight legitimate public goods, they fail to show that state-recognized marriage is a necessary or acceptable way of achieving them.

If marriage is no longer to be recognized by the state, what should replace it? Part II, 'The Marriage-Free State', answers this question. Many theorists defend relationship contracts. Some argue that enforceable relationship contracts should be available alongside existing or reformed state-recognized marriage, and available to either married or unmarried couples. Other theorists argue that relationship contracts are the best sort of legal regulation to *replace* marriage. It is this latter question that is the subject of Chapter 4: 'The Limitations of Contract'. The chapter contrasts contract and directive models of regulation, and notes that contract appears more compatible with liberty than does directive. However, this appearance is illusory since contracts can undermine liberty, directives can enhance liberty, and even a contract regime requires default directives. Moreover, there are various problems with the enforcement of relationship contracts. Specific performance is rarely appropriate in the relationship context. The alternative, fault-based compensatory alimony, risks causing injustice to vulnerable parties such as those who take on caring responsibilities (usually women) and children. Relational contract theory attempts to deal with some of these problems but has its own limitations. The chapter concludes that contract is not the best replacement for marriage.

Chapter 5, 'Regulating Relationships in the Marriage-Free State', sets out a new model for regulating personal relationships, one that relies on neither contract nor a holistic status such as marriage or civil partnership. Critics of marriage have suggested one of these two options, with most recent feminist and egalitarian work focusing on alternative holistic statuses such as Tamara Metz's Intimate Care-Giving Unions or Elizabeth Brake's Minimal Marriages. These new holistic statuses, while they improve on marriage, do not avoid a fundamental problem for egalitarians: an unjust distinction between those who have, and those who lack, that status. Instead, the chapter sets out three features of regulation in the marriage-free state. First, it is piecemeal not holistic: relationship functions are regulated separately, without assuming bundling or an ideal-typical relationship format. Second, it proceeds via practices not status: regulation applies to those who are acting in certain ways rather than being dependent on a status that must be formally acquired. Third, liberty is secured by opting out of default regulations rather than opting in. This model of regulation is compared with alternatives found in both political philosophy and legal practice.

Finally Chapter 6, 'Marriage in the Marriage-Free State', considers the extent to which the state should seek to regulate any private religious or secular marriages that citizens might enter into. In the marriage-free state citizens could still take part in religious or secular marriage ceremonies. This is why the marriage-free state is not a marriage-free society. It does not follow, however, that the state should take no interest at all in such marriages, since they may take place in the context of oppression or injustice. The chapter sets out the case for intervention in marriages that are not recognized by the state, drawing on the model of liberal intervention in cultural practices set out in my first book *Sex, Culture, and Justice: The Limits of Choice.*

\* \* \* \* \*

It is increasingly common for political philosophers to distinguish between ideal and non-ideal theory. There are a number of ways of making this distinction. It is sometimes a distinction between situations of full and partial compliance with the demands of justice. It is sometimes a distinction between considering and ignoring issues of implementation, such as whether a policy would command a democratic mandate in any given polity or whether, in particular political circumstances, it might bring about unintended consequences. It is sometimes a distinction between considering and ignoring the realities of power, violence, and inequality in society. These different ways of making the distinction may overlap.

*Against Marriage* is a work of ideal theory in the sense that it does not discuss the likelihood of its proposals being taken up by voters or politicians. Its mode of persuasion is philosophical. I do not offer suggestions as to how to transition to the marriage-free state via the democratic electoral system of any polity. Moreover, while I engage in discussion of legal change and analyse the work of many legal theorists, the discussion is not confined to any particular legal jurisdiction or framework. This is a work of political philosophy rather than of law.

*Against Marriage* is also a work of ideal theory in the sense that it does not claim to have accounted for all the unintended consequences of the marriage-free state. As I note at various points in the book, abolishing state-regulated marriage may be counter-productive in some social and historical contexts, such as if it is done as a way of avoiding giving equal rights to lesbians and gays, or if it is done without providing adequate legislative protection for the vulnerable. There may be times, that is, when the marriage-free state is worse than the best *politically-feasible* alternative. Chapter 1 offers more detailed discussion of this question.

However, *Against Marriage* is certainly *not* a work of ideal theory in the final sense: one that ignores realities of power. On the contrary, the book is firmly cognizant of prevailing structures of power, violence, and inequality. Its starting point is that marriage is an institution that has been both the result and the cause of profound inequality: a mechanism for entrenching structures of privilege and exclusion, power and oppression, hierarchies of gender and race, and heteronormativity. The state has, of course, been both an instrument of oppression and an instrument of liberation. It has brutally upheld inequality, using law and violence to maintain patriarchy, colonialism, slavery, and class. And it has provided the means for dismantling these structures, albeit only partially. This book assumes that the state rather than anarchy is the route to equality and liberation: reform rather than bloody revolution, peace rather than violence. For some this may seem naïve or complicit. But a commitment to peaceful transition in no way precludes profound critique. Reform can be radical. *Against Marriage* demolishes an enduring, popular institution, but it does so with optimism.

# PART I

# Against Marriage

# 1

# Marriage as a Violation of Equality

Feminists have long criticized the institution of marriage. Historically, it has been a fundamental site of women's oppression, with married women having few independent rights in law. Currently, it is associated with the gendered division of labour, with women taking on the lion's share of domestic and caring work and being paid less than men for work outside the home. The white wedding is replete with sexist imagery: the father 'giving away' the bride; the white dress symbolizing the bride's virginity (and emphasizing the importance of her appearance); the vows to obey the husband; the minister telling the husband 'you may now kiss the bride' (rather than the bride herself giving permission, or indeed initiating or at least equally participating in the act of kissing); the reception at which, traditionally, all the speeches are given by men; the wife surrendering her own name and taking her husband's. ⟶ feminist example

Despite decades of feminist criticism the institution resolutely endures—though not without change. The most significant change has been in the introduction of same-sex marriages and civil unions in countries such as the UK, the Netherlands, Belgium, the Nordic countries, Ireland, Spain, France, Canada, and the USA. In the USA in particular, same-sex marriage has recently been a fiercely contested and central part of political debate, with many states alternately allowing and forbidding it as the issue passed between the legislature, the judiciary, and the electorate, until the issue was settled at the federal level with a Supreme Court ruling.[1]

If marriage is to exist as a state-recognized institution then it must, as a requirement of equality, be available to same-sex couples. There is a great deal to celebrate in recent moves to widen marriage, and it is hard not to be touched

---

[1] In the 2012 US elections citizens of Maine, Maryland, Minnesota, and Washington voted to allow same-sex marriage or civil union. President Obama publicly endorsed gay marriage during the campaign. Previously several states, such as Hawaii and California, had voted against same-sex marriage. The Supreme Court Case *Obergefell v Hodges* (576 US, 2015) ruled that state bans on same-sex marriage were unconstitutional.

by the scenes of same-sex couples rejoicing as they are finally allowed to marry.[2] But even these welcome reforms do not go far enough.

Feminists have been the main critics of the institution of marriage.[3] Feminists attack marriage from several different angles, which can leave the feminist position somewhat conflicted on whether reforms such as same-sex marriage render the institution just. As I argue in this chapter, the best way to meet feminist and egalitarian concerns is to support the abolition of state-recognized marriage.

---

[2] See, for example, Matt Stopera, '60 Awesome Portraits of Gay Couples Just Married in New York State' Buzzfeed (25 July 2011) at http://www.buzzfeed.com/mjs538/portraits-of-gay-couples-just-married-in-new-york#.pnZwZWdzz.

[3] There are many feminist critiques of marriage, some of which reject the institution wholesale and some of which argue for its reform. These include, but are not limited to, the following, listed in chronological order of first publication: Mary Wollstonecraft, A Vindication of the Rights of Woman (London: Constable and Company Ltd, 1996 [1792]); John Stuart Mill, On Liberty and the Subjection of Women (Ware: Wordsworth, 1996 [1859 and 1869]); Emma Goldman, 'Marriage and Love' in her Anarchism and Other Essays (Createspace, 2011 [1910]); Simone de Beauvoir, The Second Sex (London: Vintage, 1997 [1949]); Betty Friedan, The Feminine Mystique (London: Penguin Books, 1963); Sheila Cronan, 'Marriage' in Anne Koedt, Ellen Levine, and Anita Rapone (eds), Radical Feminism (New York: Times Books, 1973 [1970]); Shulamith Firestone, The Dialectic of Sex (London: The Women's Press, 1979); Marjorie M. Shultz, 'Contractual Ordering of Marriage: A New Model for State Policy' in California Law Review 70(204) (1982); Lenore J. Weitzman, The Marriage Contract: Spouses, Lovers and the Law (London: Free Press, 1983); Carole Pateman, The Sexual Contract (Cambridge: Polity Press, 1988); Paula L. Ettelbrick, 'Since When is Marriage a Path to Liberation?' in Mark Blasius and Shane Phelan (eds), We Are Everywhere: A Historical Sourcebook of Gay and Lesbian Politics (London: Routledge, 1997 [1989]); Susan Moller Okin, Justice, Gender, and the Family (New York: Basic Books, 1989); Martha Albertson Fineman, The Neutered Mother, The Sexual Family, and Other Twentieth Century Tragedies (London: Routledge, 1995); Claudia Card, 'Against Marriage and Motherhood' Hypatia 11(3) (1996); Jane Lewis, The End of Marriage? Individualism and Intimate Relations (Cheltenham: Edward Elgar, 2001); Janet C. Gornick, 'Reconcilable Differences in The American Prospect Online (25 March 2002) at http://prospect.org/article/reconcilable-differences; Petra Boynton, 'Abiding by The Rules: Instructing Women in Relationships' Feminism & Psychology 13(2) (2003); Virginia Braun, 'Thanks to my Mother... A Personal Commentary on Heterosexual Marriage' in Feminism & Psychology 13(4) (2003); Sarah-Jane Finlay and Victoria Clarke, '"A Marriage of Inconvenience?" Feminist Perspectives on Marriage' in Feminism & Psychology 13(4) (2003); Merran Toerien and Andrew Williams, 'In Knots: Dilemmas of a Feminist Couple Contemplating Marriage' in Feminism & Psychology 13(1) (2003) Maria Bevacqua, 'Feminist Theory and the Question of Lesbian and Gay Marriage' in Feminism & Psychology 14(1) (2004); Anne Kingston, The Meaning of Wife (London: Piatkus, 2004); Celia Kitzinger and Sue Wilkinson, 'The Re-branding of Marriage: Why We Got Married Instead of Registering A Civil Partnership' in Feminism & Psychology 14(1) (2004); Martha Albertson Fineman, 'The Meaning of Marriage' in Anita Bernstein (ed.), Marriage Proposals: Questioning a Legal Status (New York: New York University Press, 2006); Nancy D. Polikoff, Beyond (Straight and Gay) Marriage: Valuing All Families Under the Law (Beacon Press, 2008); Brook J. Sadler, 'Re-Thinking Civil Unions and Same-Sex Marriage' in The Monist 91(3/4) (2008); Tamara Metz, Untying the Knot: Marriage, the State, and the Case for their Divorce (Princeton: Princeton University Press, 2010); Elizabeth Brake, Minimizing Marriage: Marriage, Morality, and the Law (Oxford: Oxford University Press, 2012).

Consider the following:

My current position on marriage is that I am against it.... Politically, I am against it because it has been oppressive for women, and through privileging heterosexuality, oppressive for lesbians and gay men.[4]

In this quote, and in feminist argument more generally, we can identify two distinct critiques of marriage. Both are common and yet in tension. The first states that traditional marriage is bad because it oppresses women. The implication of this critique is that being married makes women *worse* off. The second critique is that traditional marriage is bad because it privileges heterosexuality. The implication is that being married makes people, both men and women, *better* off: it provides benefits that are unjustly denied to lesbians and gays. But these critiques seem contradictory. If marriage oppresses at least some of its participants, why would lesbians and gays want to participate in it? On the other hand, if marriage ought to be extended to lesbians and gays because it confers privilege, what have feminists been complaining about all this time? And yet the two critiques are found together in the writings of many feminists.

This split in common feminist critiques of marriage explains why it can seem so difficult to develop a coherent feminist position and to be sure which sorts of reforms are progressive and which are reactionary. It explains, that is, the troubling ambiguities expressed by Merran Toerien and Andrew Williams, who label themselves a 'feminist couple'. 'In short,' they write, 'we want to get married and we do not.'[5]

## 1.1  Marriage as Oppressive to Women

Consider first the argument that marriage oppresses women, through a brief overview of the history of feminist criticism of the institution. Marriage has often been a trap for women, a state of imprisonment and sometimes brutality that they must endure, escape, or eschew. That is to say, marriage has played a significant role in maintaining the wider regime of gender inequality, since it has been used to consolidate legal, economic, cultural, and symbolic oppression by confining women to a private sphere in which they are seriously disadvantaged. Those significant women in history whom we know about are often victims or refusers of marriage. Consider, for example, Saint Radegund, one of the three

---

[4] Braun, 'Thanks to my Mother' p. 421. See also Finlay and Clarke, 'A Marriage of Inconvenience?' pp. 417–18.
[5] Toerien and Williams, 'In Knots' p. 435.

patron saints of Jesus College, Cambridge. Radegund was born in the first century as a German princess, but was captured by the Frankish King Chlothar I as a war prize when she was 11 or 12. Chlothar forced her to marry him when she became 18. The experience was not pleasant, to put it mildly: 'Chlothar was rough, brutal, unfaithful, and often drunk',[6] and he ordered the murder of her only surviving relative, her brother. Radegund fled the marriage and sought the protection of the Church, for religious life was one of the few activities that allowed women to live with neither marriage nor censure.

Or consider Queen Elizabeth I whose mother, Anne Boleyn, was executed by serial wife-killer King Henry VIII. At first Elizabeth was excluded from rule as her father had his marriage with her mother annulled, rendering her illegitimate. She came to the throne in 1558 on the death of her half-sister, Queen Mary I. Elizabeth's reign was dominated by discussions of her marriage, and her refusal ever to marry earned her the nickname 'The Virgin Queen' and a cult following.

Early feminists criticized marriage with the full force of condemnation reserved for the most grievous injustice. For John Stuart Mill in 1869 marriage was 'the primitive state of slavery lasting on',[7] a condition secured by wives' legal subordination to their husbands in every respect. In England at the time that Mill was writing, the system of coverture was in place, according to which married women were subordinate and subsumed to their husbands in law. So wives legally ceded all their property, as well as custody and control of their children, to their husbands, were under a legal duty to obey their husbands, were unable to vote or divorce, and could legally be raped by their husbands. Mill described women's legal duty to submit to marital sex as 'the lowest degradation of a human being, that of being made the instrument of an animal function contrary to her inclinations'.[8]

Some aspects of English coverture were reformed soon after Mill published *The Subjection of Women*. In 1870 the Married Woman's Property Act allowed women to keep property acquired after marriage, and a further Act in 1882 gave them rights over the property they owned prior to marriage. But English women had to wait until 1891 to be given the legal right not to be imprisoned by their husbands, and until 1991 (that's not a misprint) to be given the legal right not to be raped in marriage. Divorce laws were unequal until 1923.[9]

---

[6] Jesus College, 'St Radegund' at http://www.jesus.cam.ac.uk/about-jesus-college/history/pen-portraits/st-radegund/https://www.jesus.cam.ac.uk/college/about-us/history/people-note/st-radegund.
[7] Mill, *The Subjection of Women* p. 121.       [8] Mill, *The Subjection of Women* p. 146.
[9] See St Andrew's University, 'Women and the Law in Victorian England' at http://www.st-andrews.ac.uk/~bp10/pvm/en3040/women.shtml. I am using the word 'rape' here in a

Emma Goldman, who was born in Russia but emigrated to the USA, agreed with Mill that marriage subjected women to men. In 1910 she wrote:

Marriage is primarily an economic arrangement, an insurance pact. It differs from the ordinary life insurance agreement only in that it is more binding, more exacting. Its returns are insignificantly small compared with the investments. In taking out an insurance policy one pays for it in dollars and cents, always at liberty to discontinue payments. If, however, woman's premium is a husband, she pays for it with her name, her privacy, her self-respect, her very life, 'until death doth part'. Moreover, the marriage insurance condemns her to life-long dependency, to parasitism, to complete uselessness, individual as well as social.[10]

Simone de Beauvoir argued in 1949 that marriage remained deeply unequal. On her analysis, marriage is required of women for two reasons: first, they must provide children and marriage provides the socially acceptable context for childbearing, and second, 'woman's function is also to satisfy a male's sexual needs and to take care of his household'.[11] Marriage imposes both benefits and burdens on men and women, 'but there is no symmetry in the situations of the two sexes; for girls marriage is the only means of integration in the community, and if they remain unwanted, they are, socially viewed, so much wastage'.[12] For women, de Beauvoir notes, marriage was the only way to experience sex and motherhood without punishing social disapproval. 'For all these reasons a great many adolescent girls—in the New World as in the Old—when asked about their plans for the future, reply as formerly: "I want to get married." But no young man considers marriage his fundamental project.'[13] Nonetheless, the reality of marriage was horrific for many women: 'the girls concerned had been too carefully brought up, and since they had no sexual education, the sudden discovery of eroticism was too much for them.... Today many young women are better informed; but their willingness remains formal, abstract; and their defloration is still in the nature of a rape.'[14]

By the 1960s women's situation had changed. During World War II women in western countries had experienced unprecedented equal opportunities at work, with jobs previously reserved for men now having to be done by women. But the end of the war saw men's return, bringing social pressure for women to return to the home so that men could have 'their' jobs back. In *The Feminine Mystique* in

non-legal sense, since legally it was impossible for married women to be raped by their husbands prior to 1991. An act of forced sex between a husband and wife did not, legally, count as rape.

[10] Goldman, 'Marriage and Love' p. 89.   [11] de Beauvoir, *The Second Sex* p. 447.
[12] de Beauvoir, *The Second Sex* p. 447.   [13] de Beauvoir, *The Second Sex* p. 451.
[14] de Beauvoir, *The Second Sex* pp. 460–1.

1960 Betty Friedan wrote about 'the problem that has no name:...the strange stirring, a sense of dissatisfaction, a yearning that women suffered in the middle of the twentieth century in the United States'.[15] The cause of this problem, Friedan argued, was the 'mystique of feminine fulfilment'[16] which dictated that women should dream only of becoming housewives. This dream left no room for personal development, for career success, for female *personhood*:

The new mystique makes the housewife-mothers, who never had a chance to be anything else, the model for all women; it presupposes that history has reached a final and glorious end in the here and now, as far as women are concerned. Beneath the sophisticated trappings, it simply makes certain concrete, finite, domestic aspects of feminine existence—as it was lived by women whose lives were confined, by necessity, to cooking, cleaning, washing, bearing children—into a religion, a pattern by which all women must now live or deny their femininity.[17]

For Friedan, the solution was not to abandon marriage but for women to integrate marriage and motherhood with a career and, most fundamentally, for each woman to 'think of herself as a human being first'.[18]

Changing norms of sexual behaviour for women in the 1960s and 1970s may have gone some way towards weakening the grip of marriage. But marriage remained an institution subject to feminist critique. Second wave feminists continued to see marriage as a source of women's inequality. Sheila Cronan, radical feminist and founding member of Redstockings, decried the deceits of the marriage vows. As she put it in 1970, 'The marriage contract is the only important legal contract in which the terms are not listed.'[19] On the one hand marriage vows commit the parties to do things in which the courts take no interest, such as love each other. On the other hand, marriage vows fail to mention obligations which were legally enforced, such as the wife's duty to submit to sex with her husband. As already noted, the criminal act of rape could not occur within marriage in England and Wales until 1991, in the House of Lords case of *R v R*; the UK is by no means an outlier in waiting until the last gasps of the twentieth century to give women the legal right to refuse sex with their husbands.

Cronan's critique of marriage was not confined to marital rape. She argued, as Mill had one hundred years earlier, that married life is akin to slavery since 'being a wife is a full-time job for which one is not entitled to receive pay. Does this not constitute slavery?'[20] True, marriage is consented to, but this fact only makes its

---

[15] Friedan, *The Feminine Mystique* p. 15.  [16] Friedan, *The Feminine Mystique* p. 18.
[17] Friedan, *The Feminine Mystique* p. 43.  [18] Friedan, *The Feminine Mystique* p. 344.
[19] Cronan, 'Marriage' p. 218.    [20] Cronan, 'Marriage' p. 217.

enslavement 'more cruel and inhumane'.[21] Women's consent to marriage is borne not of their autonomy but of social construction:

Marriage has existed for so many thousands of years—the female role has been internalized in so many successive generations. If people are forced into line long enough, they will begin to believe in their own inferiority and to accept as natural the role created for them by their oppressor. Furthermore, society has been structured so that there is no real alternative to marriage for women. Employment discrimination, social stigma, fear of attack, sexual exploitation are only a few of the factors that make it nearly impossible for women to live as single people.... Also, marriage is so effectively described in such glowing terms that young girls rush into it excitedly, only to discover too late what the real terms of the marriage contract are.[22]

For socialist feminist Juliet Mitchell, writing in 1971, marriage formed part of the generally oppressive, socially-constructed model of a family. As she puts it:

[T]oday women are confined within the family which is a segmentary, monolithic unit, largely separated off from production and hence from social human activity. The reason why this confinement is made possible is the demand for women to fulfil these three roles: they must provide sexual satisfaction for their partners and give birth to children and rear them. But the family does more than occupy woman: it produces her.[23]

Part of the problem, for Mitchell, is that state-recognized marriage 'is utterly simple and rigid': it admits only one ideal-type of relationship, despite the fact that 'inter-sexual and inter-generational relationships are infinitely various'.[24]

Other radical feminist critics of marriage in this period include Kate Millett, for whom 'Patriarchy's chief institution is the family.'[25] Shulamith Firestone goes one step further, declaring in 1979 that 'love, perhaps even more than childbearing, is the pivot of women's oppression today'.[26] Firestone's critique echoes aspects of Friedan's critique of housewifery:

(Male) Culture was built on the love of women, and at their expense. Women provided the substance of those male masterpieces; and for millennia they have done the work, and suffered the costs, of one-way emotional relationships the benefits of which went to men and to the work of men.[27]

Artist Sally Swain's excellent book *The Great Housewives of Art* deftly and humorously illustrates this point, adapting famous paintings to show the activities of hidden women. So Mrs Degas vacuums the floor while *en pointe* in full

---

[21] Cronan, 'Marriage' p. 217.    [22] Cronan, 'Marriage' pp. 217–18.
[23] Juliet Mitchell, *Woman's Estate* (London: Verso, 2015 [1971]) p. 151.
[24] Mitchell, *Woman's Estate* p. 151.
[25] Kate Millett, *Sexual Politics* (London: Abacus, 1972) p. 33.
[26] Firestone, *The Dialectic of Sex* p. 121.    [27] Firestone, *The Dialectic of Sex* p. 122.

ballerina's outfit, Mrs Monet's attempts to clean the pond are evident only by a net surreptitiously probing the waterlilies, Mrs Klimt sews a patchwork quilt behind the head of her husband, who nuzzles her neck oblivious to her labour, and Mrs Pollock simply can't seem to find anything anymore.[28]

From the 1980s, perhaps inspired by the growth of neoliberalism in Margaret Thatcher's Britain and Ronald Reagan's USA, feminist critiques of marriage had taken a new turn. Feminists such as Martha Fineman, Marjorie Shultz, Elizabeth Kingdom, and Lenore Weitzman argued that marriage could be improved for women by being made more properly contractual.[29] The problem with marriage, as these writers saw it, was that it was a contract whose terms were set by the state, and in the most unequal fashion. Equality could be achieved either by allowing people to supplement marriage with contract, or by replacing marriage with contract. Thus Fineman argued for 'the abolition of marriage as a legal category and, with it, the demise of the entire set of special rules attached to it',[30] to be replaced by contracts. Contract thinking was not universal amongst feminists of this period, though. One landmark critic of both marriage and contracts was Carole Pateman, in her 1988 book *The Sexual Contract*. I devote Chapter 4 to critical analysis of relationship contracts.

Susan Moller Okin also criticized marriage in this period without turning to contracts. In 1989 she developed a sustained attack on what she called 'vulnerability by marriage'. She argued that 'marriage has earlier and far greater impact on the lives and life choices of women than on those of men, with girls less likely to aspire to prestigious occupations or feel able to contemplate being happily independent',[31] and marshalled a variety of evidence to show that marriage left women emotionally and practically vulnerable. Okin argued for a thorough overhaul of marriage law and practice, including proposals for obligatory egalitarian division of income between breadwinners and housewives during marriage and after divorce.[32]

Such changes are not easy. Changes to marriage law in favour of gender equality are hard-won victories resting on the suffering of many women, and changes in social norms concerning domestic labour are extremely hard for even

---

[28] Sally Swain, *The Great Housewives of Art* (New York: HarperCollins, 1988).

[29] See, for example, Weitzman, *The Marriage Contract*; Shultz, 'Contractual Ordering of Marriage'; Elizabeth A. Kingdom, 'Cohabitation Contracts: A Socialist-Feminist Issue' in *Journal of Law and Society* 15(1) (1988); Fineman, *The Neutered Mother*; Fineman, *The Autonomy Myth: A Theory of Dependency* (New York: New Press, 2005); Fineman, 'The Meaning of Marriage'; Fineman, 'Why Marriage?' in *Virginia Journal of Social Policy and the Law* 9(1) (2001).

[30] Fineman, 'Why Marriage?' p. 261.

[31] Okin, *Justice, Gender, and the Family* p. 142; see also Kingston, *The Meaning of Wife*.

[32] See also Gornick, 'Reconcilable Differences'.

feminist women and would-be egalitarian couples to achieve.[33] Nonetheless, proposals such as Okin's suggest that marriage can in principle be egalitarian, even though this would require radical social and legal change.[34]

Other late twentieth-century feminists were more sceptical. Claudia Card published 'Against Marriage and Motherhood' in 1996. On her analysis, the very idea of marriage as a state-awarded licence giving claims over another person's property and person is profoundly problematic, for it exposes individuals to each other and creates legal barriers to separation. In doing so, marriage inevitably leaves its participants (especially women) vulnerable to abuse. As Card puts it: 'For all that has been said about the privacy that marriage protects, what astonishes me is how much privacy one gives up in marrying.... Anyone who in fact cohabits with another may seem to give up similar privacy. Yet, without marriage, it is possible to take one's life back without encountering the law as an obstacle.'[35]

There is no denying that marriage oppressed women when it was the legal instrument of gender inequality. If wives cannot own property, be the legal guardians of their children, resist attack or rape or imprisonment from their husbands, or be entitled to equal rights at school and work, then marriage is a straightforward instrument of women's oppression. But liberal democracies in the twenty-first century have generally abolished these explicit inequalities of marriage, so what of the institution now? Does the feminist critique retain force?

The feminist critique can be divided into what I call practical and symbolic effects. This distinction is not rigid but indicates the difference between ways in which marriage might affect individuals' material or legal status and ways in which it consolidates or instantiates social norms or ideological values.

The first feminist critique of marriage has always been that it has practical effects on women that make them worse off. The end of legal inequality in marriage has not meant the end of actual inequality. Practical, empirical harms to women resulting from marriage include the contingent facts that marriage tends to reinforce the gendered division of labour, which itself means that women earn less and are less independent than men; that it reinforces the idea that women do most of the housework, even if they work outside the home, which saps their energies and dignity; and that domestic violence may be exacerbated by

---

[33] Pepper Schwartz, *Love between Equals: How Peer Marriage Really Works* (New York: The Free Press, 1994); Arlie Russell Hochschild and Anne Machung, *The Second Shift: Working Parents and the Revolution at Home* (London: Piatkus, 1990).

[34] Kitzinger and Wilkinson adopt this optimistic view in 'The Re-branding of Marriage' p. 135.

[35] Card, 'Against Marriage and Motherhood' p. 12.

marital concepts of entitlement and ownership.[36] Elizabeth Brake assesses the data from the USA and argues that 'marriage continues to perpetuate elements of women's oppression, understood as the diminishment of their life opportunities through the interaction of systematic legal, social, and economic forces', in particular 'spousal violence and economic dependence derived from gendered spousal roles'.[37] In the UK, sociologists Sara Arber and Jay Ginn analyse data relating to 32,000 people and conclude 'A major stumbling block to women's equality both in the labour market and the domestic sphere is the influence of the normative ideology of gender roles in marriage.'[38] They point to a mutually-reinforcing relationship between the fact of material gender inequality (the wage gap) and the marital ideology of husband-as-breadwinner: each apparently justifies and exacerbates the other. 'Failure to contest this normative structure,' they write, 'is a major factor in the perpetuation of women's disadvantaged position in British society.'[39]

One issue is whether these practical oppressions are the result of marriage, or cohabitation, or heterosexual relationships, or relationships in general. There are complex connections between gendered oppression, heteronormativity, and marriage, and it is beyond the scope of this book to provide a complete analysis.[40] But the status quo, in which marriage is recognized by the state and understood by state and society as the default mode for adult life, means that we cannot draw a neat dividing line between what happens in marriages and what happens elsewhere, in heterosexual or same-sex relationships, in cohabiting or casual relationships, in monogamous or polygamous relationships. Marriage is the norm, and the ideal: the situation that the state assumes, defines, regulates, and recommends. As we shall see shortly, the same-sex marriage movement is understood by many to be a demand for assimilation and normalization.

Nonetheless, there are some important differences between marriage and non-marriage in terms of practical effects. One example is housework. Various studies show that marriage increases the gender inequality of housework. Sanjiv Gupta analyses data from the USA and finds that both marriage and cohabitation

---

[36] Kingston, *The Meaning of Wife* pp. 158–61. See also Lewis, *The End of Marriage*.

[37] Brake, *Minimizing Marriage* p. 114.

[38] Sara Arber and Jay Ginn, 'The Mirage of Gender Equality: Occupational Success in the Labour Market and within Marriage' in *The British Journal of Sociology* 46(1) (1995) p. 26.

[39] Arber and Ginn, 'The Mirage of Gender Equality' p. 21.

[40] Many feminists argue that sexism and heterosexism are fundamentally connected. See, for example Radicalesbians, 'The Woman-Identified Woman' [1970] in Blasius and Phelan (eds), *We Are Everywhere*; Judith Butler, *Gender Trouble* (London: Routledge, 1999); Susan Moller Okin, 'Sexual Orientation, Gender, and Families: Dichotomizing Differences' in *Hypatia* 11(1) (1996).

significantly increase women's hours of housework and decrease men's.[41] He argues that these results 'constitute strong evidence for a causal relationship between marital status and housework time'.[42] Scott South and Glenna Spitze compare six different kinds of households in the USA: never married and living with parents, never married and living independently, cohabiting, married, divorced, and widowed. They find that women do more housework than men across the board, but that 'the gender gap is highest among married persons'.[43] Men's hours of housework remain consistent whether married or single (they increase where men are divorced or widowed), but women's hours are higher when cohabiting and higher still when married. The authors argue that wives' increased housework is not explained by children or reduced hours of paid work, and attribute it instead to the increased power of the normative requirement to 'display gender' that marriage brings.[44]

Another example is domestic violence. Michael Johnson and Kathleen Ferraro argue that domestic violence can best be understood if distinctions between different categories of violence are made. 'Common Couple Violence' or CCV 'arises in the context of a specific argument in which one or both of the partners lash out physically at the other'.[45] CCV does not usually escalate and is most likely to be mutual, although men are somewhat more likely to be the perpetrators than are women. It is found in marriage, but also in cohabitation and dating relationships, and is not confined to opposite-sex couples. But 'Intimate Terrorism' or IT *is* correlated with marriage. In IT, violence is used 'as merely one tactic in a general pattern of control. The violence is motivated by a wish to exert general control over one's partner. IT involves more per-couple incidents of violence than does CCV, is more likely to escalate over time, is less likely to be mutual, and is more likely to involve serious injury.'[46] Some studies find that IT is more common in marriage than in cohabitation or dating relationships, leading Johnson and Ferraro to wonder whether marriage, 'although not a license to hit, is for some people a license to terrorize'.[47] What we can say is that, even where

[41] Sanjiv Gupta, 'The Effects of Marital Status Transitions on Men's Housework Performance' in *Journal of Marriage and the Family* 61 p. 709.

[42] Gupta, 'The Effects of Marital Status Transitions' p. 710.

[43] Scott J. South and Glenna Spitze, 'Housework in Marital and Nonmarital Households' in *American Sociological Review* 59(3) (1994) p. 327.

[44] South and Spitze, 'Housework in Marital and Nonmarital Households' p. 344.

[45] Michael P. Johnson and Kathleen J. Ferraro, 'Research on Domestic Violence in the 1990s: Making Distinctions' in *Journal of Marriage and the Family* 62(4) (2000) p. 949.

[46] Johnson and Ferraro, 'Research on Domestic Violence' p. 949.

[47] Johnson and Ferraro, 'Research on Domestic Violence' p. 952.

domestic violence takes place in non-marital relationships, it is connected to tropes of ownership and control that are distinctively marital.

The state recognition of marriage also has implications more broadly, since it shores up the notion of the couple-headed household as ideal family form, which in turn shores up the system that makes children and work difficult to combine—what Joan Williams refers to as the clash between the norm of the ideal worker and the norm of parental care.[48] These clashing norms thus make life even harder for unmarried people as compared with married ones, since they strengthen the ideas that work does not have to take account of caring responsibilities, that children are harmed if their mothers work outside the home, and that people should not rely on state benefits. These ideas are compatible only within a family structure based on traditional marriage, with a breadwinning husband and a housewife, and yet they provide the cultural, legal, and financial structures within which everyone must operate.

The extent to which marriage is associated with practical oppression or disadvantage for women depends on particular laws and sociological facts. In past incarnations of marriage, when the institution left women with few or no rights over their bodies, possessions, children, and lives, practical feminist critiques were particularly salient. But feminists have also always argued that marriage disadvantages women symbolically, by casting women as inferior. This theme recurs in several of the historical feminist critiques just surveyed. It is still deeply relevant today.

Pierre Bourdieu describes this form of symbolic effect as 'symbolic violence'. Symbolic violence affects thoughts rather than bodies, and is inflicted upon people with their complicity.[49] In other words, symbolic violence occurs when, through social pressures, an individual feels herself to be inferior or worthless. One particularly pernicious form of symbolic violence that marriage enacts on women in contemporary western societies is the sense that they are flawed and failing if unmarried. Many heterosexual women see single life as a temporary phase preceding marriage, and being single for longer or when older is construed as sad and shameful, and at least partially the fault of the single woman herself.[50] A particularly striking example of this sort of pressure can be found in *The Rules*,

---

[48] Joan Williams, *Unbending Gender: Why Family and Work Conflict and What To Do About It* (Oxford: Oxford University Press, 2000).

[49] Pierre Bourdieu, *Masculine Domination* (Cambridge: Polity Press, 2001); Pierre Bourdieu and Loïc Wacquant, *An Invitation to Reflexive Sociology* (Cambridge: Polity Press, 1992).

[50] Anna Sandfield and Carol Percy, 'Accounting for Single Status: Heterosexism and Ageism in Heterosexual Women's Talk about Marriage' in *Feminism & Psychology* 13(4) (2003); Jill Reynolds and Margaret Wetherell, 'The Discursive Climate of Singleness: The Consequences for Women's Negotiation of a Single Identity' in *Feminism & Psychology* 13(4) (2003).

the best-selling self-help book that instructs women to secure marriage by following a strict set of guidelines such as not telephoning men, not describing their own sexual desires or asking them to be met, and not minding when men are angry. Women wishing to ignore, let alone criticize, *The Rules* are sharply admonished:

If you think you're too smart for The Rules, ask yourself 'Am I married?' If not, why not? Could it be that what you're doing isn't working? Think about it.[51]

J. Jack Halberstam provides many examples of the portrayal of marriage as ultimate destiny for women in popular culture. The pinnacle of this form, of course, is the romantic comedy. In the average 'rom com' marriage is both women's downfall and their ultimate aim: protagonists have to overcome various pitfalls on their way to the altar, such as commitment-phobic men, choosing the wrong man, choosing the wrong dress, choosing the wrong bridesmaids, choosing the wrong bridesmaids' dresses . . . The aim always has to be marriage, though, spurred on by the fear of spinsterdom. As Halberstam puts it 'The wedding is the cum shot of the romantic comedy.'[52]

We might ask whether it would matter if women felt pressure to enter into marriage if it were the case that the practical aspects of marriage were egalitarian. In other words, if marriage no longer disadvantaged women practically, would it matter if women were pressured to enter it symbolically? We might have a number of autonomy- and diversity-based objections to such pressure, which would apply to both women and men. But one way in which pressure to enter into even reformed marriages might particularly harm women (and thus be of particular concern to feminists) is through the simple fact that marriage has *historically* been an extremely sexist institution. Even if these historical oppressions have been reformed, such that wives are equal to husbands in law, marriage remains an institution rooted in the subjection of women.[53]

The question of whether the patriarchal history of an institution continues to taint its modern incarnations even if the explicitly patriarchal aspects have been

---

[51] Ellen Fein and Sherrie Schneider, *The Rules: Time Tested Secrets for Capturing the Heart of Mr Right* (London: Thorlens, 1995) p. 120. For a feminist who is not too chastised to criticize *The Rules*, see Boynton, 'Abiding by The Rules'.

[52] J. Jack Halberstam, *Gaga Feminism: Sex, Gender, and the End of Normal* (Boston, MA: Beacon Press, 2012) p. 115.

[53] See Pateman, *The Sexual Contract*; Card, 'Against Marriage and Motherhood'; Toerien and Williams, 'In Knots' p. 434; Sheila Jeffreys, 'The Need to Abolish Marriage' in *Feminism & Psychology* 14(2) (2004); Richard H. Thaler and Cass R. Sunstein, *Nudge: Improving Decisions about Health, Wealth and Happiness* (New Haven, CT: Yale University Press, 2008) p. 219.

reformed is a vexed one.[54] It seems obvious that institutions need not remain unjust forever, beyond the abolition of that which initially made them unjust. For example, cotton picking in the USA and chimney sweeping in the UK were once done by slaves and children respectively, both unjust forms of labour; and democratic participation was denied to women in the UK (and elsewhere) until the extension of the suffrage in the early twentieth century. But cotton picking, chimney sweeping, and democracy are not inherently unjust once slavery, child labour, and sex discrimination are abolished: the injustice does not outlive its concrete manifestation. Why, an objector might ask, should marriage be any different?

The question of whether an unjust institution remains unjust after reform invokes two key issues: participation and meaning. First, consider participation. It is possible for an institution to be unjust only because participation in it is on unequal terms; in these cases, equal participation removes the injustice. The example of democracy is like this. The ideal of democracy is government by the people, and participation in a society of equals. The male-only suffrage is unjust precisely because it excludes women from the category of 'the people', reflecting and perpetuating a context in which they are treated unequally. If women are the only group excluded from the vote then changing the situation to allow women to participate ends the injustice, because their participation changes the institution of voting from one that is exclusionary and based on inequality to one that is inclusive and egalitarian. The same is not true if women are not the only group excluded from voting. If a multi-racial society initially allows only white men to vote and then opens the suffrage to include white women, the move is in some sense an improvement. But opening the vote to white women in such a society does not make the institution of voting just if people of colour remain excluded from it.

So too for marriage. Like democracy, marriage may be rendered more just if it is opened up to more people: introducing same-sex marriage is an improvement on traditional marriage. But introducing same-sex marriage does not make the institution of marriage just if other people are excluded from it and the benefits it provides. The move to same-sex marriage still excludes people in non-monogamous relationships, and people who are in monogamous relationships but who do not want to solemnize those relationships through the institution of marriage for reasons such as religion, culture, politics, uncertainty, or one person's reluctance.

---

[54] Pateman's argument strongly implies that no reform could render marriage non-patriarchal since the very idea of contracting parties is deeply embedded in insurmountably patriarchal concepts. See Pateman, *The Sexual Contract* pp. 184–5.

This group also includes people who are not in stable sexual or personal relationships at all but who could still benefit from things such as tax breaks, immigration rights, health insurance, or pension rights. These are rights that individuals may legitimately want to assign to friends, relatives, or cohabitants: anyone with whom one has a non-conjugal yet significant relationship. Including same-sex couples in the category of people who may participate in and benefit from marriage is thus not sufficient to rectify the participatory injustice.

The second issue, particularly pertinent in the case of marriage, is that of meaning. Return to the examples of cotton picking and chimney sweeping. These activities do not remain unjust if their association with slavery and child labour is removed, because there is nothing inherently unjust about the activities of picking cotton and sweeping chimneys. It would, of course, be possible for the injustice of those professions to persist, if people who worked in them were denied adequate wages or safety equipment or faced unfair working conditions. But it is in principle possible for those activities to be performed in fair conditions for fair pay.

It follows that cotton picking and chimney sweeping can in principle be performed justly. One way of seeing this is to note that many welfare states, such as the one in the UK, provide unemployment benefit only if no job is available to the claimant. That may or may not be a just arrangement (the movement for basic income argues that it is not). But if it were a just arrangement then it would not be unjust to require a fit, able-bodied person to take a job as a chimney sweep or a cotton picker or else lose unemployment benefits, as long as those jobs were fairly paid and properly regulated.

The same is not true of all jobs. It would *not* be compatible with justice to require someone to take a job as a prostitute or else lose benefits, and this injustice would persist even if being a prostitute were fairly paid and properly regulated. First, the injustice of prostitution is largely based on the deep and ancient gender inequality associated with that practice, a gender inequality that persists in society at large. Prostitution has always been an activity providing male access to women's bodies, based on a model of human sexuality that places men's needs over women's and that regards prostituted women as debased objects for use. Paying prostituted women fairly does not undermine those deep-seated cultural meanings of the practice. Second, prostitution makes sense only in a context of wider gender inequality, one in which many women lack realistic alternative options for achieving financial independence such that prostitution may appear the best, or only, option. Improving conditions for prostituted women, though laudable in and of itself, does not change the context of inequality that makes prostitution exist as a gendered phenomenon. Third, one's sexuality and one's sexual organs are deeply private and intimate, and it is a profound and crucial part of our cultural understanding of sex that it must be fully consensual if it is not to be criminal and abusive. Improving conditions for prostitution does not remove the profound injustice of being forced to have sex in order to survive.

For all these reasons, it would not be acceptable for the state to require people to take jobs in prostitution or else lose benefits, even if prostitution were fairly paid and properly regulated. State-mandated prostitution would worsen and not mitigate the idea that it is appropriate for men to use women's bodies for sexual satisfaction, and it would not undermine the idea that women's bodies are appropriately considered as objects for use. Even if men were also required to take such jobs where possible the situation would still be unjust, because there would not be such a demand for male prostitutes as female prostitutes (and so it would be less likely that men would in fact have to take such a job), and because a prostituted man is not regarded as a debased object for use and abuse in the same way as a prostituted woman. Male prostitution does not undermine gender inequality generally. And finally, even if we ignore the gendered aspects of prostitution, the privacy and intimacy of sex and the necessity for it to be fully consensual mean that it would still be unjust to require anyone to have sex with other people indiscriminately in order to survive.

State-recognized marriage shares many of the meaning-based features of prostitution, even though marriage is not nearly as unjust as state-mandated prostitution would be. First, like prostitution marriage is an institution that is largely based on ancient and enduring inequality between women and men, one that stems from and reinforces a gendered society in which women are viewed as objects for male ownership and use. Second, its location within a wider system of gender equality means that marriage, like prostitution, is more central to women's life chances than it is to men's. The persistence of the gender pay gap and discrimination against women in the workplace, both of which worsen considerably when women become mothers, mean that women are much more dependent than men are on marriage and the financial support of a spouse.[55] The persistence of cultural pressures on women to get married means that women are much more likely to feel that they have to get married in order to be valuable. But it is unjust if women's ability to combine work and motherhood, the social bases

---

[55] See TUC, *The Motherhood Pay Penalty* (March 2016) at https://www.tuc.org.uk/sites/default/files/MotherhoodPayPenalty.pdf. The report concludes that 'cultural factors—negative views of women's commitment to work after having children and positive views of fathers in the workplace, probably associated with the traditional male breadwinner role—are at play' (p. 5).

of women's self-respect, and the benefits which are associated with marriage, are all dependent on participation in a particular form of sexual relationship.

What makes marriage distinctive is that it is an institution entered into not only for the practical benefits it may bring but also because of the meanings it represents, something discussed in more detail in Chapter 2. Couples may marry so as to obtain various practical benefits, but a key aspect of most marriages is the statement the couple make about their relationship. For the marrying couple and for society in general, the symbolic significance of marriage is at least as important as its practical aspects, as demonstrated in debates about same-sex marriage discussed next.

Thus the state recognition of marriage is state intervention in, and control of, the meaning of marriage. As Tamara Metz puts it, 'the "establishment of marriage" highlights the state's integral role in reproducing and relying on belief in a particular, comprehensive account and institutional form of intimate life'.[56] This being the case, it is impossible to escape the history of the institution. Its status as a *tradition* ties its current meaning to its past. This feature of marriage makes the issue of what the institution really does represent, what meanings it carries, particularly pertinent.

It is possible for practices to change their meanings, such that those that were once associated with injustice can be transformed into practices of liberation and equality. For example, the pink triangle was initially used by the Nazis as a symbol of stigma for those prisoners in concentration camps who were deemed to be gay, but it has since been reclaimed by the gay rights movement as a symbol of empowerment.[57] As we shall see in Section 1.2, there is significant debate within feminism and the gay rights movement as to whether same-sex marriage will have a progressive or reactionary effect.

## 1.2 Marriage as Heterosexist

As noted at the outset, the number of countries that recognize same-sex marriage has increased dramatically in recent years. However, for the vast majority of its history, marriage has been an institution reserved for different-sex couples, assumed to be heterosexual. Thus the second major strand of feminist critique of marriage is that it is heterosexist.

According to this critique marriage *benefits* those who enter into it. Thus feminists, who favour gender equality and oppose discrimination on the grounds

---

[56] Metz, *Untying the Knot* p. 11.
[57] For further discussion see http://www.pink-triangle.org.

of both sex and sexuality, must oppose marriage as long as it is denied to same-sex couples.[58] Many feminists campaign for the extension of marriage to same-sex couples, and some argue that extending marriage to lesbians and gays would transform the institution.

Once again, this line of argument can be separated into practical and symbolic strands. Practically, marriage privileges heterosexuality if it is denied to same-sex couples and if the law is structured so as to give married couples particular rights that are denied to unmarried couples. Such laws discriminate against not only same-sex couples but all unmarried individuals (whether single or in a relationship). In the UK, for example, spouses and registered partners (who must be same-sex) do not have to pay inheritance tax when inheriting each other's property, unlike those in any other form of relationship, and until recently marriage was available only to different-sex couples. Material benefits such as this lead Thomas Stoddard to advocate same-sex marriage 'despite the oppressive nature of marriage historically, and in spite of the general absence of edifying examples of modern heterosexual marriage'.[59]

Heterosexual-only marriage also has discriminatory *symbolic* effects. By recognizing heterosexual marriage, the state confers legitimacy and approval on such partnerships and denies it to gay and lesbian ones. Thus Maria Bevacqua, a lesbian feminist, argues:

The exclusion of a portion of the population from a major social institution creates a second-class citizenship for that group. This is a humiliating experience, whether as individuals we feel humiliated or not.[60]

Bevacqua's insistence that the humiliation is independent of the feelings of the humiliated emphasizes the deeply symbolic nature of the institution. Marriage presents and represents a particular symbolic meaning that transcends individuals' subjective self-understandings and experiences. Instead, it appeals to supposedly shared social understandings of value, understandings that can fail to respect minority and historically-oppressed groups. In particular, marriage reinforces the idea that the monogamous heterosexual union is the (only) sacred form of relationship.

Stoddard argues that marriage is 'the centrepiece of our entire social structure' and notes that the US Supreme Court has called it 'noble' and 'sacred'.[61]

---

[58]   Toerien and Williams, 'In Knots' p. 434.

[59]   Stoddard, 'Why Gay People Should Seek the Right to Marry' in Blasius and Phelan (eds), *We Are Everywhere* p. 754.

[60]   Bevacqua, 'Feminist Theory' p. 37.

[61]   Stoddard, 'Why Gay People Should Seek the Right to Marry' p. 756.

Understandably he 'resents' and 'loathes' the fact that, according to the Court at the time he was writing, lesbians and gays were not deemed able to enter into such noble and sacred relationships.[62] Like Bevacqua, Stoddard believes that legalizing same-sex marriage is a crucial egalitarian step, even if many gays and lesbians have no desire to marry. Indeed, Stoddard argues that same-sex marriages would also benefit heterosexual women, as they would serve the feminist purpose of 'abolishing the traditional gender requirements of marriage' and thus divesting the institution of 'the sexist trappings of the past'.[63]

According to these feminist critiques, then, marriage oppresses both those heterosexual women who do or could participate in it and those lesbians and gays who could not; and it does so in ways that are both practical and symbolic. But these criticisms can conflict in their implications for marriage reform, rendering the debate exceedingly complicated. Consider, for example, whether it would be desirable from an egalitarian perspective to legalise same-sex marriage.

## 1.3  Is Same-sex Marriage Egalitarian?

I stated earlier that, if marriage is to be recognized by the state at all, then equality requires the recognition of same-sex marriage. But perhaps that claim was too hasty. With the various feminist critiques in mind, we can now see that the issue is by no means clear-cut.

Reserving marriage for different-sex couples is, according to the feminist critiques considered so far, symbolically oppressive to both women and gay men. If same-sex couples are allowed to marry, it is not clear whether its oppressiveness will rub off onto lesbians and gays, making them worse off, or whether the anti-patriarchy of queer lives and culture will rub off onto marriage, making all women better off.

Feminists and advocates of gay rights have argued both ways but, in the current political climate, pro-marriage voices prevail. The simplest egalitarian argument in favour of same-sex marriage is that it is needed to rectify an inequality of civil rights and practical benefits. This issue is particularly salient in those polities which connect a great deal of rights and duties to marriage. The USA is paradigmatic here, as marriage is crucial in many areas such as health insurance, welfare payments, housing, and immigration.[64] So Margaret Morganroth Gullette writes that she was transformed from 'a rebellious critic of the institution

---

[62] Stoddard, 'Why Gay People Should Seek the Right to Marry' p. 756.
[63] Stoddard, 'Why Gay People Should Seek the Right to Marry' p. 757.
[64] See Brake, *Minimizing Marriage* for an overview of the privileges of marriage in the US context.

into a vocal and explicit advocate' as the result of 'recognizing and honoring the growing desire of some of my lesbian friends and relatives to enjoy the protections that marriage now extends only to heterosexuals'.[65] For Joan Callahan, since the complete abolition of marriage is a long way off, same-sex marriage is a 'central way to work on defeating systemic homophobia and heterosexism, while immediately affording equal crucial rights and goods of many sorts to sexual and gender minorities'.[66] This is the sense in which we can initially state that egalitarians should support same-sex marriage, if marriage exists at all.

But the egalitarian case for same-sex marriage does not rest only on the practical legal benefits that *accompany* marriage, for many of those could be provided to unmarried people on equal terms (and since there is an equally pressing inequality of service provision for those who are unmarried by choice). Instead, the basic argument for same-sex marriage on the grounds of equality is that the *right to marry*, pure and simple, must be equally available to all.

The idea that the right to marry is both intrinsically valuable and sometimes illegitimately denied is grounded in recent historical experience. For example, restrictions on interracial marriage were in place in Nazi Germany and South African apartheid. In the USA slaves were not able to legally marry, and slave families were subject to permanent separation at the whims of their owners.[67] The end of slavery did not mean the end of unequal marriage by race, for many states retained antimiscegenation laws prohibiting interracial marriage. In 1967 the landmark Supreme Court case *Loving v Virginia* struck down those laws as unconstitutional for violating equal protection. In his ruling Justice Warren described marriage as 'one of the vital personal rights essential to the orderly pursuit of happiness by free men... one of the "basic civil rights of man", fundamental to our existence and survival'.[68] In its ruling in *Obergefell v Hodges* in 2015 the Court once again affirmed the centrality of marriage:

[T]he annals of human history reveal the transcendent importance of marriage. The lifelong union of a man and a woman always has promised nobility and dignity to all persons, without regard to their station in life.... Its dynamic allows two people to find a

---

[65] Margaret Morganroth Gullette, 'The New Case for Marriage' in *The American Prospect Online* (5 March 2004), http://www.prospect.org.

[66] Joan Callahan, 'Same-Sex Marriage: Why It Matters—At Least for Now' in *Hypatia* 24(1) (2009) p. 73.

[67] Brake, *Minimizing Marriage* pp. 11, 125–9; Katherine Franke, *Wedlocked: The Perils of Marriage Equality—How African Americans and Gays Mistakenly Thought the Right to Marry Would Set Them Free* (New York: New York University Press, 2015).

[68] Justice Warren, 'Race and the Right to Marry' in Andrew Sullivan (ed.) *Same-Sex Marriage Pro and Con: A Reader* (New York: Vintage, 2004) p. 89.

life that could not be found alone, for a marriage becomes greater than just the two persons. Rising from the most basic human needs, marriage is essential to our most profound hopes and aspirations.[69]

Article 12 of the European Convention of Human Rights is entirely devoted to the right to marry: 'Men and women of marriageable age have the right to marry and to found a family, according to the national laws governing the exercise of this right.'[70]

So marriage is often considered, even in liberal democratic states, to be central to human flourishing. The experience and legacy of institutional racism and heterosexism in marriage lends support to what I call the basic egalitarian claim for same-sex marriage:

*The basic claim*: if different-sex marriage exists, then the principle of equal rights requires the recognition of same-sex marriage.

The philosophical issue at stake is whether *equal rights* require same-sex marriage or, to put it in reverse, whether restricting recognition to different-sex marriage just is to instantiate unequal rights. This question might seem easy to answer but, like all philosophical questions, it is not.

The idea of marriage equality can be stated simply: if heterosexuals can marry then lesbians, gays, and bisexuals should be able to marry as well. This apparent simplicity is echoed in the fact that many supporters of same-sex marriage describe themselves as supporters of 'marriage equality'.[71] On this reasoning, then, denying same-sex marriage is denying equal rights. Thus Alex Rajczi claims that a case for same-sex marriage can be built on only 'widely-accepted political principles' of equal opportunity:[72] 'there is not one single thing wrong with homosexuality, and so gay people should never be treated differently from anyone else'.[73]

The basic claim that equality requires same-sex marriage is one with a great deal of appeal for feminists and other egalitarians.[74] But many have argued

---

[69] *Obergefell v Hodges* (2015) at http://www.supremecourt.gov/opinions/14pdf/14-556_3204.pdf p. 3.
[70] European Convention on Human Rights at http://www.echr.coe.int/Documents/Convention_ENG.pdf.
[71] See, for example, Australian Marriage Equality (http://www.australianmarriageequality.org); Human Rights Campaign (http://www.hrc.org/campaigns/marriage-center); Irish Marriage Equality (www.marriageequality.ie); LGBTQ Nation (http://www.lgbtqnation.com/tag/gay-marriage/); Marriage Equality USA (http://www.marriageequality.org); Advocate (http://www.advocate.com/marriage-equality).
[72] Alex Rajczi, 'A Populist Argument for Legalizing Same-Sex Marriage' in *The Monist* 91(3/4) (2008) p. 475.
[73] Rajczi, 'A Populist Argument' p. 498.
[74] A sustained discussion of a version of the basic claim is found in Ralph Wedgwood, 'The Fundamental Argument for Same-Sex Marriage' in *The Journal of Political Philosophy* 7(3) (1999).

against the basic claim. For example, Richard McDonough argues that traditional, different-sex-only marriage should not be equated with *heterosexual* marriage. Different-sex-only marriage gives every single person regardless of sexuality the exact same, equal right: to marry a person of a different sex. This right is not, he claims, worthless to lesbians, gays, and bisexuals, since many of them have in fact had successful marriages to people of a different sex. For McDonough, people 'are free to argue for the right to marry persons of the same sex, but this must be an argument for a *new* right, for the right which they want is not "the same" one already possessed by heterosexuals'.[75] Same-sex marriage is not, then, a requirement of equality in the most basic sense, and so the basic claim fails.

One response to McDonough's argument is to say that it misdescribes the right that is at stake. It may be true that, under traditional marriage, everyone has the right to marry a person of a different sex. But the importance of the right to marry is not captured by the idea of an interest in marrying a person of a different sex. After all, antimiscegenation laws gave every person the right to marry someone of their own race, but that way of stating the right to marry does not capture its intrinsic importance.

Instead, we must construe the right to marry more carefully. There are various ways of doing so: it could be a right to marry whichever consenting person you choose,[76] or a right that belongs to a couple as couple,[77] or the right to marry for love.[78] Similar conceptual issues arise in all cases, so we can consider just one option. What is valuable, let us assume, is the right to marry the person with whom you are in sexual love. Since heterosexuals will, by definition, be in sexual love with people of a different sex, the availability of different-sex marriage gives them the right to marry for sexual love. Bisexuals have the right to marry for sexual love in some cases but not all; that is to say, they are permitted to marry only some kinds of people with whom they may be in sexual love. But since gays and lesbians feel sexual love only for people of the *same* sex, then they do *not* have the right to marry for sexual love without same-sex marriage.

---

See also Benjamin A. Gorman, 'Brief Refutations of Some Common Arguments Against Same-Sex Marriage' in *American Philosophical Association Newsletter on Philosophy and Lesbian, Gay, Bisexual, and Transgender Issues* 4(1) (2004).

[75] Richard McDonough, 'Is Same Sex Marriage an Equal Rights Issue?' in *Public Affairs Quarterly* 19(1) (2005) p. 53.

[76] Wedgwood, 'The Fundamental Case for Same-Sex Marriage' p. 240.

[77] Reginald Williams, 'Same Sex Marriage and Equality' in *Ethical Theory and Moral Practice* 14(5) (2011).

[78] Andrew Lister, *Public Reason and Political Community* (London: Bloomsbury, 2013) p. 137.

The usual counter-argument at this point runs as follows. If equality requires that same-sex couples have the right to marry for love, then it also follows that polygamists have the right to marry for love, and adult incestuous couples have the right to marry for love, such that there is a slippery slope from same-sex marriage to polygamy and incest. For example, William Bennett asks rhetorically 'why on earth' an advocate of same-sex marriage would 'exclude from marriage a bisexual who wants to marry two other people? After all, exclusion would be a denial of that person's sexuality. The same holds true of a father and daughter who want to marry. Or two sisters. Or men who want (consensual) polygamous arrangements.'[79]

A great deal of the political, legal, and philosophical literature on same-sex marriage has thus been devoted to the idea of whether the equality arguments for same-sex marriage do entail the recognition of other sorts of marriage and, if so, whether that would be a bad thing. One notable response comes from Jonathan Rauch, who argues that lesbians and gays want the possibility of marrying for love but that that possibility does not have to be unlimited. 'What homosexuals are asking for,' he writes, 'is the right to marry, not anybody they love, but somebody they love, which is not at all the same thing.'[80] Rauch therefore argues that same-sex marriage does not entail support for polygamy, since polygamy is essentially a demand to be able to marry more than just some(one)body.[81] In a similar vein, John Corvino gives many examples of what he calls the PIB argument—the argument that recognition of homosexuality leads inexorably to recognition of polygamy, incest, and bestiality. He rejects this argument on the grounds that there is no reason why homosexuality is more closely connected to PIB

---

[79] William Bennett, 'Leave Marriage Alone' in Sullivan (ed.), *Same-Sex Marriage* p. 275. Bennett is wrong, of course, if he means to suggest that bisexuals cannot be monogamous. For other arguments that same-sex marriage is a slippery slope to the recognition of morally-suspect sexualities see John Finnis, 'Marriage: A Basic and Exigent Good' in *The Monist* 91(3/4) (2008); Hadley Arkes, 'The Role of Nature' in Sullivan (ed.), *Same-Sex Marriage*; Charles Krauthammer, 'When John and Jim Say "I Do"' in Sullivan (ed.), *Same-Sex Marriage*; Patrick Lee, 'Marriage, Procreation, and Same-Sex Unions' in *The Monist* 91(3/4) (2008). Polygamy and incest do not exhaust the morally-suspect sexualities that are used in this argument but they are the most commonly-used. Some versions of the argument include bestiality.

[80] Jonathan Rauch, 'Marrying Somebody' in Sullivan (ed.), *Same-Sex Marriage* p. 286.

[81] For the argument that a line can be drawn isolating same-sex marriage from morally-suspect or harmful sexualities, such that there is no slippery slope, see Williams, 'Same Sex Marriage and Equality'; Andrew Sullivan, 'Three's A Crowd' in Sullivan (ed.), *Same-Sex Marriage*; Rauch, 'Marrying Somebody'; John Corvino, 'Homosexuality and the PIB argument' in *Ethics* 115(3) (2005); Andrew F. March, 'What Lies Beyond Same-Sex Marriage? Marriage, Reproductive Freedom and Future Persons in Liberal Public Justification' in *Journal of Applied Philosophy* 27(1) (2010); Stephen Macedo, *Just Married: Same-Sex Couples, Monogamy, and the Future of Marriage* (Princeton, NJ: Princeton University Press, 2015).

than heterosexuality. Sexual practices, for Corvino, 'ought to be evaluated in terms of their relative contribution to human flourishing...there is no reason to presuppose that homosexuality is more like PIB in this contribution than heterosexuality'.[82] Other egalitarians disagree. Ronald Den Otter, for example, argues that support for same-sex marriage *does* entail support for plural marriage, but that this is not an argument against same-sex marriage since plural marriage is morally unproblematic and deserves recognition.[83]

What this debate highlights is that we cannot debate marriage without making value judgements about what marriage really is and why it is valuable.[84] The basic claim rests on the premise that same-sex relationships are the same as different-sex relationships *in some relevant characteristic*. We therefore need to ask what the relevant characteristic of marriage is: what is it about marital relationships that makes them valuable and worthy of state recognition? The answer we give to this question will determine how extensive marriage should be. If what is valuable about marital relationships is their heterosexuality then we should endorse traditional marriage (and possibly extend it to heterosexual incestuous couples). If it is procreation then we should reserve marriage for those couples who are able and willing to procreate, which may include same-sex couples using IVF, sperm donation, or surrogate mothers, and include polygamous marriage, but exclude even different-sex couples who cannot or do not procreate. If it is love or care then we should extend marriage to all loving and caring relationships, whether sexual or not. If it is stability and commitment then we should extend marriage to all but make divorce much more difficult. If it is monogamy then we should recognize monogamous relationships of whatever sex, but should be less willing to consider remarriage after divorce. And so on.

The important point is that even the basic claim from equality cannot be made without considering the meaning of marriage; and the meaning of marriage, as with all other social, cultural, and legal institutions, is inevitably social. We are

---

[82]   Corvino, 'Homosexuality and the PIB Argument' p. 533.

[83]   Ronald C. Den Otter, *In Defense of Plural Marriage* (Cambridge: Cambridge University Press, 2015). For other examples of the argument that same-sex marriage does lead to the recognition of some other sexualities, such as polygamy or polyamory, but that this is not to be feared morally see Dennis Altman, 'Sexual Freedom and the End of Romance' in Sullivan (ed.), *Same-Sex Marriage*; Cheshire Calhoun, 'Who's Afraid of Polygamous Marriage? Lessons for Same-Sex Marriage Advocacy from the History of Polygamy' in *San Diego Law Review* 42 (2005); Andrew F. March, 'Is there a Right to Polygamy? Marriage, Equality and Subsidizing Families in Liberal Public Justification' in *Journal of Moral Philosophy* 8(2) (2011); Alex Rajczi, 'A Populist Argument for Legalizing Same-Sex Marriage'; Martha C. Nussbaum, *From Disgust to Humanity: Sexual Orientation and Constitutional Law* (Oxford: Oxford University Press, 2010); Sonu Bedi, *Beyond Race, Sex, and Sexual Orientation: Legal Equality without Identity* (Cambridge: Cambridge University Press, 2013).

[84]   This point is emphasized in Wedgwood, 'The Fundamental Case for Same-Sex Marriage'.

not the sole authors or arbiters of the meanings of our practices. Our practices mean, to a significant extent, what they mean in the society in which they and we are situated. So we are once again returned to the question of what marriage means, and whether its patriarchal meanings are strengthened or overcome by the movement towards same-sex marriage.

We have already seen that, for Stoddard, same-sex marriage is needed not just to rectify inequality but also for what he assumes will be its more general progressive effects. Cheshire Calhoun also argues that same-sex marriage is necessary as it marks that homosexuality is no bar to full citizenship.[85] On the other hand, Paula Ettelbrick predicts the triumph of patriarchy and reaction: 'marriage will not liberate us as lesbians and gay men. In fact, it will constrain us, make us more invisible, force our assimilation into the mainstream, and undermine the goals of gay liberation',[86] she writes. Nancy Polikoff agrees: 'Everything in our political history suggests that a concerted effort to achieve the legalization of lesbian and gay marriage will valorize the current institution of marriage... [and] work to persuade the heterosexual mainstream that lesbians and gay men seek to emulate heterosexual marriage as currently constituted.'[87]

For Katherine Franke, the repressive effects of same-sex marriage extend to society as a whole: 'Not only have some advocates of same-sex marriage abandoned any effort to promote respect, non-discrimination, and recognition of diverse family forms, but they have veered in the direction of portraying families with non-married parents as a site of pathology, stigma, and injury to children,'[88] she writes. 'Letting same-sex couples into the club leaves in place the bias and shame suffered by those who can't or won't fulfil the criteria for membership.'[89] For Franke the deeply normative nature of marriage, which same-sex marriage strengthens rather than undermines, can be seen by looking at those who defend same-sex marriage from a conservative standpoint: 'When the conservatives sign up for marriage equality, they do so because it dawns on them that their interests in traditional family values, in the nuclear family, in privatizing dependency, and in bourgeois respectability are stronger than their homophobia.'[90]

Franke also worries that many same-sex couples, particularly gay men, wish to engage in prenuptial agreements that circumvent requirements such as alimony.

---

[85] Cheshire Calhoun, *Feminism, the Family, and the Politics of the Closet: Lesbian and Gay Displacement* (Oxford: Oxford University Press, 2000).

[86] Ettelbrick, 'Since When is Marriage a Path to Liberation?' p. 758.

[87] Nancy D. Polikoff, 'We Will Get What We Ask For: Why Legalizing Gay and Lesbian Marriage Will Not "Dismantle the Legal Structure of Gender in Every Marriage"' in *Virginia Law Review* 79(7) (1993) p. 1541.

[88] Franke, *Wedlocked* p. 113.      [89] Franke, *Wedlocked* p. 108.

[90] Franke, *Wedlocked* p. 203.

These prenups may be quite appropriate for the structure of those relationships, if they do not take the traditional gendered form of breadwinner and dependent homemaker, since standard divorce law would lead to an unjust distribution of assets. But their increased use 'risk[s] undermining or weakening the justice-enhancing traditions that women's rights advocates have worked hard to build into marriage'.[91]

Card is another prominent feminist critic of same-sex marriage. She argues that, while it is unjust that marriage is denied to lesbians and gays, the injustice of the institution as a whole means that lesbians and gays should not fight for the right to marry—just as white women should not have fought for the (equal) right to be slave-owners:

Let us not pretend that marriage is basically a good thing on the ground that durable intimate relationships are. Let us not be eager to have the State regulate our unions. Let us work to remove the barriers to our enjoying some of the privileges presently available only to heterosexual married couples. But in doing so, we should also be careful not to support discrimination against those who choose not to marry and not to support continued state definition of the legitimacy of intimate relationships. I would rather see the state *deregu*late heterosexual marriage than see it begin to regulate same-sex marriage.[92]

Similarly, Judith Butler argues that the basic claim for equal civil rights obscures symbolic injustice. 'The petition for marriage rights,' she argues, 'seeks to solicit state recognition for nonheterosexual unions, and so configures the state as withholding an entitlement that it really should distribute in a non-discriminatory way, regardless of sexual orientation. That the state's offer might result in the intensification of normalization is not widely recognized as a problem within the mainstream lesbian and gay movement.'[93] Butler insists that this intensification of normalization is both evident and troubling. The idea that marriage is the only way to sanction homosexuality is 'unacceptably conservative',[94] and the attempt to use same-sex marriage to rectify heterosexism 'brings with it a host of new problems, if not new heartaches'.[95] Butler's worry is that state recognition for same-sex marriage will further delegitimate non-marital relationships and forms of life, an effect that would be particularly troubling for the queer community.

---

[91]  Franke, *Wedlocked* p. 223.        [92]  Card, 'Against Marriage and Motherhood' p. 6.

[93]  Judith Butler, 'Is kinship always already heterosexual?' in *differences: A Journal of Feminist Cultural Studies* 13(1) (2002) p. 16.

[94]  Butler, 'Is kinship always already heterosexual?' p. 21.

[95]  Butler, 'Is kinship always already heterosexual?' p. 26. See also Samuel A. Chambers and Terrell Carver, *Judith Butler and Political Theory: Troubling Politics* (London: Routledge 2008).

Sheila Jeffreys also argues that marriage must be abolished as a legal category since it has inescapably sexist symbolic meanings. According to Jeffreys, 'when lesbians and gay men demand marriage they shore up a foundational practice of male dominance.... I do not think that marriage can be saved and made into a neutral and egalitarian institution that would be open to either heterosexuals or lesbians and gay men.'[96]

Ann Ferguson describes her own situation, in which her Muslim son-in-law convinced his wife (Ferguson's daughter) to prevent their child from seeing Ferguson on the grounds that she was in a lesbian relationship. For Ferguson, '[i]n this and other cases of queer chosen kinship no legal changes by themselves to the structure of marriage will remove the stigma of violating the heterosexual normativity required for legitimate kinship. Only a pluralist culture that accepts the sexual rights of those who deviate from the heterosexual norm will do this.'[97] And Ferguson echoes the worry of theorists such as Ettelbrick and Butler that same-sex marriage may in fact be harmful, by 'creat[ing] a new hierarchy—the socially acceptable gay marrieds versus the queer abjected'.[98] Ferguson's conclusion is not that same-sex marriage can never be compatible with equality, but that there is no necessary correlation between the two, 'and engaging in it may indeed lead to a worse situation in some contexts'.[99] Whether it helps or harms depends on the legal, economic, social, and citizenship status of those who are affected by it. Same-sex marriage is thus a 'morally risky' institution and support for it is always problematic, whether that support is for creating it as a state-recognized institution or participating in it where it exists.

As Halberstam puts it:

So, to summarize: marriage is an agenda forced upon LGBT groups by the widespread opposition to gay marriage, and while some gays and lesbians choose to marry, it's not a cause that lies at the heart of the queer community. Marriage flattens out the varied terrain of queer social life and reduces the differences that make queers, well, queer, to legal distinctions that can be ironed out by the strong hand of the law.[100]

What does this discussion show? Does it show that feminists are hopelessly confused, because they believe that marriage is both bad and good, both liberatory and oppressive, both patriarchal and egalitarian? Or does it show that feminism is

---

[96] Jeffreys, 'The Need to Abolish Marriage' p. 330.
[97] Ann Ferguson, 'Gay Marriage': An American and Feminist Dilemma' in *Hypatia* 22(1) (2007) p. 43.
[98] Ferguson, 'Gay Marriage' p. 48.      [99] Ferguson, 'Gay Marriage' p. 51.
[100] Halberstam, *Gaga Feminism* p. 114.

an incoherent doctrine, a social movement without unity? No. Confusion and disagreement are inevitable features of the human condition, but there is a way to make sense of all the feminist arguments on marriage considered here. Both advocates and opponents of same-sex marriage—those, that is, who are feminist or at least egalitarian—share the view that traditional, different-sex-only marriage is deeply problematic. Egalitarians identify the problem as one of inequality; feminists refine it as patriarchy.

We started with an apparent puzzle. Feminists argue that marriage is oppressive to both its (female) participants and its (lesbian and gay) non-participants. The solution to this puzzle is that marriage, as an institution, just is oppressive. Quite possibly, *if the institution of marriage exists*, it is better to be married than not. Even more plausibly, *if the institution of marriage exists*, it is better to be legally permitted to enter it than to be excluded from it. But the fact that marriage might be the best or only way to securing a variety of social, economic, and legal goods does not undermine the fact that the *very existence of the institution* is oppressive. In other words, it might be that women are better off if marriage does not exist at all; but if marriage does exist they are better off married than unmarried. On this account juxtaposing marriage's oppressiveness to women and to lesbians and gays are two sides of the same coin. Marriage is oppressive to women as compared to a world without marriage. It is oppressive to deny same-sex marriage only insofar as that institution does exist. The common thread is that the existence of marriage oppresses, and its removal liberates.

This analysis fits with some of the examples of oppression just given. The symbolic pressure on women to marry, and the idea that they are worthless if unmarried, means that *if marriage exists* women are better off married than unmarried. This view is compatible, then, with the idea that it is harmful to be denied access to marriage *if the institution exists for others* and confers practical or symbolic benefits. But there is no necessary harm if the state refuses to recognize marriage at all.[101]

The natural implication is that equality is best served if marriage ceases to exist as an institution. Abolishing the institution satisfies all feminist critiques, and is thus a policy implication around which feminists should unite.

---

[101] The European Declaration of Human Rights protects the right to marry, a right which has also been seen as fundamental in US constitutional law. Insofar as the right to marry is a genuine right, it is best understood as the right to form committed partnerships, and to enjoy protection from undue legal interference in those relationships, rather than as a right to have one's marriage recognized as a special and privileged legal status.

## 1.4 Civil Union

Some egalitarians declare that, even if traditional marriage is oppressive, there is room for a reformed, gender-neutral, sexuality-neutral, breaking-with-history marriage—marriage, perhaps, that is named something else. This sort of instinct may explain why many egalitarians who oppose marriage argue in favour of civil unions as an alternative.[102] The ideal of a civil union is the ideal of marriage untainted by patriarchy or religion. Civil unions may be an accompaniment to marriage or a replacement for it; if an accompaniment, they may be available to all (as in France and the Netherlands) or available to same-sex partners only (as in the UK, though this looks set to change in 2019[103]).

Civil unions have two advantages from the feminist point of view: first, they give all couples (including same-sex couples) access to the practical benefits of marriage and second, the idea of a civil partnership breaks away from the patriarchal symbolism of historically-oppressive marriage. Some feminists also argue that same-sex civil partnerships will benefit heterosexual women, whether married or not, by undermining both the hegemony of marriage and the idea that traditional gender roles must prevail within it. Indeed, one way of breaking away from the patriarchal history of marriage might be to offer civil partnerships to all couples regardless of sex. The status of civil partnership would thus be doubly egalitarian: it would emphasize equality between different- and same-sex couples since both could enter into it, and it would emphasize equality between men and women by breaking from patriarchal history and by imposing equal terms on each member of the partnership.

Susan Shell argues that liberals should support a dual regime, with marriage reserved for different-sex couples and civil unions available for same-sex couples. Shell argues that this is a liberal solution because it goes some way towards satisfying both traditionalists and libertarians, and thus captures the liberal requirement of reasonableness, understood as making reasonable accommodation for others' moral commitments. Lesbians and gays should be able to adopt children without prejudice, and to have access to some of the benefits of

---

[102] See, for example, March, 'What Lies Beyond Same-Sex Marriage?'; Sadler, 'Re-thinking Civil Unions'; Thaler and Sunstein, *Nudge*; Polikoff, *Beyond (Straight and Gay) Marriage*; Lawrence Torcello, 'Is State Endorsement of Any Marriage Justifiable?' in *Public Affairs Quarterly* 22(1) (2008).

[103] In 2018 Rebecca Steinfeld and Charles Keidan of The Equal Civil Partnerships Campaign won their case in the UK Supreme Court, with the Court ruling that it is discriminatory for civil partnerships to be available to same-sex couples only. At the time of writing, the Civil Partnerships, Marriages and Deaths (Registrations Etc.) Bill, a Private Members' Bill by Tim Loughton MP, is making its way through Parliament. See http://equalcivilpartnerships.org.uk and *R (Steinfeld and Another) v Secretary of State for International Development* UKSC 32 (2018), 3 WLR 415 (2018).

marriage, but marriage itself should be retained for different-sex couples and defined as a union that 'automatically entails joint parental responsibility for any children generated by the woman'.[104]

But this policy of distinguishing civil partnership from marriage has various disadvantages. If the title 'marriage' is reserved for different-sex relationships the institution of civil partnerships *entrenches* the gendered nature of marriage, since the idea that marriage must be between a man and a woman is reinforced, and with it traditional gender roles and controversial meanings (such as Shell's idea that marriage is defined by procreation). Moreover, the fact that marriage symbolically oppresses lesbians, gays, and bisexuals remains, since the discriminatory and hierarchical distinction between different- and same-sex couples is unchanged if only different-sex couples may marry.

This partly explains why the usual trajectory of legal reform in liberal democracies[105] is as follows:

1. Marriage for different-sex couples only. No recognition of same-sex partnerships.
2. Marriage for different-sex couples only. Civil unions for same-sex couples only.
3. Marriage extended to same-sex couples.
4. Abolition of civil unions.

The move from stage 1 to stage 2 allows the state to extend legal rights to homosexual couples without seeming to undermine the traditional and special status of marriage. After some years of same-sex civil unions, the idea of same-sex marriage gains popular acceptance, and so the state moves from stage 2 to stage 3. Stages 3 and 4 may occur simultaneously but are generally close together. Robert Wintemute calls this the '"Wintemute law of registered partnership laws": they are always, everywhere in the world, introduced primarily to address the absence of any legal recognition of same-sex marriage, *while continuing to exclude them from marriage*, and not to create an alternative for all couples.'[106] He cites South Africa as a notable exception for its introduction of same-sex marriage and civil partnerships for all at the same time in 2006. Another exception is Greece, which

---

[104] Susan M. Shell, '"The liberal case against gay marriage' in *The Public Interest* (Summer 2004) p. 22.

[105] Countries that have progressed through all four stages include Denmark, Iceland, Norway, Sweden, Finland, Slovenia, Ireland, and parts of the USA (Connecticut, Delaware, New Hampshire, Rhode Island, Vermont, Washington State). See Robert Wintemute, 'The Future of Civil Partnerships in England and Wales' presented at The Future of Registered Partnerships Durham-Cambridge Conference (University of Cambridge, 10–11 July 2015).

[106] Wintemute, 'The Future of Civil Partnerships'.

is 'alone in all European countries'[107] in introducing registered partnerships for different-sex couples only.

In some jurisdictions this use of civil unions is quite explicit. In Ireland, for example, Article 41.3.1 of the Constitution expressly stipulates 'The State pledges itself to guard with special care the institution of Marriage, on which the Family is founded, and to protect it against attack.' Brian Tobin argues that the 2015 Marriage Equality Referendum that legalized same-sex marriage in Ireland thereby rendered same-sex civil partnerships unconstitutional, since now they compete with, and undermine, marriage. Ironically, the more popular civil partnerships are the more they violate the constitution.[108]

Questions about the ideal trajectory of reform are interesting but impossible to settle here.[109] It may be that the move to recognize same-sex marriage is an important or even necessary step on the path to equality, since public debates and legal change on this issue play a vital role in galvanizing public acceptance of homosexuality and equal rights. Or, it may be that the move to same-sex marriage is ultimately conservative, silencing calls for universal civil unions or the marriage-free state. Most likely this will be different for different societies. I make no recommendations, then, for the precise path towards the marriage-free state. But I do propose the following ranking of stopping-places.[110] The nearer a society is towards the top of the list, the better.

1. The marriage-free state.
2. Civil unions[111] for same-sex and different-sex couples. No state recognition of marriage.
3. A choice between civil unions and state-recognized marriage for both same-sex and different-sex couples.
4. Marriage for both same-sex and different-sex couples.

---

[107] Dafni Lima, 'Draft National Report: Greece' presented at The Future of Registered Partnerships.

[108] Brian Tobin, 'The Future of Registered Partnerships in the Republic of Ireland' presented at The Future of Registered Partnerships.

[109] For discussion of this issue see William K. Eskridge, Jr, *Equality Practice: Civil Unions and the Future of Gay Rights* (New York: Routledge, 2002).

[110] I am unsure where to place the status quo in the UK: marriage for same-sex and opposite-sex couples; civil unions for same-sex couples only. It might go at position 3.5, because it improves on option 4 by adding the valuable choice of civil union for same-sex couples; or it might go at position 4.5, because it detracts from position 4 by deviating from equality.

[111] In this ranking 'civil unions' is short for 'civil unions or some other well-designed replacement for marriage, such as those statuses based on caregiving and proposed by feminists'. I discuss examples of these alternative statuses throughout the book.

5. Marriage for different-sex couples only; civil partnerships for same-sex couples only.
6. Marriage for different-sex couples only.

Civil unions are better than marriage, then, but they are not the ideal form of regulation for two main reasons. The first is that they still entail *bundling* rights and duties which, as I argue in Chapter 2, is problematic as it does not fit many relationships. The second is that, like marriage, civil unions maintain inequality between partnered and unpartnered people. I explore this inequality in Section 1.5.

## 1.5 Inequality between Married and Unmarried People

The central egalitarian problem with civil unions is that they do nothing to challenge the hierarchy that marriage enacts between being partnered and being single. Thus Celia Kitzinger and Sue Wilkinson argue:

By re-branding as 'civil partnership' a union that is otherwise identical to opposite-sex civil marriage, civil partnerships achieve the symbolic separation of same-sex couples from the state of 'marriage'. They grant same-sex couples the possibility of legal conformity with institutional arrangements which formally recognize heterosexual intimacy while effectively excluding us from that very institution. The irony is that this separation is positively valued by many feminists and LGBT activists because it is the *symbolism* of marriage—and not the civil institution itself—that is the target of their critique.[112]

Lisa Dettmer argues that the gay marriage movement risks exacerbating inequality, not solving it, because marriage is a system for discriminating against the unmarried and because rich people are more likely to be married than poor people. She cites a study by Lisa Duggan which found that the majority of LGBT people in California were not in stable partnerships. However, 'white, wealthy gay men are the most partnered population in California. And, for instance, Black lesbians are the least partnered and the most likely to have children.'[113] The implication is that same-sex marriage is an issue that benefits the already advantaged.

Of course, not every campaign and worthwhile cause is about the very worst off: it is perfectly reasonable for egalitarians to care about equal rights at all stages of an income distribution. But same-sex marriage is not something that simply

---

[112] Kitzinger and Wilkinson, 'The Re-branding of Marriage' p. 144.
[113] Lisa Dettmer (quoting Lisa Duggan), 'Beyond Gay Marriage: the assimilation of Queers into neoliberal culture' at https://www.academia.edu/11879158/Beyond_Gay_Marriage_the_assimilation_of_Queers_into_neoliberal_culture p. 28.

benefits the already-advantaged; it also harms the already-disadvantaged. Indirectly, campaigns for gay marriage took focus and funding away from campaigns and programmes that were crucial to poor LGBT people, such as those providing health care and housing.[114] And Franke suggests that the whiteness of the gay marriage movement helped that cause and did so at the expense of perpetuating:

the negative reputation African Americans suffer when it comes to marriage.... When judges, policy makers, or the media are persuaded that same-sex couples are sufficiently similar to different-sex couples when it comes to marriage, that recognition of shared identity is premised upon the specter of a constitutive outsider that gay couples are not like. And what they are not like is African Americans (even though, of course, many lesbians and gay men are African American).... A conception of marriage as the pinnacle of mature personhood and mutual responsibility is ... saturated with racial and gender stereotypes.[115]

It is worth noting that the existence of tax and other benefits for married couples in some jurisdictions does not simply mean that unmarried individuals cannot access a benefit. If that benefit is a tax break or similar it imposes a measurable *cost* on those who do not receive it, since their tax burden will necessarily be higher than it would be if the benefit did not exist for others. In other words, the move from tax equality to tax breaks for the married cannot be Pareto-optimal: the benefit for the married can be achieved only at the expense of the unmarried.[116]

More directly, marriage itself discriminates against the unmarried. The egalitarian demand for same-sex marriage is a demand for access to the material and symbolic privileges of marriage. Achieving same-sex marriage does nothing to undermine, and may even strengthen, the connection between marriage and benefits that ought to be universal.[117] As Dettmer puts it, 'While marriage is being rewarded, other ways of organizing family, relationships and sexual behaviour do not receive these benefits and are stigmatized and criminalized. In short, people are punished or rewarded depending on whether or not they marry.'[118]

For Polikoff this point can be put simply: '"Couples", meaning two people with a commitment grounded on a sexual affiliation, should not be the only unit that counts as a family.'[119] Polikoff therefore argues for an approach that would value

[114] Dettmer, 'Beyond Gay Marriage' pp. 19–20.    [115] Franke, *Wedlocked* pp. 204–6.

[116] David M. Estlund, 'Commentary on Parts I and II' in David M. Estlund and Martha C. Nussbaum (eds), *Sex, Preference, and Family: Essays on Law and Nature* (Oxford: Oxford University Press, 1997) p. 163.

[117] Card makes this point in 'Against Marriage and Motherhood'.

[118] Dettmer, 'Beyond Gay Marriage' p. 6.

[119] Polikoff, *Beyond (Straight and Gay) Marriage* p. 4.

all families equally, including those headed by same-sex couples, by single parents, and those without children. 'When law makes marriage the dividing line, it harms all unmarried people, including those with children. The harm is the dividing line.'[120]

The problem runs deep. It is not just the symbolism of marriage as founded on heterosexuality that is retained within civil unions, but the practical and symbolic hierarchy between coupled and uncoupled people of all sexualities. Brake terms this privileging of the sexually monogamous committed dyad 'amatonormativity', and argues that 'amatonormative discrimination is wrong for the same reasons that other forms of arbitrary discrimination are wrong':

The similarities between exclusive amorous relationships, friendships, and adult care networks can involve mutual support, intimacy, and caretaking that provide emotional fulfilment and are grounds for moral approbation. But not only do friendships and care networks lack social recognition, their members are systematically subjected to stereotyping and discrimination.[121]

Brake's critique of amatonormativity might lead us to be suspicious of framing egalitarian aims in terms of the family, as Polikoff does: this term, too, might exclude some care and relationship networks that deserve equal consideration.

Brake invokes a variety of non-traditional relationships to highlight the limits of amatonormativity, such as 'urban tribes, best friends, quirkyalones, polyamorists and revolutionary parents'.[122] But it is not just 'alternative' lifestyles such as these that are excluded. In 1971 Mitchell wrote of the range of familiar yet diverse relationship forms that exist but are obscured by the 'monolithic' institution of marriage:

Couples—of the same or of different sexes—living together or not living together, long-term unions with or without children, single parents—male or female—bringing up children, children socialized by conventional rather than biological parents, extended kin groups, etc.—all these could be encompassed in a range of institutions which match the free invention and variety of men and women.[123]

The social significance of these alternative relationship forms can be seen by considering the comparative data on the proportion of children born out of wedlock. This statistic varies significantly by country. In Columbia, Peru, and Cuba the figures are 74 per cent, 69 per cent, and 68 per cent; in China, India,

---

[120] Polikoff, *Beyond (Straight and Gay) Marriage* p. 123.
[121] Brake, *Minimizing Marriage* p. 97.
[122] Brake, *Minimizing Marriage*, p. v.  [123] Mitchell, *Women's Estate* p. 151.

Saudi Arabia, and Egypt the figure is less than 1 per cent.[124] But in Western liberal democracies there is more uniformity, with the proportion of children born out of wedlock generally around the 40–50 per cent mark. In 2017 in England and Wales 48.1 per cent of children were born to mothers who were neither married nor in a civil partnership;[125] in 2017 in the USA 39.8 per cent of children were born to unmarried mothers;[126] in Denmark 50 per cent of children are born out of wedlock.[127] So marriage cannot any longer be described as the normal situation for bringing up children in western liberal democracies.

So, the 'diverse care networks' to which Mitchell and Brake refer are traditional, mainstream, and significant in number. In the USA they are also more prominent in black communities. Franke details how, for African Americans,

the nuclear family has never been the most common way they have arranged their family lives. Instead, black families have tended to be predominately female-headed, and rather than relying upon a single wage earner for financial stability and a single homemaker for domestic stability, they have drawn from a broad network of aunts, grandmothers, close friends, and others to provide support to both mothers and children.[128]

A focus on the married couple as the paradigmatic form of family relationship and the paradigmatic source of stability is, on this analysis, racist as well as sexist.

## Conclusion

In case a reader is unconvinced by the argument to this point, let me offer a final observation. Perhaps you think that it is possible for marriage to be compatible with equality; perhaps you think that some suitably-reformed version can avoid the associations with patriarchy and heterosexism and can avoid (somehow!) being inappropriately biased towards committed coupledom. In that case you might not think that the marriage-free state has been shown to be *necessary*. Or you might not think it yet—there are many more arguments to come. But even at this early stage I hope to have shown that there are reasons for an egalitarian to be

[124] Social Trends Institute, 'The Sustainable Demographic Dividend' at http://www.sustaindem ographicdividend.org. Other countries for which data are provided here include South Korea, Taiwan, Japan, Indonesia at 1–5%; Italy at 18%; Germany and Australia at 32% and 33%; New Zealand at 47% and Sweden at 55%.

[125] Office of National Statistics, *Births in England and Wales, 2017* at http://www.ons.gov.uk.

[126] Centers for Disease Control and Prevention, 'Percentage of Births to Unmarried Mothers by State' at https://www.cdc.gov/nchs/pressroom/sosmap/unmarried/unmarried.htm. Numbers vary widely by state, from 18.5 per cent in Utah to 53.5 per cent in Mississippi.

[127] Ingrid Lund-Andersen, 'Registered Partnerships in Denmark' presented at The Future of Registered Partnerships.

[128] Franke, *Wedlocked* p. 90.

suspicious of marriage, and that alone ought to provide a *prima facie* case for the marriage-free state.

The basic egalitarian case against marriage that this chapter has set out is that it is an institution founded on patriarchy and heteronormativity, that its reform to include same-sex couples does not do enough to make it egalitarian since the very idea of marriage remains rooted in forms of intimacy that are associated with heterosexual and male privilege, and that even a radically-reformed marriage or civil union inevitably brings about inequality between those who are partnered and those who are not. All of these arguments are returned to and strengthened in the book as a whole. Chapter 2 turns to the question of what the state is doing when it engages in the act of *recognizing* marriage. What does marriage mean?

# 2

# Marriage as a Violation of Liberty

[W]hat one is wanting when one wants 'state recognition' for marriage and what one is not wanting when one wants to limit the scope of that recognition for others are complex wants. The state becomes the means by which a fantasy becomes literalized: desire and sexuality are ratified, justified, known, publicly instated, imagined as permanent, durable. And, at that very moment, desire and sexuality are dispossessed and displaced, so that what one 'is,' and what one's relationship 'is' are no longer a private matter; indeed, ironically, one might say that through marriage, personal desire acquires a certain anonymity and interchangeability, becomes, as it were, publicly mediated and, in that sense, a kind of legitimated public sex. But more than that, marriage compels, at least logically, universal recognition: everyone must let you into the door of the hospital; everyone must honor your claim to grief; everyone will assume your natural rights to a child; everyone will regard your relationship as elevated into eternity. And in this way, the desire for universal recognition is a desire to become universal, to become interchangeable in one's universality, to vacate the lonely particularity of the nonratified relation and, perhaps above all, to gain both place and sanctification in that imagined relation to the state.[1]

Traditional marriage violates equality. While marriage can be reformed so as to mitigate some of its inequalities, equality is best served by the abolition of state-recognized marriage. I defended this claim in Chapter 1. It is a claim that has long been made by feminists who criticize marriage for its patriarchal past and present, pointing out that marriage is an institution that oppresses both the heterosexual women it embraces and the lesbians and gays it traditionally excludes.

In this chapter I consider the additional reasons against the state recognition of marriage that derive from considerations that are specifically liberal. Liberals share feminists' commitment to equality, and thus all liberals ought to be troubled by

---

[1] Judith Butler, 'Is kinship always already heterosexual?' in *differences: A Journal of Feminist Cultural Studies* 13(1) (2002) pp. 22–3.

the way that state-recognized marriage undermines equality between women and men, between people of different sexualities, between married and unmarried adults, and between children.[2] Most egalitarian liberals accept that there is something unjust about state-recognized marriage that is open only to different-sex couples, and happily endorse same-sex marriage.[3] As Tamara Metz puts it, liberals tend to 'downplay or ignore marriage's meaning side'.[4] But liberals should oppose the very existence of state-recognized marriage, not just its promotion.

State-recognized marriage can undermine individual autonomy in a way that is problematic for comprehensive liberals such as John Stuart Mill, who notes the troubling similarity between marriage and voluntary slavery.[5] But marriage should also be objectionable to liberals because state recognition of it involves the state endorsing a particular way of life and particular views about what makes life valuable. These views are controversial at best.

Perfectionist or comprehensive liberals have no principled objection to the state promoting particular ways of life, if those ways of life are valuable and therefore can contribute towards autonomous or rational choices. For example Mill argues that 'Human beings owe to each other help to distinguish the better from the worse, and encouragement to choose the former and avoid the latter'.[6] Despite being a staunch critic of the marriage laws of his time he did not believe that abolition was necessary to secure liberty: for him 'nothing more is needed for the complete removal of the evil [of marriage] than that wives should have the same rights, and should receive the same protection of law in the same manner, as all other persons'.[7] He gives no indication that he would be unhappy with the state continuing to recognize and promote marriage if it were equalized in this way.

---

[2] For an argument that specifically liberal equality requires the abolition of state-recognized marriage see Véronique Munoz-Dardé, 'Is the Family to be Abolished Then?' in *Proceedings of the Aristotelian Society* XCIX (1999) p. 53.

[3] For a good example see Martha Nussbaum, *From Disgust to Humanity: Sexual Orientation and Constitutional Law* (Oxford: Oxford University Press, 2010).

[4] Tamara Metz, *Untying the Knot: Marriage, the State, and the Case for their Divorce* (Princeton: Princeton University Press, 2010) p. 48.

[5] John Stuart Mill, 'On Liberty' in *Utilitarianism, On Liberty, Considerations on Representative Government* ed. Geraint Williams (London: Everyman, 1993) p. 172ff. Comprehensive liberals usually deploy arguments about the compatibility of autonomy and commitment in an attempt to salvage marriage. Mill gestures at the importance of legitimate expectations as a reason not to allow marriages to be dissolved at will, but does not seriously consider the idea that marriages should not be formed in the first place. (Mill, 'On Liberty' p. 173.) See also Joseph Raz's defence of commitments such as marriage from an autonomy-prioritizing perfectionist liberal perspective in his *The Morality of Freedom* (Oxford: Oxford University Press, 1998) and discussion in Clare Chambers, *Sex, Culture, and Justice* (University Park, PA: Penn State University Press, 2008) ch. 7.

[6] Mill, 'On Liberty' p. 144.    [7] Mill, 'On Liberty' p. 174.

Similarly Joseph Raz is a perfectionist liberal who argues that the state can and should promote a range of valuable social forms, so that individuals may autonomously choose between them. He explicitly states that marriage is one such valuable social form and that it requires state recognition, such that lesbians and gays are not adequately autonomous if they may only cohabit, not legally marry.[8]

In the book as a whole I hope to show that perfectionist and comprehensive liberals are wrong to endorse state-recognized marriage as compatible with liberal egalitarian autonomy. They are wrong because, as we saw in the last chapter, marriage is an institution with a decidedly inegalitarian tradition and associated meanings, and because even reformed marriage discriminates against the unmarried. This chapter develops the notion of the meaning of state-recognized marriage, and so its arguments are relevant to comprehensive and perfectionist liberals. But the main target of this chapter is political liberals, who endorse neutrality between conceptions of the good. I argue that state-recognized marriage is a violation of political liberal neutrality, and so political liberals in particular cannot endorse it. Nonetheless, I am not a political liberal. Insofar as I am a liberal my liberalism is much more comprehensive than it is political, a position that I have defended elsewhere.[9] My reason for discussing political liberalism here is twofold: first many, perhaps the majority, of contemporary political philosophers who identify themselves as liberal defend a version of political liberalism; and second, I wish to show that political liberals have a particular reason to reject state-recognized marriage.

## 2.1 State-recognized Marriage versus the Marriage-Free State

There are various alternatives to traditional marriage. But the contrast that is significant for political liberalism is not between traditional and reformed marriage, or between marriage and some alternative status such as civil union. Instead, the relevant contrast is between state recognition of any special status for personal relationships, and the piecemeal regulation of the marriage-free state.

Marriage, so-called, is particularly problematic for political liberalism since its traditional status, bringing with it entrenched and controversial views about meaning and value, makes it more fully non-political than alternative statuses such as civil union. Yet even civil union and its equivalents have perfectionist features, which can be seen by contrasting a state which recognizes marriage or

---

[8] Raz, *The Morality of Freedom* p. 206.    [9] Chambers, *Sex, Culture, and Justice.*

civil union with the marriage-free state. In general marriage is a formalized relationship type and status, sanctified or certified by a religion, state, or similar authority. In the rest of this chapter 'marriage' means marriage or civil union or a similar alternative, 'marriage so-called' means a recognized relationship status using the name 'marriage', and 'traditional marriage' means marriage so-called that is reserved for different-sex couples and which may include additional gendered aspects.

The state recognizes marriage in the relevant sense when it provides a bundle of rights and duties to married people because they are married, such that access to those rights and duties requires opting in to marriage.[10] This definition of state recognition has two parts. First, state-recognized marriage gives the members of a marrying couple a *bundle* of rights and duties. For example, depending on the jurisdiction, they may acquire rights to inheritance without tax, next-of-kinship rights, rights to financial support from each other, rights concerning children, and so on, regardless of their particular financial circumstances, their shared understanding of their relationship, or whether they are parents. The rights and duties of marriage include those pertaining to divorce. In many liberal democracies, the rights and duties pertaining to divorce are the most significant aspect of the marriage bundle. Second, these rights are given to the couple *because* they are married, a special status that can only be acquired by *opting in* to it. They do not acquire the rights and duties by choosing each in turn, or because there is some other feature of their relationship that merits them. Under state-recognized marriage a distinction is made in law between couples in functionally identical relationships (with regards to matters such as shared property, parental status, care, and dependency) according to their marital status. Married co-parents may have different rights to unmarried co-parents; married property-owners may have different rights to unmarried property-owners.

The alternative is the marriage-free state. It allows people to engage in private religious or secular ceremonies of marriage, but accords these no legal status. The

---

[10] This idea of state recognition does not exhaust the ways in which a state might take an interest in marriage. A state may also take an interest in marriage by defining and setting limits on it: stating who may and may not enter into a marriage and which procedures must be followed for a relationship to become a marriage. A marriage-free state might refrain from showing this sort of interest in the institution but it is not a requirement of a society counting as marriage-free that it so refrains, for a marriage-free state might take an interest in setting limits on even private marriages, as discussed in Chapter 6.

Another important way the state might interact with marriage is by registering and enquiring about its existence, for example on official forms. A marriage-free state will not do this for any purpose other than monitoring the prevalence of private marriage, or applying such regulations to private marriage as may be required by justice (such as a prohibition on marrying children).

state does regulate key areas of personal relationships, such as those concerning children, shared property, immigration, and next-of-kinship, but does so in a piecemeal fashion. Anyone with children is subject to the regulations concerning children; anyone with shared property is subject to the regulations concerning shared property, and so on.[11] Crucially, such regulation does not operate via a status such as marriage.

In a marriage-free state people who are in relationships still have a set of rights and duties. For example, a couple that shares property or children will have a set of rights and duties concerning that property or those children. However the couple has those rights and duties simply by virtue of sharing property or children. In order to be eligible for rights and duties people must be actually engaging in the relationship practice to which those rights relate. No discrimination is made between the rights allocated to 'couples with children' and those allocated to '*married* couples with children'. To take another example, if there are good normative reasons not to require inheritance tax for transfers between life partners, or between people who share a home, then a marriage-free society will not levy inheritance tax on transfers between *any* life partners, or *any* people who share a home. Moreover, in the marriage-free state there is no assumption that any one relationship attracts a complete bundle of rights. Each relationship attracts only those rights that specifically pertain to its own unique circumstances.

The marriage-free state demonstrates that the state can regulate relationships according to justice, thereby securing desiderata such as gender equality, support for care, and protection for vulnerable parties, without a special status such as marriage or civil union.[12] It is therefore possible for the state to avoid making a problematic legal and symbolic distinction between those who are married or civil partners, and those who are not. As I shall argue, this is to be preferred from the standpoint of political liberal neutrality.[13] The rest of this chapter focuses

[11] The content and form of these regulations is not discussed in this chapter: separate arguments would be needed both to identify each area of state interest and to specify what the just regulations should be. I discuss the format of my proposed regulation in detail in Chapter 5.

[12] The marriage-free state is not the only method for regulating relationships without marriage. Nancy Polikoff provides both a useful analysis of diverse international legal regimes, and a proposal she terms 'Valuing all Families', in her *Beyond (Straight and Gay) Marriage: Valuing All Families Under the Law* (Boston, MA: Beacon Press, 2008). Polikoff's proposal has some similarities with mine, such as the need to apply legal regulations to relationships according to each individual law's purpose; however, her proposal differs from mine in retaining civil partnerships (p. 131ff).

[13] There is a distinction, although not a firm one, between the state *recognizing* a status called 'marriage' and the state *promoting* that status. Above and beyond recognition the state might provide incentives for couples to marry, such as tax breaks or special privileges, or active state promotion of marriage through campaigns or education in public schools. Promotion is a stronger departure from state neutrality than recognition alone, and so will need stronger reasons if it is to be justified. However, the distinction between recognition and promotion is not firm: recognition

not on positive arguments for the marriage-free state (that is the focus of Part II of the book) but on arguing in more detail that political liberals should reject the alternative.

## 2.2 Political Liberalism: Neither Comprehensive nor Perfectionist

For John Rawls and other political liberals, state action must be capable of public justification. Under conditions of liberalism, the burdens of judgement mean that there will be reasonable disagreement about conceptions of the good. In order to achieve the necessary standard of public justification, state action must not be based on a value judgement that makes sense only from the perspective of some particular conception of the good. To put this another way: state action must not be justified by reference to reasons that conflict with some reasonable conception of the good.

This basic tenet of political liberalism can be stated in several different ways. It is common to contrast the *political* nature of political liberalism with the *comprehensive*, and with the *perfectionist*.

Comprehensive liberalism usually refers to a variety of liberalism that is based on claims about what makes a life valuable, or what contributes to human flourishing.[14] According to comprehensive liberals, liberal values such as autonomy and equality are required because human lives that contain them go better than lives that do not. Political liberalism, in contrast, makes no claims about what is valuable in human life. It asserts only that liberal values are required by justice, that they are in some sense the fairest way of adjudicating conflict and ordering society.

The phrase 'comprehensive conception of the good', or 'comprehensive doctrine' (these two are, I think, interchangeable) is an extremely common term in Rawlsiana, and it is natural to think that the term 'comprehensive' means the same here as in 'comprehensive liberalism', and is properly contrasted with the term 'political'. If the term were used in the same way we might say that a conception of the good becomes comprehensive if it concerns itself with matters of human flourishing and the good life. But this definition alone would make a distinction between a comprehensive and a non-comprehensive conception of

---

alone is a form of promotion, since it attaches state approbation to one form of relationship. Thus even recognition alone is a departure from neutrality that can be justified only if political reasons can be adduced.

[14] John Rawls, *Political Liberalism* (New York: Columbia University Press, 1993) p. 175.

the good nonsensical, because any conception of the *good* (as opposed to a conception of the *right*) concerns itself by definition with human flourishing.

This explains why when Rawls defines the phrase 'comprehensive doctrines' he refers not only to the *content* of those doctrines but also to their *scope* or *detail*. For Rawls:

A conception ... is comprehensive when it includes conceptions of what is of value in human life, as well as ideals of personal virtue and character that are to inform much of our nonpolitical conduct (in the limit our life as a whole). ... A doctrine is fully comprehensive when it covers all recognized values and virtues within one rather precisely articulated scheme of thought; whereas a doctrine is only partially comprehensive when it comprises certain (but not all) nonpolitical values and virtues and is rather loosely articulated.[15]

Jonathan Quong, a defender of political liberalism, also emphasizes the importance of scope[16] and emphasizes the significance of the multiplicity of judgements when he writes:

Comprehensive doctrines will have a complete and determinate ordering of judgments. To simplify, we can suppose that for all issues a–z, a comprehensive doctrine will take a position (e.g. either a or –a) and rank these judgments in order of priority. Comprehensive doctrines will thus necessarily conflict or else they will be identical.[17]

So, all conceptions of the good concern human flourishing rather than political values of justice. Every person has a conception of the good just insofar as every person makes any judgement at all about what makes their life, or human life in general, valuable or good. A person's conception of the good becomes fully comprehensive not by including any particular value judgement, but rather by including a great many value judgements; indeed, by including an *exhaustive set* of value judgements.

It is not clear that there are any fully comprehensive doctrines according to this definition. Even a religion, surely the most likely candidate for a comprehensive doctrine,[18] does not 'cover all recognized values and virtues': no religion specifies all matters of aesthetic judgement, for example, such as whether stringed instruments are preferable to woodwind or whether gardening is superior to watercolours. It is not even clear that any or most religions offer guidance on more

---

[15] Rawls, *Political Liberalism* p. 175.

[16] Jonathan Quong, *Liberalism without Perfection* (Oxford: Oxford University Press, 2011) p. 13.

[17] Quong, *Liberalism without Perfection* p. 29.

[18] 'There is a tendency for religious and philosophical conceptions to be general and fully comprehensive; indeed their being so is sometimes regarded as an ideal to be realized.' (Rawls, *Political Liberalism* p. 175.)

mainstream and pressing matters of human flourishing such as whether the arts should receive public funding, or whether the UK should be a member of the European Union, or how to vote in a referendum on Scottish independence.

If there are no truly comprehensive doctrines then the political liberal insistence that liberalism must not rely on such doctrines is rather inconsequential. More problematically, it is unclear what it means to say that some state action is, or is not, based on a comprehensive doctrine. For according to this interpretation what makes a conception of the good comprehensive is not merely the subject-matter or content of its judgements but also the volume of those judgements. Any individual judgement simply lacks its own status as comprehensive or not: it gains that status only by being situated, for some group or individual, alongside other judgements in a fully exhaustive set of judgements.

It follows that the judgement 'in order to have value, a life must include reading the Bible' is not a comprehensive doctrine since it is not in itself a fully articulated, exhaustive doctrine containing judgements on all possible matters. If a person were to hold that judgement as part of a fully articulated, exhaustive doctrine then it would, for that person, be a judgement based on a comprehensive doctrine. But another person might hold only that judgement, in which case it would not be based on a comprehensive doctrine, for this second person's doctrine says nothing about many, many other values or practices (including whether one should attempt to live one's life according to Biblical teachings). In contrast, a person or group that could present a complete and determinate ordering of judgements would thereby have a comprehensive doctrine, even if that doctrine included as its first and most important judgement 'a life goes well if it is lived with maximal freedom'.

For a policy to be ruled out by political liberalism what matters is that the policy should be capable of justification to all those who hold reasonable conceptions of the good. For political liberals this justificatory potential requires neutrality and anti-perfectionism. As Quong puts it, a political liberal will 'avoid making perfectionist judgments and metaphysical claims' and 'will only appeal to values or other moral ideas that do not contradict the claims of any conception of the good life, insofar as that conception is a just one'.[19]

Perfectionism, then, is another contrast to political liberalism. Perfectionism argues that the state should act so as to promote some conception of the good or non-political value. Political liberalism adheres to non-perfectionism, or state neutrality. It does not justify state action by referring to claims about what is valuable or good for people. As the above quote from Quong shows, this means

---

[19]   Quong, *Liberalism without Perfection* p. 14.

that if a policy is to be acceptable to political liberalism it must meet two criteria. It must not be justified by reference to perfectionist judgements about human value. And it must be compatible with all reasonable conceptions of the good.[20]

## 2.3  Marriage as Non-neutral

Marriage can be endorsed by those with a variety of conceptions of the good, since those who endorse marriage can differ over matters pertaining to other values. That is why marriage can be endorsed by people with different religions or none. But it is not a neutral, political institution since it appeals to values that could not be endorsed by everyone with a reasonable conception of the good, and since state recognition of it is necessarily perfectionist.

The simplest way of showing that state-recognized marriage does not meet this test is by showing that there are reasonable conceptions of the good that are incompatible with it.[21] Consider the following examples of reasonable conceptions of the good that are incompatible with state recognition of marriage since they reject assumptions that underpin the special treatment thereby given to marriage:

- *Nonmonogamy*: it is better for a life to contain polyamorous relationships.
- *Bohemianism*: it is better to pursue an unconventional lifestyle with few permanent ties.
- *Feminism*: it is better to reject institutions that are or have been central to patriarchy.
- *Pragmatism*: it is better for a life to contain relationships that are structured in such a way as to best enable the wellbeing of those in the relationship, and this will vary for different people.
- *Celibacy*: a life is better without sexual relationships.

These positions are all reasonable since none of them necessarily conflict with political liberal tenets such as the conception of citizens as free and equal and a commitment to public reason and state neutrality. That is to say, they can all be held in conjunction with anti-perfectionism, since none of them imply that

---

[20] It should be clear by now that whether a conception of the good is reasonable does not depend on whether it is comprehensive: both comprehensive and non-comprehensive conceptions of the good could be reasonable or unreasonable. A conception of the good becomes comprehensive according to its scope; it becomes reasonable according to its adherents' willingness to tolerate other conceptions of the good and to refrain from making perfectionist claims about state implementation of their conception.

[21] This basic neutrality argument against state-recognized marriage is also made by Michael Sandel in his *Justice: What's the Right Thing to Do?* (London: Penguin, 2010) p. 256ff.

legislative preference should be given to their respective value judgements. But they are all incompatible with the state recognition of marriage, because they all conflict with the value judgements inherent to that recognition.

The point is not that a political liberal state must forbid anything that is incompatible with some conception of the good. A political liberal state should permit marriages, without granting them legal status. Nor is it that the state cannot grant official recognition to anything that not all people want to do. The state must recognize parents, for example, in the sense of defining who counts as a parent and stipulating parental rights and duties, even though not all people want to be parents. The point is rather that the political liberal state cannot base its recognition or regulation on *values* that conflict with some reasonable conceptions of the good. So it could not legitimately stipulate that only married or heterosexual people could be parents unless some neutral case for doing so could be found, for example if it were true that only married or heterosexual people could meet the needs of children. This reason, if true, would be acceptable to the political liberal since meeting the needs of children is a value that does not conflict with any reasonable conception of the good. Similarly, the political liberal state could not recognize and assign a status without adequate political justification or public reason. So it could not legislate for who counts as a 'board game player', for example, unless some bizarre political circumstances made such an assignation necessary for justice.

There are three ways[22] in which the state recognition of marriage rests on values which are incompatible with some reasonable conceptions of the good, and therefore violates political liberal neutrality:

---

[22] Potential support for a fourth conflict between state-recognized marriage and state neutrality can be found in Rawls's definition of a 'comprehensive doctrine'. According to Rawls, a doctrine is comprehensive 'when it includes conceptions of what is of value in human life, and ideals of personal character, as well as ideals of friendship and of familial and associational relationships' (Rawls, *Political Liberalism* p. 175). Marriage is nothing if not an ideal of familial and associational relationships: it is a claim that a certain sort of relationship should be considered as uniquely deserving of status and privilege. Of course, state-recognized marriage (once reformed away from its patriarchal excesses) can admit of variety: married couples can have children or not, live together or not, be religiously or racially similar or not, and so on. But this acceptance of variety does not detract from the comprehensive nature of marriage, for marriage cannot exist without a definition of which sorts of relationship may count as marital, and such a definition is inevitably a claim about value in relationships and family life.

There is something odd in this claim that ideals of family life are inevitably comprehensive, since it is at odds with the idea that a doctrine becomes comprehensive by virtue of scope rather than content. A political liberal could, and perhaps should, jettison this claim. I include it here for the sake of completeness rather than by way of offering a decisive objection.

1. *Meaning.* Traditional marriage is a cultural practice that has a particular, profound, weighty, and controversial meaning. Its historical and current significance to many people involves metaphysical and perfectionist claims that can reasonably be rejected by others. These controversial meanings affect any state use of the concept of marriage.

2. *Bundling.* State-recognized marriage allocates a bundle of rights and duties to those who marry. The assertion that this bundle belongs together constitutes a conception of the good life. State recognition of that bundle is inescapably perfectionist and non-neutral.

3. *Hierarchy.* The opting-in requirement of state recognition enacts a hierarchy between marriage and non-marriage, which violates both equality and neutrality.

I explore each in turn in Sections 2.3.1 to 2.3.3.

### 2.3.1 Meaning

Marriage has a social meaning, and this social meaning involves shared assumptions about what marriage typically entails. This social meaning, Ralph Wedgwood argues, is what enables us to communicate about our marital status: when someone says she is married we have a reasonably clear idea about the sort of relationship she means.[23] Of course, not all marriages are the same, and the particular cultural context may give a broad or specific meaning to marriage. Wedgwood suggests that the meaning of marriage in liberal societies involves sexual intimacy, economic and domestic cooperation, and a mutual commitment to the relationship. These principles, although compatible with diversity, are by no means neutral between reasonable conceptions of the good. They therefore invoke a conception of human flourishing that is decidedly non-political.

The non-political nature of the meaning of marriage can be clearly seen by considering conservative objections to same-sex marriage. These do not give public reasons for heterosexual exclusivity, or prioritize the heterosexual exclusivity of political values such as tax and other legal rights. Instead they emphasize the non-political importance of retaining heterosexuality's symbolic hegemony by reserving the word 'marriage' for different-sex couples. So David Gutman argues that the sanctity of heterosexuality means that the state should let 'homosexuals have their special unions, and the civil rights that properly go with them;

---

[23] Ralph Wedgwood, 'Is Civil Marriage Illiberal?' in Elizabeth Brake (ed.), *After Marriage* (Oxford: Oxford University Press, 2016).

but we should not grant those unions the title and sacramental status of Marriage'.[24] Although he does not put it in these terms, Gutman's claim is that there are public reasons for granting equal rights to same-sex couples, but not for doing so via the content-laden, meaningful, non-neutral concept of *marriage*.

Similarly, the statement against same-sex marriage made by the President and Vice President of the Catholic Bishops' Conference of England and Wales declares:

> The roots of the institution of marriage lie in our nature. Male and female we have been created, and written into our nature is this pattern of complementarity and fertility.... [N]either the Church nor the State has the power to change this fundamental understanding of marriage itself. Nor is this simply a matter of public opinion.[25]

This statement of marriage is inescapably perfectionist and metaphysical, appealing as they do to such controversial claims as human nature and the good life. For these Catholic bishops it is not possible to use the term 'marriage' to apply to same-sex relationships without conflicting with the conception of the good.

Note, moreover, that the advocates of these claims are not willing to allow that there are different conceptions of marriage. Gutman does not say, 'Well, there is my sort of sanctified heterosexual marriage, which is what I want to defend and engage in, and then there is an alternative conception of marriage that can be open to same-sex couples and which others can endorse.' The Catholic bishops do not say, 'This is the meaning of *Catholic* marriage, and marriage cannot mean anything else *for Catholics*.' All see marriage as one thing, and see it as vital that its meaning is not diluted by state recognition of same-sex marriage.

This commitment to the word 'marriage' is not confined to those who oppose same-sex marriage. In 2013 the UK Coalition Government passed a bill allowing same-sex couples to marry or enter into civil partnerships. David Cameron, the Conservative Prime Minister at the time, opposed the option of allowing different-sex civil partnerships alongside marriage. Although UK civil partnerships are almost identical to marriage, legally speaking, Cameron argued in Parliament that it was important to protect the term 'marriage' by making marriage the only option for different-sex couples:

> [F]rankly I am a marriage man. I am a great supporter of marriage. I want to promote marriage, defend marriage, encourage marriage, and the great thing about last night's vote

---

[24] David Gutman, 'Against Gay Marriage' in *The American Spectator* (15 June 2010) at https://spectator.org/39416_against-gay-marriage/.

[25] Most Reverend V. Nichols and Most Reverend P. Smith, 'A Letter on Marriage from the President and Vice-President of the Bishops' Conference of England and Wales' in *The Independent* (6 March 2012).

is that two gay people who love each other will now be able to get married. That is an important advance. We should be promoting marriage, rather than looking at any other way of weakening it.[26]

One wonders if Cameron slipped into betraying his ambivalence when talking about any *other* way of weakening marriage, since the implication is that he feels that same-sex marriage weakens the institution, despite his claim to the contrary.

Within the philosophical literature, same-sex marriage has recently been opposed by arguments from what is usually called 'new natural law'. For example, Gerard Bradley argues that state recognition of marriage is based on 'an objective common good'[27] which, for him, is that 'marriage is the morally normative and uniquely appropriate legal context for sexual relations and for children to come to be'.[28] It follows, for Bradley, that homosexual sex is always 'morally wrong' as it 'instrumentalize[s] sex' and lacks the distinctively procreative character that gives marital sex its value.[29] Bradley concludes that same-sex marriage is wrong as it lacks proper marital standing, and that civil unions are impermissible as they undermine marriage by competing with it. Similar arguments are found in the writings of a variety of other new natural lawyers.[30]

For Ann Ferguson, the value-laden nature of marriage plays out as a tension in American values or American national identity. This identity, as she understands it, 'is both heterosexual-family-oriented and individualistic; so, in this sense, there is a conflict of values that gay marriage brings to the fore'.[31] On the one hand, same-sex marriage fits perfectly with the liberal idea of civil rights, individual freedom and pluralism; but on the other hand, marriage is generally understood as doing more than simply providing these rights and freedoms.

---

[26] *Hansard* (6 February 2013) Column 268 Q1 [141634].

[27] Gerard V. Bradley, 'What's in a Name? A Philosophical Critique of "Civil Unions" Predicated Upon a Sexual Relationship' in *The Monist* 91(3/4) (2008) p. 614. For criticism of new natural law see Adèle Mercier, 'On the Nature of Marriage: Somerville on Same-Sex Marriage' and 'Mercier's reply to Lee' both in *The Monist* 91(3/4) (2008); John Corvino, 'Homosexuality and the PIB Argument' in *Ethics* 115(3) (2005); Andrew Lister, *Public Reason and Political Community* (Bloomsbury, 2013); Brook J. Sadler, 'Public or Private Good? The Contested Meaning of Marriage' in *Social Philosophy Today* 26 (2011); Stephen Macedo, *Just Married: Same-Sex Couples, Monogamy, and the Future of Marriage* (Princeton, NJ: Princeton University Press, 2015). Both sides are represented in John Corvino and Maggie Gallagher, *Debating Same-Sex Marriage* (Oxford: Oxford University Press, 2012).

[28] Bradley, 'What's in a Name?' p. 613.     [29] Bradley, 'What's in a Name?' p. 621.

[30] See, for example, Patrick Lee, 'Marriage, Procreation, and Same-Sex Unions' in *The Monist* 91(3/4) (2008); John Finnis, 'Marriage: A Basic and Exigent Good' in *The Monist* 91(3/4) (2008); Margaret Somerville, *The Ethical Imagination: Journeys of the Human Spirit* (Montreal: McGill–Queen's University Press, 2008). For criticism of new natural law see the works cited in note 27.

[31] Ann Ferguson, 'Gay Marriage: An American and Feminist Dilemma' in *Hypatia* 22(1) (2007) p. 40.

As Ferguson puts it, 'the "American way of life" is portrayed as so dependent on our intimate sexual and reproductive choices that private life must be made a public political issue, and wrong choices here are seen to undermine our national identity'.[32]

The fact that the state recognition of marriage necessarily reflects and promotes a significant, substantive, and controversial *meaning* is why it is not enough to simply dismiss the arguments of traditionalists as nonsensical. Some advocates of same-sex marriage claim that it would have no effect on traditional marriage. 'If you're against same-sex marriage,' this argument runs, 'then don't have one.' Martha Nussbaum argues in this way. She considers conservative arguments in favour of traditional marriage and finds them both normatively unappealing and conceptually perplexing:

> [W]hy should it be thought that recognition of same-sex marriage would ruin heterosexual marriages? It is difficult even to identify the logic behind this thought. Is the idea that heterosexuals are so unhappy with the institution of marriage that they will all rush out and choose same-sex unions if they are made available? Surely that is highly unlikely. Or is the idea that in some nebulous way the institution will be degraded or demeaned, made shameful, by contact with that which is shameful? This seems the more likely of the 'defense of marriage' idea, and yet the mechanism by which something 'good' becomes shameful by proximity to something allegedly shameful is reminiscent of the magical thinking involved in disgust, with its core ideas of contamination and contagion.[33]

While I share Nussbaum's normative distaste for these homophobic arguments I do not share her failure to understand their underlying logic. Nussbaum rejects as 'magical' the idea that same-sex marriage would undermine the special status of heterosexual marriage, since she can see no way in which a heterosexual couple's marriage would be affected by other people's same-sex unions. However, once we have recognized the profoundly symbolic nature of marriage, this process is obvious. The very function that marriage serves within both a society and a state is to legitimate and prioritize certain sorts of relationships, to demarcate them as worthy of special consideration, validity and respect. As we saw in Chapter 1, it is this symbolic privileging of marriage that lies behind many feminist critiques of it, since they assert that marriage is shackled to deeply patriarchal gender relations. But if marriage is a symbolic institution it follows that allowing same-sex couples to participate changes the nature of the symbol. The more diversity is permitted within the scope of the privileged institution, the

---

[32] Ferguson, 'Gay Marriage' p. 39.
[33] Martha Nussbaum, *Hiding From Humanity: Disgust, Shame and the Law* (Princeton, NJ: Princeton University Press, 2004) pp. 258–9.

less approbation is reserved for any one particular form. Those couples whose marriages are founded on the belief of the particular sanctity and specialness of the heterosexual couple will certainly find that the meaning of their marriage changes if same-sex marriages are permitted. Indeed, that is precisely the hope of feminists who argue in favour of same-sex marriage: that marriage's traditional oppression of women will be mitigated by the fundamental change in the symbolism of the institution. It is also the fear of supporters of gay rights who oppose same-sex marriage: that marriage has been used 'to redefine what it means to be gay'.[34] Nussbaum may certainly normatively dispute right-wing objections to this symbolic shift, but she should not dismiss them as nonsensical or superstitious.

It follows, then, that state recognition of marriage so-called necessarily conflicts with some conceptions of the good. Insofar as marriage is allowed to remain true to its traditional and patriarchal past, it conflicts with feminist and other egalitarian conceptions. But, if it is reformed, it conflicts with the conceptions of the good of those who revere its traditional meaning, a meaning that they see as sacred and inviolable. As Lawrence Torcello puts it, 'we cannot genuinely imagine any definition of marriage that does not in some sense call upon a comprehensive notion of the meaning of marriage',[35] whether that meaning is a restrictive religious or natural law definition, or the more inclusive definition favoured by advocates of same-sex marriage. This conflict need not worry comprehensive or perfectionist liberals, or non-liberal egalitarians and feminists. But it is fatal for political liberals. The best way to solve this intractable conflict is for marriage and its meaning to cease to be determined, or recognized, by the state.

Now, of course the political liberal state should refrain from enacting policies which rest on values that conflict with conceptions of the good only if those conceptions are *reasonable*. When religions or new natural lawyers want to impose their traditional views of marriage on others via the coercive power of the

---

[34] Katherine Franke, *Wedlocked: The Perils of Marriage Equality—How African Americans and Gays Mistakenly Thought the Right to Marry Would Set Them Free* (New York: New York University Press, 2015) p. 21. Franke argues that this redescription of what it means to be gay is a mixed blessing. The movement for same-sex marriage emphasizes homosexual assimilation, that same-sex couples can and do conform to heterosexual assumptions and family forms. In the USA this shift has brought general acceptance and destigmatization, something that has not happened for African Americans. But this gain, Franke argues, is costly, for it risks entrenching gendered and heterosexist norms at the heart of gay relationships and increasing the stigma of non-conforming behaviour.

[35] Lawrence Torcello, 'Is the State Endorsement of Any Marriage Justifiable? Same-Sex Marriage, Civil Unions, and the Marriage Privatization Model' in *Public Affairs Quarterly* 22(1) (2008) p. 51. One way of seeing the inevitable controversy involved in defining marriage in any particular way is to look at the sociological literature on personal relationships, which contains a number of competing perspectives on the nature of contemporary coupledom and family life. For an overview see Val Gillies, 'Family and Intimate Relationships: A Review of the Sociological Research' (South Bank University, 2003) at http://www1.lsbu.ac.uk/ahs/downloads/families/familieswp2.pdf.

state then they are unreasonable, and the political liberal state must not accommodate them. But a supporter of traditional marriage could argue that marriage should
not be recognized by the state, which would make their conception of it reasonable
and would make state recognition of some alternatively-configured marriage
unreasonable. This is because state recognition of non-traditional marriage
would be invoking the traditional, honorific term 'marriage' in a way that conflicted
with that reasonable traditional understanding. Compare the term 'rabbi'. A
political liberal state should not create and confer a status of 'rabbi' defined as
'people qualified to issue parking tickets' because, although the issuing of parking
tickets is reasonable and within the state's purview, using the term 'rabbi' for that
function conflicts with the reasonable view of Jewish people for whom the term has
a specific, traditional, and honorific meaning. The same is true of marriage.

As Metz argues, '[t]he fact that public use of "the 'm' word" is at the center of
many of today's marriage battles is, therefore, significant' since it demonstrates
the constitutive nature of the institution.[36] When the state uses the concept
of marriage it directly engages with the controversial and non-political question
of what marriage 'really' means. For Metz this makes marriage laws 'hyperconstitutive' as opposed to merely instrumental, 'for meaning cultivation and belief
formation are their integral functions'.[37] On Metz's account only marriage so-called,
as opposed to alternatives like civil union, has this hyperconstitutive feature.
Later in this chapter I question that conclusion. But it is certainly true that there
are particular problems with the state recognizing marriage so-called, since
it thereby summons existing non-political understandings of the term and
maintains continuity with the institution's profoundly patriarchal history and
traditions.[38] The meaning of this traditional cultural practice is not freestanding,
capable of being changed at will. The mere fact that marriage is understood by
many as a thickly metaphysical doctrine makes it problematic for political
liberals; the fact that the institution is traditionally oppressive and hierarchical
adds to the problem.[39] It follows that any form of state recognition that uses the
term 'marriage' is inescapably non-neutral.

---

[36] Metz, *Untying the Knot* p. 93.     [37] Metz, *Untying the Knot* p. 94.

[38] Carole Pateman, *The Sexual Contract* (Cambridge: Polity Press, 1988); Claudia Card, 'Against
Marriage and Motherhood' in *Hypatia* 11(3) (1996); Merran Toerien and Andrew Williams, 'In
Knots: Dilemmas of a Feminist Couple Contemplating Marriage' in *Feminism & Psychology* 13(1)
(2003) p. 434; Richard H. Thaler and Cass R. Sunstein, *Nudge: Improving Decisions about Health,
Wealth and Happiness* (New Haven, CT: Yale University Press, 2008) p. 219; Sheila Jeffreys, 'The
Need to Abolish Marriage' in *Feminism & Psychology* 14(2) (May 2004) p. 330; Polikoff, *Beyond
(Straight and Gay) Marriage* p. 132.

[39] My argument on this point has similarities with that of radical feminist Sheila Jeffreys, who
argues that marriage must be abolished as a legal category since it has inescapably sexist symbolic

It can hardly be disputed that the state recognition of marriage constitutes a value judgement in contemporary liberal societies. Marriage is upheld and recognized not as a merely instrumental status but as a valuable way of life, an important milestone, a celebration, as the earlier quote from David Cameron shows. To be sure, the content of the value judgement can change across time and place: state-recognized marriage need not retain the traditional prioritization of heterosexual monogamous coupledom over alternative relationship and family forms. But even if same-sex marriage is allowed, state recognition still prioritizes coupledom, monogamy, permanence, and sexual relationships.[40] Alternative brandings or versions of marriage may deviate from one or more of these features, but the more they deviate the less they become recognizable as versions of marriage.

Some liberals may find the idea of endorsing committed coupledom personally unproblematic, if such endorsement is uncoupled from the blatantly discriminatory features of traditional marriage. But political liberal neutrality does not allow the state to endorse any conception of the good, however appealing it may seem.[41]

The value judgement inherent in any form of state-recognized marriage has fundamental implications for political liberalism. If there is to be any difference between a committed monogamous sexual partnership and a marriage, it is because the state grants special approbation and symbolic significance to marriages that it denies to other relationships.[42] By defining and maintaining a recognized form of relationship known as 'marriage', rather than simply regulating relationships in a piecemeal fashion as occurs in the marriage-free state, the

---

meanings. According to Jeffreys, 'when lesbians and gay men demand marriage they shore up a foundational practice of male dominance....I do not think that marriage can be saved and made into a neutral and egalitarian institution that would be open to either heterosexuals or lesbians and gay men.' (Jeffreys 'The Need to Abolish Marriage' p. 330.)

[40] For a sustained critique of this feature of marriage, particularly its requirement of monogamy, see Card, 'Against Marriage and Motherhood' and Elizabeth F. Emens, 'Just Monogamy?' in Mary Lyndon Shanley (ed.), *Just Marriage* (Oxford: Oxford University Press, 2004).

[41] Metz puts this point as follows: 'marital status is...recognition intended to alter behavior by altering belief. The conferring authority must represent and defend a comprehensive story about the relationships (between the individuals in the couple and between the couple and the community) that it labels. The public performance of these accounts transforms by enacting, celebrating, and calling for public defense of the shared understandings they express.' (*Untying the Knot* pp. 114–15.) See also the works cited in note 38.

[42] As Thaler and Sunstein put it, 'when people marry, they receive not only material benefits but also a kind of official legitimacy, a stamp of approval, from the state' (*Nudge* p. 218). As Sonu Bedi puts it, 'Marriage is a morally special status. By conferring it, the state takes a side in what ought to be each individual's personal decision about how to live' (Sonu Bedi, *Beyond Race, Sex, and Sexual Orientation: Legal Equality without Identity* (Cambridge: Cambridge University Press, 2013) p. 229).

state endorses some conceptions of the good above others, and does so by appealing to values that some reasonable conceptions of the good reject.

### 2.3.2 Bundling

Controversy about the meaning of marriage might be side-stepped by replacing state-recognized marriage with some alternative status, such as civil union. For example, Andrew March argues that political liberals must reject marriage in favour of civil unions. He starts by assuming that 'it is justified for a [political] liberal state to recognize some forms of domestic partnerships or families in the first place' but provides no argument for this justification, or for the compatibility of political liberalism and such recognition. One argument he gives for preferring civil union to marriage is just as problematic for civil union. March writes, correctly, 'if *all the state offered to anyone* was legal status as a civil union then there could be no complaint of unfairness or disrespect by those offered a status less than marriage.'[43] But even reformed or re-named marriage, though preferable to traditional marriage, violates neutrality since in recognizing it the state endorses a conception of the good and denies endorsement to those who are not in the mandated form of relationship.

Similarly, Torcello writes that since 'to define marriage is always to define it comprehensively' it follows that 'all that can properly be justified by the state in terms of public reason is a civil union in *both* same-sex and heterosexual cases'.[44] But Torcello, like March, does not consider that it is not just the name 'marriage' which makes state recognition of it problematic from a political liberal point of view. He notes that polygamy and incest could be ruled out only if there are 'compelling public reasons'[45] to do so, and he states, rightly, that marriage has metaphysical and comprehensive meanings that do not apply to civil union. But it is not just meaning that makes state-recognized marriage problematic from a public reason perspective. The bundling feature of state-recognized marriage or civil union makes either status a conception of the good: a claim about the sorts of functions and interactions that belong together, and which properly change a relationship between two people into a capital-R Relationship, given an honorary title.[46] As we saw in Chapter 1, this bundling fails to capture many actual relationships, and may be discriminatory in reflecting the relationship practices of some socioeconomic, racial, or cultural groups more than others.

---

[43] March 'What Lies Beyond Same-Sex Marriage?' p. 41.
[44] Torcello, 'Is the State Endorsement of Any Marriage Justifiable?' p. 52.
[45] Torcello, 'Is the State Endorsement of Any Marriage Justifiable?' p. 54.
[46] For a similar critique of bundling see Brake, *Minimizing Marriage*.

State-recognized marriage involves giving a married couple a bundle of rights and duties covering various aspects or practices of a relationship (a) because they are married, (b) regardless of whether the couple does in fact perform those practices, and (c) that do not apply to other relationships that *do* include those practices. This bundling makes sense only from within a conception of the good that assumes that certain relationship practices should go together, and which prioritizes unifying those practices over and above supporting them individually. And the more areas of life are bundled together by the state in the institution of marriage the more controversial, perfectionist, and non-political that state action becomes. For example, in some polities marriages must be consummated or be liable to annulment, a requirement that stems from religious interpretations of marriage and is endorsed by the new natural lawyers. The consummation requirement means that the state stipulates not merely that sex is a valuable part of many relationships, but also that a relationship that is in all other respects identical to marriage does not qualify for recognition and legal protection if it has not also included at least one act of sexual intercourse.[47]

Of course, any particular relationship might bundle together a variety of practices. Such relationships will attract a bundle of rights and duties by virtue of actually combining a number of practices. They do not acquire that bundle by state fiat, though, and it is the state's role in bundling that is problematic for a political liberal.

Some might reply that the state could recognize marriage, or civil unions, as a *convenient but not exclusive* way for people to access bundles of rights and duties. It would not be exclusive since these rights and duties need not be denied to those in unrecognized relationships. There are various options for structuring such a legal regime, but the key point of this proposal is that it would be possible for two couples to have identical legal rights and duties but for one couple to have accessed those via marriage or civil union, while the other accessed them through some other means. This proposal is preferable to traditional marriage. But political liberals should not be happy with this situation either, since in this case the state recognizing some relationships but not others as marriages or civil unions is even more clearly recognition in the symbolic sense: recognition bringing with it approbation. For if there are various ways to acquire rights and duties what else can the state be doing by attaching a special label to one of them?

---

[47]  The introduction of same-sex marriage to the UK in 2014 brought with it an anomaly: without consummation a different-sex marriage is voidable, but the same is not true for a same-sex marriage. For discussion see Jonathan Herring, 'Why Marriage Needs To Be Less Sexy' in Joanna Miles, Perveez Mody, and Rebecca Probert (eds), *Marriage Rites and Rights* (Oxford: Hart Publishing, 2015).

The political liberal state should not be in the business of according some but not all relationships labels that offer approbation and symbolic status, particularly if those labels are traditional and deeply resonant.

### 2.3.3 Hierarchy

State recognition of marriage, or an alternative status such as civil union, means that the state enacts a hierarchy between those with and those without that status. This hierarchy may be both practical and symbolic. It is practical if there is a material difference between those who have and those who lack the relevant status, for example in polities where married couples are given special tax breaks.[48] It is symbolic as the formalized, ceremonial act of naming some relationships and not others gives those named relationships a veneer of state-sanctioned respectability and approbation.

The ceremonial aspect is important here. Marriage is not recognized by the state merely in the sense of the state setting out rules to identify who counts as married; it is recognized by virtue of a formalized, state-run or endorsed ceremony, one that is cast as the celebratory conferral of an honorific status. It is thus unlike other state-recognized statuses which lack ceremonial aspects, such as parent, or those such as felon which do have ceremonial aspects (the court judgment) but explicitly do *not* confer honour.

The opting-in feature of state-recognized marriage or civil union is also particularly relevant. State recognition means that the state withholds certain rights and duties from those who have not opted in to the relevant status, even if their relationships are otherwise identical. This is a problem both for couples who choose not to marry, and for people who are excluded from marriage. Every form of marriage enacts discrimination. Traditional marriage discriminates between heterosexual and homosexual couples, but even reformed versions of marriage discriminate between monogamy and non-monogamy, between sexual relationships and other relationships, between permanent and temporary relationships. This discrimination is made evident by the variety of reasonable conceptions of the good that are incompatible with state-recognized marriage, some examples of which were given above. As Polikoff writes, 'When law makes marriage the dividing line, it harms all unmarried people, including those with children. The harm is the dividing line.'[49] Even a reformed version of state-recognized marriage enacts hierarchy. Such a hierarchy violates both liberal equality and political liberal neutrality.

---

[48] The practical hierarchy enacted by marriage, even if same-sex marriage is allowed, is documented in detail in Polikoff, *Beyond (Straight and Gay) Marriage*. See also Linda McClain, *The Place of Families* (Cambridge, MA: Harvard University Press, 2006) pp. 198–200.

[49] Polikoff, *Beyond (Straight and Gay) Marriage* p. 123.

## 2.4 Political Liberalism and Other Statuses

State-recognized marriage thus violates political liberal neutrality. But it does not follow that the political liberal state cannot recognize *any* forms of status. Marriage and civil union are problematic since they combine the three features of meaning, bundling, and hierarchy. But it is hard to think of another status that combines these features. There are few other state-recognized statuses that have a culturally-privileged and historically-significant symbolic meaning, that provide a bundle of rights and duties, *and* that allow functionally-identical people to choose whether to acquire those rights and duties by opting in, enacting a hierarchy between those who opt in and those who do not.

For example, driving a car brings with it a bundle of duties: to insure one's vehicle, to obey the rules of the road, and so on. But there is no special state-recognized status of 'driver' that one must opt into before these rights and duties apply. Anyone who is driving a car is subject to them. To be sure, the state may stipulate that people who wish to drive must be licensed, and to that extent distinguishes between 'drivers' and 'people (unlawfully) driving'. But people unlawfully driving do not thereby gain an exemption from the rules of the road, or find themselves subject to different speeding limits. So state regulation of 'drivers' is different from state recognition of marriage or civil union, according to which two couples may be in identical relationships except for their marital or civil union status and be subject to different rights and duties for reason of that status alone. It does not enact a hierarchy between 'drivers' and mere people who drive, and it does not constitute claims about driving that conflict with any reasonable conception of the good.

Second, the crucial question for political liberals is always whether a status can be justified by reference to political as opposed to perfectionist or metaphysical values. It may be appropriate for the state to recognize and regulate statuses such as 'judge' or 'politician', and to ascribe bundles of rights and duties to such statuses. Indeed, such statuses may even share the ceremonial naming rituals that add to the non-political nature of marriage. But it is not possible to be a person in a position of judging a court case, or an elected political representative, without being a state-recognized 'judge' or 'politician'. That is to say, no hierarchy is enacted between a state-recognized 'judge' and a non-recognized person judging a court case, because all judges have to be recognized by the state. And the statuses of judge and politician are clearly political in the Rawlsian sense, and the bundles of rights and virtues that the state might stipulate and recognize can be justified by reference to the political roles that judges and politicians play. No reasonable conception of the good conflicts with the idea of a trained and certificated judiciary.

Another example of a state-recognized status that sometimes has a ceremonial aspect is citizenship. In the UK and elsewhere, citizenship ceremonies are offered to new citizens (those who do not have citizenship from birth). These ceremonies may, like civil marriages, be held in public buildings and conducted by public officials. They have a celebratory aspect, including guests, certificates, oaths, and refreshments. In these respects they are very like civil marriages. But the status of 'citizen' is very clearly a political status, and not one that rests on values that are incompatible with reasonable conceptions of the good. Some *particular* conceptions of citizenship might be non-neutral, and so a political liberal state would not include things such as a religious or racial aspect to citizenship. But the mere concept of citizenship is compatible with all reasonable conceptions of the good from a political liberal perspective.

Other statuses, not so intimately bound up with affairs of state, usually lack the ceremonial naming and with it the intimations of value of marriage. Recognition of them is therefore more minimal and functional, and public reasons can be provided for what recognition there is. The reason to recognize the status of 'driver' is not that driving is an inherently valuable activity or that there is some difference between a state-recognized 'driver' and a mere person who drives a car; the reason is that the activity of driving is itself something that requires regulation if it is to be done safely. Similarly, the state sets out grounds on which someone becomes an 'employer' not to confer any particular approbation on that activity, but to ensure that there is a clear allocation of rights and duties with respect to things such as tax and provision of workers' rights: requirements of justice rather than elements of the good life.

No such claims can be made about marriage. Relationships do not need state recognition if they are to be performed safely or in line with justice, and the state does not need to stipulate who counts as being in A Relationship. Of course, some *elements* of relationships require regulation if justice is to be done: there must be laws against domestic violence, laws about distribution of property between partners in case of separation or dispute, laws about children, and so on. Such laws are provided piecemeal in the marriage-free state. But justice requires that these laws apply to all people in the relevant circumstances, not just to married people. There is no justice-based reason for the state to distinguish between married and unmarried people: it would do so only if it wished also to appeal to the specialness of marital status.[50]

---

[50] Rawls suggests that such an appeal could never be fully political since 'the political virtues must be distinguished from ... those appropriate to roles in family life and to the relations between individuals' (Rawls, *Political Liberalism* p. 195).

So far I have argued that marriage is a non-political institution (in the Rawlsian sense, not the feminist sense), one which conflicts with some reasonable conceptions of the good, and one towards which the politically liberal state should therefore be neutral.[51] Section 2.5 questions what the requirements of neutrality are.

## 2.5 Strict and Lax Neutrality

If marriage is non-political and state recognition of it is an act of perfectionism, it follows that a politically liberal state must be neutral with respect to marriage by refraining from recognizing it. However, it is important to note that political liberalism requires not neutrality of *effect* but neutrality of *justification*, a feature Rawls highlights:

Even though political liberalism seeks common ground and is neutral in aim, it is important to emphasize that it may still affirm the superiority of certain forms of moral character and encourage certain moral virtues.... [I]deas of the good may be freely introduced as needed to complement the political conception of justice, so long as they are political ideas, that is, so long as they belong to a reasonable political conception of justice for a constitutional regime. This allows us to assume that they are shared by citizens and do not depend on any particular comprehensive doctrine.[52]

This passage suggests that state recognition of marriage might be acceptable, even though it rests on a controversial conception of the good, as long as it could be justified on grounds separate from that conception.

Similarly, Charles Larmore defends neutrality as follows:

a political decision ... can count as neutral only if it can be justified without appealing to the presumed intrinsic superiority of any particular conception of the good life. So long as a government conforms its decisions to this constraint, therefore, it will be acting neutrally.... Of course, some ends (e.g. the establishment of a state religion) are impermissible, because there can be no neutrally justifiable decision to pursue them. But any goals for whose pursuit there exists a neutral justification are ones that a liberal state may pursue.[53]

---

[51] As Carlos A. Ball writes in connection with same-sex marriage: 'to accept a particular type of human relationship, in a moral sense, is to endorse a particular conception of the good, and this political liberalism cannot do. A legal recognition of homosexual relationships would not only entail toleration of such relationships; it would also constitute a recognition that same-sex relationships are normatively valuable.' It is interesting that Ball does not note that precisely the same is true of heterosexual relationships. (Carlos A. Ball, 'Moral Foundations for a Discourse on Same-Sex Marriage: Looking Beyond Political Liberalism' in *The Georgetown Law Journal* 85 (1996–7) p. 1875.)

[52] Rawls, *Political Liberalism* p. 195.

[53] Charles E. Larmore, *Patterns of Moral Complexity* (Cambridge: Cambridge University Press, 1987) p. 44.

Larmore's account also suggests that policies that appear to prioritize a conception of the good can be compatible with neutrality if another justification can be found. But this strategy seems rather disingenuous. Could we not justify any policy simply by inventing a spurious but neutral justification, when really we are motivated by non-neutral considerations?[54]

Indeed, Rawls seems to think that even the policy of state religion that Larmore rules out could, in principle, be justified on neutral grounds. Rawls writes:

[L]et's consider the question of school prayer. It might be thought that liberal position on this question would deny its admissibility in public schools. But why so? We have to consider all the political values that can be invoked to settle this question and on which side the decisive reasons fall. . . . With some care, many if not all of these arguments [about school prayer] can be expressed in terms of the political values of public reason.[55]

Thus Rawls endorses the idea that political liberalism can support a policy just so long as one can find a justification for that policy that does not rest on a conception of the good or, to put it another way, a justification that is compatible with all reasonable conceptions of the good.[56] This is the process of public reason. The question that arises is just how weighty that justification or public reason needs to be.

Imagine that a society is debating the issue of school prayer. In support of school prayer citizens cannot argue that it is good because prayer is required by God, for that would be a reason based on a particular conception of the good and

---

[54] For discussion of this objection see Micah Schwartzman, 'The Sincerity of Public Reason' in *The Journal of Political Philosophy* 19(4) (2011) pp. 375–98.

[55] John Rawls, 'The Idea of Public Reason Revisited' in his *The Law of Peoples* (Cambridge, MA: Harvard University Press, 1999) p. 165.

[56] I assume that the question of state-recognized marriage would be debated according to public reason at the legislative stage, rather than being one of the constitutional essentials to be decided behind the veil of ignorance. In contrast to this assumption, Ball discusses the question of how marriage might be discussed in the original position. He rather assumes that those in the original position will sanction state-recognized different-sex marriage, but he concludes that they would *not* see the need for state-recognized same-sex marriage as a precaution against finding themselves to be homosexual in a society that recognized only different-sex marriage. Same-sex marriage would not be needed, Ball argues, since '[t]he homosexual citizen . . . is presumably free, in Rawls's conception, to pursue her aims in her non-public life, but cannot bring her sense of identity, value, and morality, as a *homosexual*, into the arena of public reasoning to change those institutions that exclude her'. Ball's remarks echo much of this paper's criticism of state-recognized marriage *tout court*, but the problem with Ball's own account is that it wrongly assumes that the *heterosexual* 'sense of identity, value, and morality' can legitimately inform the original position and that public institutions can legitimately be 'constructed with the assumption that all citizens are heterosexual'. In fact the position of lesbians, gays, bisexuals, and heterosexuals is equivalent: no sexuality can legitimately be assumed, and public institutions cannot justly be instituted based on the value of one form of sexuality rather than another or none. (All quotations from Ball, 'Moral Foundations for a Discourse on Same-Sex Marriage' p. 1890.)

incompatible with many other reasonable doctrines. So other, public reasons must be given, for example that school prayer teaches children to sit still and concentrate. This is a public reason since quiet concentration is a skill that is useful for learning generally, whatever one's conception of the good. To put it another way, the idea that children should learn the skill of sitting still and concentrating does not conflict with any reasonable doctrine.

Assume for the sake of argument that school prayer does indeed teach quiet concentration, but that it does so no better than other activities such as non-religious meditation or listening to classical music. Could a Rawlsian political liberal then endorse school prayer?

The answer to this question depends on how we interpret the neutrality requirement. There are two possibilities.[57] On the first interpretation, which I call *lax neutrality*, a policy counts as neutral between conceptions of the good just so long as there exists some justification for the policy that does not rest on advocating some conception of the good. That justification does not have to be particularly weighty. It simply has to be true. By 'particularly weighty' I mean two things. First, the justification does not have to objectively outweigh other justifications. It does not matter if other groups of deliberators would decide against school prayer and in favour of classical music. Nor does it matter if research were to show that classical music is *better* at teaching quiet concentration than school prayer. School prayer simply has to have some beneficial effect. Second, the justification does not have to be sufficiently strong to overcome any objections associated with the policy's association with a particular doctrine. That is to say, for lax neutrality it is of no relevance if school prayer involves the decidedly non-neutral activity of praying to a particular deity such as the Christian God. As long as there exists some public reason for the policy it is acceptable.

The alternative interpretation, *strict neutrality*, takes a different approach. Strict neutrality starts by noting that school prayer is *prima facie* non-neutral, since it involves an activity that is so closely entwined with a particular conception of the

---

[57] Andrew Lister draws attention to a different way of problematizing the neutrality requirement, via the closely-related idea of public reason. He distinguishes what he calls the coercion model and the reasons-for-action model of public reason. According to the coercion model, all laws must be approved of by all reasonable doctrines, with the default situation in the case of disagreement being no legislation. On this view, 'no institution of civil marriage will pass the test of being acceptable to all reasonable points of view, forcing us to default to not having any such institution' (Lister, *Public Reason and Political Community* p. 25). But Lister prefers the reasons-for-action model, according to which 'public reason's neutrality involves an exclusion of contested premises, not a refusal to adopt any law that some reasonable comprehensive doctrine disagrees with, based on its total balance of reasons'. (Lister, *Public Reason and Political Community* p. 25.) Showing that state-recognized marriage violates public reason on this reasons-for-action model is more tricky, but that is the task I attempt in the remainder of this and subsequent chapters.

good that it involves actively affirming that conception (one is not actually praying unless one is attempting to communicate with and worship God). Strict neutrality thus requires that any acceptable policy on school prayer should have a sufficiently weighty justification. In particular, acceptable policy must have a justification that is weighty enough to overcome that *prima facie* non-neutrality. So, on strict neutrality the fact that school prayer is an activity that involves active affirmation of a particular conception of the good is a hefty strike against it. If school prayer is to be justified overall then some overriding reason will have to be found in its favour: for example, that it is the *only way* of teaching children quiet concentration and that quiet concentration is a vital skill,[58] or that prayer is so much more effective than other methods that the policy can be justified on neutral grounds *all things considered*. According to strict neutrality a policy is legitimate only if the deliberators endorse that policy *and* if it is reasonable for them to conclude that the justifications in support of the policy are sufficiently weighty.

The distinction between strict and lax neutrality can be clearly seen by considering a society in which it had been uncontroversially demonstrated that school prayer does teach quiet concentration, but that it does so less well than non-religious meditation. School prayer in such a society would be compatible with lax neutrality, since there is *a* public reason in favour of it, but it would be incompatible with strict neutrality, since (1) the public reason in favour of school prayer actually tells in favour of meditation and, more importantly, (2) the public reason in favour of school prayer is not strong enough to offset the *prima facie* non-neutrality of the activity.

It is not immediately clear which version of neutrality Rawls endorses, as textual support can be found for both. His discussion of school prayer quoted earlier suggests lax neutrality, since it mentions the possibility of finding neutral reasons in favour of school prayer and suggests that these could be sufficient to justify the policy. If political liberalism does indeed require merely lax neutrality then state-recognized marriage might seem relatively unproblematic for political liberals: it is permissible as long as deliberators who support it can find some arguments that are compatible with public reason and that do not appeal to the non-political value of a conception of the good.

Wedgwood argues that marriage can be compatible with political liberalism, based on lax neutrality. He writes 'marriage is justified simply because, in

---

[58] If quiet concentration were not a vital skill, and if it could be taught only via school prayer, then we might conclude that the end of quiet concentration is itself not neutral and should be abandoned. (After all, if only school prayer could develop it, it is hard to see how it could be useful for many other conceptions of the good.)

societies that had a tradition of marriage, maintaining that tradition can promote the common good. According to this justification, maintaining the institution of marriage promotes the common good simply because marriage does not clearly violate any rights or cause any serious harms, and a lot of people make it part of their fundamental life-aspirations to participate in the institution.'[59] This argument may work insofar as it is confined to marriage as a *social* institution: one that is not recognized by the state. It makes a plausible case, that is, for the permissibility of marriage that is not state-recognized. But as a defence of state-recognized marriage it is weak, as it seems to allow state recognition of virtually any aspect of any conception of the good that is not inherently rights-violating or seriously harmful, merely on the basis that many people endorse it. On this lax neutrality version of political liberalism, there is nothing to prevent established religion, for example. Political liberalism understood in this way loses all distinctiveness.

As befits this conclusion, there are places where it seems more apt to interpret Rawls as advocating strict neutrality. Rawls states that public reason 'imposes very considerable discipline on public discussion' since 'not any balance of political values is reasonable'.[60] And the following excerpt is particularly pertinent to the question of marriage:

the government would appear to have no interest in the particular form of family life, or of relations among the sexes, except insofar as that form or those relations in some way affect the orderly reproduction of society over time.... Of course, there may be other political values in the light of which such a specification would pass muster: for example, if monogamy were necessary for the equality of women, or same-sex marriages destructive to the raising and educating of children.[61]

This passage suggests that the default political liberal position is that the government has 'no interest in the particular form of family life', a statement that seems to close the door on state-recognized marriage. Rawls opens it only on strict conditions: for the state to have a legitimate interest in the form of the family it must be 'necessary' for gender equality, or alternatives must be 'destructive' to children. State-recognized marriage is not permitted merely if it would be somewhat helpful to either cause, and it is important too that (unlike quiet concentration) the goals of gender equality and the protection of children are constitutional essentials, vital requirements for any just society. So this passage suggests strict neutrality: controversial policies which are closely entwined with, derived from and promoting of particular conceptions of the good are justified

---

[59] Wedgwood, 'Is Civil Marriage Illiberal?'  [60] Rawls, *Political Liberalism* p. 227.
[61] Rawls, 'The Idea of Public Reason Revisited' p. 147.

only if *sufficiently weighty* reasons in their favour can be given. Strict neutrality requires the *weighing* of public reasons, not just the *provision* of public reasons.[62]

Regardless of Rawls's own view there is reason to think that strict neutrality comes closer to the aims of political liberalism, for strict neutrality does better at securing reasonable pluralism. If the state were to mandate school prayer, or make important rights and duties contingent on living in and affirming commitment to a specific form and institution of family life, simply because it were possible to find *some* public reason in favour of those policies then the state would be unduly interfering with the legitimate choices people may make to follow alternative conceptions of the good.[63] The goal of the politically liberal state is not to perfect society or the choices of its citizens but to secure justice. Political liberalism's *raison d'être* is that citizens may legitimately be restricted in their conceptions of the good if such restriction is necessary for justice, but not simply because some conceptions are more attractive (from some non-neutral standpoint) than others.

In Chapter 3 I argue that there are in fact no particularly weighty public reasons in favour of the state recognition of marriage. That argument, if correct, is relevant to political liberals who endorse either lax or strict neutrality, but its scope changes depending on which form of neutrality is endorsed. If political liberalism requires merely lax neutrality, then discussion of potential public reasons for marriage would be directed at the deliberators within the process of public reason. However, on this interpretation one could not possibly hope to show that state-recognized marriage is unjust *because it violates neutrality*, although it would still be an unjust violation of equality. That is not surprising: if neutrality is satisfied merely by the availability of some, possibly trivial, public reason then almost nothing will be unjust in the italicized sense.

However, if political liberalism requires strict neutrality, as seems more in keeping with its *raison d'être*, then the absence of strong public reasons for marriage has more significant implications. If the justifications of state-recognized marriage are not particularly weighty, then they will be insufficient to outweigh the *prima facie* non-neutrality of endorsing one particular form of family life.

---

[62] Gina Schouten endorses the idea that political liberalism requires the weighing of reasons and not just the provision of reasons in 'Citizenship, Reciprocity, and the Gendered Division of Labor' in *Politics, Philosophy & Economics* (2015).

[63] Lax neutrality seems open to David Estlund's mischievous objection: 'I cannot help wondering if the face-to-face community of the missionary position has salutary effects on citizen empathy, and whether there might be some ingenious way to discourage other sexual positions through public policy' (David Estlund, 'Commentary on Parts I and II' in Martha Nussbaum and David Estlund (eds), *Sex, Preference, and Family* (Oxford: Oxford University Press, 1997) p. 161).

Therefore political liberals who endorse strict neutrality must conclude that the state recognition of marriage is unjust *because it violates neutrality*.

## Conclusion

I have argued the following:

1. A policy is *prima facie* ruled out by political liberalism when it is a non-neutral perfectionist policy, which is to say when it is not compatible with all reasonable conceptions of the good.
2. The state recognition of marriage is *prima facie* ruled out by political liberalism. It conflicts with various reasonable conceptions of the good, and it does so by virtue of its symbolic and historical meaning, its use of bundling, and the hierarchy it enacts between the married and the unmarried.
3. There are two forms of neutrality: strict and lax. Strict neutrality allows a *prima facie* non-neutral policy only if sufficiently weighty public reasons in its favour can be given. For a public reason to be sufficiently weighty it must be both true and important enough to outweigh the *prima facie* non-neutrality. Lax neutrality sets a lower bar: to reach it, a policy can be justified merely by the presence of some true public reason. Its *prima facie* non-neutrality is no bar.
4. I have suggested but not developed the claim that political liberals should endorse strict neutrality.

If these arguments are correct, the result is that the state recognition of marriage is *prima facie non-neutral*, and thus ruled out by political liberalism. The state recognition of marriage is permissible only if public reasons can be put forward that are sufficiently weighty to overcome this non-neutrality.

Various theorists have recently offered political liberal defences of state-recognized marriage, some of which are considered in the next chapter.[64] Any purported public reasons in defence of state-recognized marriage must meet two demanding criteria. The first is that the purported public reason must be true: there must be an empirically-defensible explanation of why the state recognition of marriage does in fact achieve the goal in question. This criterion is difficult enough to meet on its own, since there is little to no empirical evidence about the

---

[64] See, for example, Brake, *Minimizing Marriage*; Christie Hartley and Lori Watson, 'Political Liberalism, Marriage, and the Family' in *Law and Philosophy* 31 (2012); Wedgwood, 'Is Civil Marriage Illiberal?'

effects or benefits of state-recognized marriage as compared to a marriage-free state. Most accounts of the benefits of marriage are actually benefits of stable, committed, supported relationships. And even advocates of lax neutrality must face this challenge. But this chapter has focused on the second demanding criterion that a public reason-based defence of state-recognized marriage must meet. Advocates of strict neutrality must show that any purported public reason offered in favour of the state recognition of marriage is not only true, empirically, but is also sufficiently weighty to overcome the significant barrier of the non-neutrality of marriage.

# 3

# A Liberal Defence of Marriage?

Various contemporary liberals defend marriage. All liberal defences of marriage must show how state-recognized marriage is or can be compatible with equality, avoiding the critique set out in Chapter 1. Comprehensive or perfectionist liberal defenders of state-recognized marriage also have to show that marriage can be compatible with autonomy: that it sets out an appealing model of the good life without undermining individuality and choice. For political liberals, the form of autonomy that matters is political: they can support recognizing marriage only if there are public reasons for doing so that override its *prima facie* non-neutrality. Their arguments, if successful, should also appeal to perfectionist and comprehensive liberals. But the liberal arguments for state-recognized marriage are not successful, and so liberals should endorse the marriage-free state.

In this chapter I consider five potential liberal justifications of state-recognized marriage, based on communication, gender equality, caring relationships, the interests of society, and children's interests.[1] All of these arguments claim that recognizing marriage will achieve some good for individuals or society as a whole. If they are to work as liberal arguments, they must first show that the good they rely on is in fact supported by public reason and is compatible with autonomy and equality. For political liberal adherents of strict neutrality as defined in Chapter 2, this reason or good must be weighty enough to overcome the *prima facie* non-neutrality of marriage. Second, if they are to be successful, the arguments must show that state action of some kind is an appropriate way of securing the relevant good. Third, they must show that the right form of state action is the state recognition of marriage, and not some other non-conjugal regulation or provision. I argue that none of the proposed liberal arguments in favour of state-recognized marriage meet these criteria.

---

[1] Brook Sadler considers eight different public good arguments in favour of state-recognized marriage; I agree with her that those arguments are unsuccessful. See Brook J. Sadler, 'Public or Private Good? The Contested Meaning of Marriage' in *Social Philosophy Today* 26 (2011).

## 3.1 Marriage as Communicative

For Ralph Wedgwood, it is uncontroversial to state that marriage has a social meaning. For him this meaning essentially consists of assumptions about the marital relationship: it involves sexual intimacy, domestic and economic cooperation, and commitment.[2] Wedgwood argues that transmission of this shared social meaning does not violate liberal principles of neutrality or autonomy, but is instead an important liberal goal. In the following passage he directly defends the state recognition of marriage against an alternative that resembles the marriage-free state:

Without marriage law, married couples would have no such assurance that marriage will have a generally-understood social meaning, let alone that their relationship will be understood in the light of this social meaning. Suppose that individuals were allowed to enter any legally binding contracts that they wished, and non-government organizations (such as churches) were allowed to call any relationship a 'marriage' if they wished, but there were no laws that determined which relationships were marriages and which were not. The risk is that this solution might lead to widespread confusion about what it means to be married.... If we are to be assured that marriage will not cease to have a definite social meaning in this way, then marriage must be insulated from the risk of such confusion; and the most effective way to insulate marriage from this risk is for the law to determine exactly who is married, and to associate marriage with a standard package of rights and obligations.[3]

Wedgwood recognizes that it would be illiberal to *promote* this shared meaning as an ideal. But he argues that marriage can be justified in liberal terms by the fact that 'many people *want* to be married',[4] and this desire deserves respect insofar as it 'furthers a fundamental interest in *mutual understanding*'.[5] Liberals can accommodate people's deep desire to communicate their marital status, that is, because doing so does not rely on 'any controversial ideal of married life'.[6]

---

[2] Ralph Wedgwood, 'The Fundamental Argument for Same-Sex Marriage' in *The Journal of Political Philosophy* 7(3) (1999) p. 229. Wedgwood talks a lot about what 'we' think of as part of the essential meaning, claiming, for example, that heterosexuality is not part of the essential meaning of marriage. One problem with his argument is that many would disagree, so that it is problematic to talk about what 'we' mean by marriage.

[3] Wedgwood, 'The Fundamental Argument for Same-Sex Marriage' p. 233.

[4] Wedgwood, 'The Fundamental Argument for Same-Sex Marriage' p. 235. Emphasis in the original.

[5] Wedgwood, 'The Fundamental Argument for Same-Sex Marriage' p. 236. Emphasis in the original.

[6] Wedgwood, 'The Fundamental Argument for Same-Sex Marriage' p. 234. Endorsements of Wedgwood's argument are found in Andrew Lister, *Public Reason and Political Community* (London: Bloomsbury, 2013), and Stephen Macedo, *Just Married: Same-Sex Couples, Monogamy, and the Future of Marriage* (Princeton, NJ: Princeton University Press, 2015) ch. 4.

However, this argument is weak. Wedgwood does not do enough to establish that the 'risk' of non-communication is sufficiently serious. What will go wrong if people fail to eradicate confusion about whether they are married? Of course, in a society in which marriage brings with it a great many legal entitlements and duties it is important to know exactly who is married, but it would be question-begging to rely on that consideration as a reason to recognize marriage. In the marriage-free state there is no need to identify married people so as to establish legal entitlements. So the communicative ideal that Wedgwood defends must be just that: a desire to communicate a fact about your life to others, even if that fact has no legal implications.

But if the goal is communication about one's life, state recognition of marriage is both too much and not enough. It is *not enough* because telling someone that you are married leaves a whole host of questions unanswered. Is your marriage religious or secular, arranged or romantic, monogamous or open, gay or straight, procreative or childfree, happy or miserable? Just saying 'I am married' does not settle these questions. As Brook Sadler puts it, 'The law prescribes no behaviors…that must be exhibited in order to marry or to stay married. It dictates no requirements for the living arrangements of married people.'[7] The law does stipulate the conditions under which divorce may be granted, but divorces are typically only granted at the request of one or both parties. Adulterous couples, for example, may stay married if they wish. Yet Wedgwood does not describe the status quo as a situation of risky incomprehension.

On the other hand, state recognition of marriage is *too much* to satisfy the communicative ideal. People want to be able to communicate many things about themselves, but that desire neither requires nor justifies a state-recognized status. I might want it to be generally known that I am my children's mother but I do not need proof of state recognition to do that: I can simply tell people. True enough, I have my children's birth certificate as proof if I should need it, but outside the most deeply formal situations I do not need it, just as people never produce their marriage certificate when introducing their spouse in conversation. And people often have to communicate things about themselves without state assistance, relying on mere words or on symbols such as wedding rings. If I want people to know that I am a feminist, or a vegetarian, or an academic, or an only child, I simply tell them. The fact that I cannot rely on the state to endorse my claims is no impediment. My own testimony is adequate. In fact, state recognition is most useful if a relationship does not fit the shared meaning of marriage, for then a claim to be married may be met with scepticism.

---

[7] Brook J. Sadler, 'Re-Thinking Civil Unions and Same-Sex Marriage' in *The Monist* 91(3/4) (2008) p. 580.

Advocates of marriage for communicative reasons sometimes speak to the value of the public communication of commitment. On this account, marriage enables the couple to communicate their commitment to each other, and the ensuing social expectations may help married couples to keep that commitment. For example, a traditional Christian marriage service may include the following words, spoken by the Minister:

Marriage is not something that two people invent, or construct by themselves. It takes a far wider community of family and friends to make any marriage work. Each of you have been invited here today because you are a part of that community. Therefore, having heard _____ and _____ state their intentions to each other and to God in this Service of Marriage, do you, pledge to support their union and to strengthen their lives together, to speak the truth to them in love, and with them to seek a life of love for others?
The people (or the congregation) shall answer: Yes, we do.[8]

Once again, however, the state recognition of marriage is both too little and too much for this purpose. It is too *little* for the purpose of the communication of commitment because state-recognized marriage necessarily brings with it the possibility of divorce. The necessity is two-fold: first, a liberal state must include the possibility of divorce if it is not to be unacceptably restrictive and oppressive; second, since the most salient legal rights and duties attained on marriage are those pertaining to divorce, the state necessarily regulates marriage with an eye to its impermanence.

On the other hand, state recognition of marriage is too *much* for the communication of commitment since, as the Christian example shows, state recognition is not necessary for marriage to retain its strong normative connection to commitment. The symbolic aspects of public commitment can be maintained by religious and cultural expectations of married couples, and the legal aspects of public commitment can be maintained by contractual and other mechanisms of relationship regulation.

Wedgwood might reply that people *like* to know who is married and for people to know this fact about them, and this consideration is enough. Some people certainly do like that, but others do not. Men are generally not harmed by people knowing their marital status, but then it is also relatively easy for men to conceal their marital status since men customarily do not change their name or their title on marrying, and many married men do not wear a wedding ring. Women's marital status is much more public. In the simplest interaction with others in any remotely formal setting they must clarify whether they are Miss or

[8] 'A Christian Wedding Ceremony: Traditional Version' on GodWeb.org at http://www.godweb.org/marriage3.htm.

Mrs (I have recently been asked this question when buying furniture from a local business, when returning faulty merchandise to a major retailer, when making a medical appointment, and in communication with my child's school.) In the 1970s feminists promoted the use of a new title, 'Ms', to avoid this problem.[9] It was an important move and its adoption by feminists and others contributes to the cause of gender equality. However, its use is still unusual in many contexts.[10] Changing one's name on marriage, and wearing a wedding ring, is still the norm for women. But women have not been helped by this ability easily to communicate their marital status; on the contrary, discrimination against women on grounds of marital status was until recently legally sanctioned in employment and service-provision, and it remains salient.[11]

Stephen Macedo takes it as an argument in favour of same-sex marriage that he finds it 'not only awkward, but demeaning and embarrassing'[12] to have to explain that his same-sex life partner is not his business partner when purchasing joint insurance policies or bank accounts. If he were married, Macedo implies, he would not face that problem since he could ask for a bank account for himself and his husband. But couples who chose not to marry would still have to ask for a

---

[9] See Wendy Atkins-Sayre, 'The Emergence of "Ms." As a Liberatory Title' in *Women and Language* 28(1) (2005).

[10] See Paul Baker, 'Will Ms ever be as frequent as Mr? A corpus-based comparison of gendered terms across four diachronic corpora of British English' in *Gender and Language* 4(1) (2010). For discussion of controversy around the term 'Ms' see Anna Browning, 'Mrs? Or is that Ms, Miss?' on BBC News (20 March 2009) at http://news.bbc.co.uk/1/hi/7952261.stm. *The Economist* style guide dismisses Ms as 'an ugly title' in http://www.economist.com/styleguide/t#node-21532475.

[11] Legislation prior to the UK Sex Discrimination Act of 1975 had not prevented discrimination on grounds of marital status, and marriage bars were frequently in place dismissing women from their jobs upon marriage. In the UK many marriage bars were lifted during World War I but replaced afterwards; they were enforced in many industries including the Civil Service and the teaching profession. (Kate Murphy, 'A Marriage Bar of Convenience? The BBC and Married Women's Work 1923–39' in *Twentieth Century British History* 25(4) (2014).) In the USA marriage bars were common until 1950. (Claudia Goldin, 'Marriage Bars: Discrimination Against Married Women Workers, 1920s to 1050s' NBER Working Paper No. 2747 (1988).) Discrimination against married women and women of childbearing age continues, despite being illegal in the UK, with some employers choosing not to employ women who are likely to have children, which often means married women. A recent government study found that a quarter of employers thought they should be allowed to ask a woman about her plans to have children at a job interview; a quarter of women had been asked at interview whether they had young children and felt that this often affected their chances of getting a job. (Equality and Human Rights Commission, 'Pregnancy and Maternity-Related Discrimination and Disadvantage' BIS Research Paper No. 235 (2015) p. 67. Available at http://www.equalityhumanrights.com/sites/default/files/publication_pdf/Pregnancy-and-maternity-related-discrimination-and-disadvantage_0.pdf.) For discussion of three studies showing that being married disadvantages women employees but advantages male employees see Alexander H. Jordan and Emily M. Zitek, 'Marital Status Bias in Perceptions of Employees' in *Basic and Applied Social Psychology* 34 (2012). See also Kira Cochrane, 'You're fired' in *The Guardian* (23 April 2008) at http://www.theguardian.com/money/2008/apr/23/worklifebalance.discriminationatwork.

[12] Macedo, *Just Married* p. 139.

bank account for themselves and their partners and risk confusion. Would that be demeaning and embarrassing for them? Insofar as the awkwardness is the result of the lack of marital status, it is shared by all unmarried couples, gay or straight, and recognizing same-sex marriage will only worsen the situation. Insofar as the awkwardness is peculiar to same-sex couples, it surely stems from public expectations of heterosexuality rather than from the lack of same-sex marriage.[13] Being able to refer to one's partner as one's spouse would not erase any demeaning or embarrassing heteronormativity. Indeed, Katherine Franke notes that legal acceptance of same-sex marriage does not always translate into public acceptance or the elimination of homophobia, such that a gay couple 'may be at greater physical peril in many places identifying as "husbands" than if they did so as "partners"'.[14]

In any event, at least the explanation that Macedo is required to give is pertinent to the transaction: is a business or personal account required? Not so for the compulsory declarations of marital status repeatedly required of women. Women have for decades found it demeaning to have to reveal their marital status in order to enact a transaction not remotely relevant to that status.[15] In the marriage-free state anyone *could* refer to their partner as their husband or wife if they felt, like Macedo, that doing so was preferable. But the pressure to identify one's marital status would be lessened by the lack of state recognition.

Finally, Wedgwood is far too blasé about the existence of a *shared* social meaning of marriage. It is essential to his argument that what marriage means is uncontroversial and thus legitimate for liberal recognition. He refers repeatedly to what 'we' believe to be, or what 'intuitively' counts as, the essential meaning of marriage. Thus he claims that the essential core of marriage is that it is a relationship 'characterized by sexual intimacy, domestic and economic cooperation, and so on',[16] and that the existence of couples who do not live in that way is understood as an exception to the essential core that does not undermine it. On the other hand, Wedgwood claims that it is *not* part of the essential core of marriage that it is between one man and one woman, even when it is legally

---

[13] Is it just as awkward or embarrassing for an opposite-sex couple to have to explain that they are life partners rather than business partners in similar circumstances? If not, then the problem lies with heterosexism rather than the absence of marriage; if so, then the problem will continue for unmarried people, straight and gay, even after the recognition of same-sex marriage.

[14] Katherine Franke, *Wedlocked: The Perils of Marriage Equality—How African Americans and Gays Mistakenly Thought the Right to Marry Would Set Them Free* (New York: New York University Press, 2015) pp. 58–9.

[15] See, for example, Myf Warhurst, 'Mrs or Miss: why do forms require women reveal their marital status?' in *The Guardian* (8th April 2015).

[16] Wedgwood, 'The Fundamental Argument for Same-Sex Marriage' p. 230.

defined in that way. But the most casual perusal of the debate on same-sex marriage shows us that there simply is no claim about the essential meaning of marriage that is uncontroversial, certainly not the claim that the essential core of marriage does not include its heterosexuality. As Martha Fineman puts it, marriage has 'as many meanings as there are individuals entering (or not entering) the relationship'.[17]

The same mistake is made by Macedo, who spends Part 1 of his book *Just Married* detailing the myriad objections to same-sex marriage and their prominence in American political and legal debate, but then writes in Part 2 that 'it does not seem wrong to speak of a common conception of marriage'[18] which same-sex marriage does not challenge. Macedo is quite right to point out that there is a widely-held understanding of marriage that happily includes same-sex couples, but his own work shows that he is wrong to take this as an unproblematically 'common' or 'baseline' conception.[19] He worsens his case when he advocates marriage for its ability to communicate a wide range of social meanings, over and above those associated with civil partnership:

The core of a case for a law of civil marriage recognizes ... that marriage here and now has widely understood social meanings. No other relationship has the same social meaning: domestic partnerships, civil unions, and other options have unclear social meanings, and that could be exacerbated if we introduce a great deal of variety of marital and partnership forms. Status relations are public and defined in advance of our entering into them, and so, by entering, individuals can assume serious commitments of a particular and widely understood sort.[20]

As Susan Moller Okin urges us to consider in another context, 'Whose traditions? Which understandings?'[21] If marriage means something over and above civil partnership does it mean the gendered division of labour, the unhappiness of wives, the second shift performed by working women, the gendered pay gap? Does it mean, as Susan Maushart puts it, 'His marriage [or] Her marriage?'[22]

---

[17] Martha Albertson Fineman, 'Why Marriage?' in *Virginia Journal of Social Policy & the Law* 9 (1) (2001) p. 242 n. 5. Fineman gives various examples of the meanings of marriage, including 'a legal tie, a symbol of commitment, a privileged sexual affiliation, a relationship of hierarchy and subordination, a means of self-fulfillment, a societal construct, a cultural phenomenon, a religious mandate, an economic relationship, a preferred reproductive unit, a way to ensure against poverty and dependency, a romantic ideal, a natural or divined connection, a stand-in for morality, a status, or a contractual relationship.' (Fineman, 'Why Marriage?' p. 242.) For extensive critique of the idea that marriage has some clear or uncontested meaning see Elizabeth Brake, *Minimizing Marriage: Marriage, Morality, and the Law* (Oxford: Oxford University Press, 2012) ch. 6.
[18] Macedo, *Just Married* p. 90.   [19] Macedo, *Just Married* p. 90.
[20] Macedo, *Just Married* p. 91.
[21] Susan Moller Okin, *Justice, Gender, and the Family* (New York: Basic Books, 1989).
[22] Susan Maushart, *Wifework* (Bloomsbury 2001) p. 3. For Maushart, 'His marriage still works. And Hers doesn't' (p. 3).

If we assess the communicative argument for state-recognized marriage we see it fails on all three criteria set out earlier. First, the wish to communicate one's relationship status to others could be a public reason, in the sense that people may want to communicate and this does not rule out any reasonable conception of the good. However, it is not clear that the *state* can set any meaning of marriage which could be communicated without relying on a conception of the good, and so state definition of marriage for the purposes of communication does not look like something that can be supported by public reason. Moreover, the desire to be able to communicate the nature of one's relationship using just one word is not particularly weighty, so the goal of communication is insufficiently important to overcome the objections to the institution. Indeed, there are reasons to object not just to marriage but to the ease of communicating one's relationship status: for some people, usually women, the need to communicate one's relationship status through title and ring or other symbol can be discriminatory.

Second, there is no reason to think that state action is needed to enable us to communicate important things about our lives, since we are able to communicate many significant things without relying on state recognition and since people do not generally need to produce their marriage certificates in communication. People could refer to their spouses in a marriage-free state just as they do in a marriage regime. And third, there is no reason to think that the state recognition of marriage, in particular, fulfils the communicative goal, since it leaves many facts about the marital relationship obscure and does not help with communication about significant but non-marital relationships.

## 3.2 Marriage and Gender Equality

The next liberal defence of state-recognized marriage appeals to gender equality, the pursuit of which is a legitimate part of justice for all egalitarians, including political liberals, comprehensive liberals, and feminists. The gender equality argument for marriage can take a moderate or radical form. The radical form suggests that we could design a re-branded version of marriage with strongly egalitarian requirements for family life. Various models for radically egalitarian marriage exist in feminist thought and legal practice, including Okin's idea that 'both partners should have *equal legal entitlement* to all earnings coming into the household',[23] regardless of the breadwinner's willingness to share; Nancy Fraser's Universal Caregiver model according to which both women and men should

---

[23] Okin, *Justice, Gender, and the Family* pp. 180–1.

combine paid and care work;[24] Joan Williams' argument that the standard of living enjoyed by both households created by a divorce should be the same;[25] and the Swedish model of parental leave which provides for a portion of leave that may be used only by fathers, so as to encourage a more egalitarian division of parenting.[26] While not the intention of their authors, proposals like these could be used as part of a radical programme of marriage promotion, aimed at encouraging people to enter marriage and then forcing or strongly pressuring them to live equally once they got there.[27]

The moderate version of the gender equality argument for marriage appeals not to thorough-going egalitarian living but to the more modest goals of limiting vulnerability and discrimination. Thus Christie Hartley and Lori Watson argue that political liberals can support state-recognized marriage so as to undermine discrimination against same-sex couples and so as to protect people, usually women, who are made vulnerable by the breakdown of a traditionally gendered relationship.[28] Their argument from discrimination is that, in societies containing deep-seated homophobia which may be bolstered by religion, state recognition of same-sex marriage can be a powerful statement of equal citizenship and anti-discrimination. Hartley and Watson note that this effect is neither certain nor necessary: it could be that 'privatizing marriage could promote equality by removing the legitimacy-conferring power of state recognition'.[29] As we saw in Chapter 1, there is a significant debate within the gay rights movement as to whether same-sex marriage is helpful or harmful to that cause. Nonetheless, in some societies the journey to the marriage-free state may be smoothest if it goes via same-sex marriage, and in such societies it may be counter-productive to abolish state-recognized marriage as soon as it is extended to same-sex couples. Chapter 1 suggested a hierarchy of stopping-places en route to the marriage-free state, and noted that societies may need to progress at different rates.

---

[24] Nancy Fraser, 'After the Family Wage: A Postindustrial Thought Experiment' in her *Justice Interruptus: Critical Reflections on the Postsocialist Condition* (London: Routledge, 1997).

[25] Joan Williams, *Unbending Gender: Why Work and Family Conflict and What To Do About It* (Oxford: Oxford University Press, 2001) p. 233.

[26] Williams, *Unbending Gender* p. 236.

[27] This argument was put to me by Andrew Williams; another version of it is found in Jonathan Rauch, who argues that marriage is 'unmatched' in its ability to stabilize and settle young men, preventing them from committing violence. Unfortunately Rauch mentions only marriage's role in reducing the violence that men perpetrate on other men, failing to note that marriage may make it easier for men to act violently towards women. See Jonathan Rauch, *Gay Marriage: Why it is Good For Gays, Good For Straights, and Good For America* (New York: Henry Holt, 2004) p. 20.

[28] Christie Hartley and Lori Watson, 'Political Liberalism, Marriage and the Family' in *Law and Philosophy* 31 (2012).

[29] Hartley and Watson, 'Political Liberalism, Marriage and the Family' p. 204.

Hartley and Watson's argument from vulnerability starts with the fact that the traditional gendered division of labour, according to which men specialize in wage-earning and women specialize in unpaid care-giving, leaves women economically dependent and limits their autonomy. Hartley and Watson note that some people choose to live according to a gendered division of labour because they adhere to a reasonable doctrine which upholds gendered norms of family life. They argue that state recognition of such marriages can provide safeguards for women who would otherwise be vulnerable. They suggest various reforms of marriage law which could have this effect, including some of the more radical feminist proposals just mentioned.

As Hartley and Watson recognize, existing marriage does not do a particularly good job of protecting the vulnerable, in that it tends to satisfy the needs of those who are vulnerable because they are in need of care only at the expense of those who are vulnerable because they provide the care. As Martha Fineman puts it:

The market assumes an unencumbered worker and is structured accordingly, punishing those who cannot conform. The state assumes self-sufficiency on the part of the family, punishing those adults who do not conform. Society mandates the traditional, role-defined, marital family form. Even with the best of egalitarian intentions, marriages tend to slip into traditional and gendered patterns. Even the best single mother is viewed as inadequate. Within society, caretakers are required, but caretakers need resources, including time, money, energy, and accommodation from the workplace. The roles of head of household and dependent wife-caretaker provided both nurturing and economic resources. They did so, however, through the unpaid appropriation of the wife's labor—initially and most directly through the imposition of caretaking obligations to her husband and children.[30]

To Fineman's critique we might add that the gendered division of labour also prevents the breadwinner from receiving the benefits and fulfilment of participating fully in family life.

Fineman's argument, and those of many other feminists,[31] emphasizes that marriage cannot be the sole or even the central medium for rectifying gender inequality. An egalitarian division of labour within a marriage cannot succeed if work and welfare are not compatible with significant caring responsibilities. Most jobs require an ideal worker, able to attend for hours longer than a child can be at school or flourish without parental attention. In countries like the USA and the UK there is little or no welfare provision for stay-at-home parents: parents must either return to work, leaving their children with others, or rely on a

---

[30] Fineman, 'Why Marriage?' pp. 270–1.
[31] For example Williams, *Unbending Gender*; Fraser, 'After the Family Wage', Okin, *Justice, Gender, and the Family*.

breadwinning partner.[32] In the UK proposals to remedy this situation, even those from left-of-centre parties, revolve around the provision of extra childcare rather than legislation to allow for more flexible working or the provision of state support for full-time carers.[33] Focusing on marriage to bring about gender equality of this sort misses the main limitation to it, which is outside rather than inside the family. As Williams puts it:

exclusive reliance on the redistribution of family work has proved a failure.'... As long as employers are free to marginalize anyone who does not perform as an ideal worker, and the ideal worker is defined as someone with immunity from family work, most men feel as if they have little choice to resist demands to share equally in household work.... Contemporary proposals need to recognize that gender redistribution cannot work in isolation.[34]

The central problem with bringing about gender equality via marriage, though, is not that it will not work. The central problem is that even if it works, it will work only for married women.

The moderate and the radical versions of the argument deploy different levels of equality. Proponents of the moderate argument are trying to secure the basic equality that is a fundamental requirement of equal citizenship. They want women to be able to enter relationships and take on caring responsibilities without suffering economic dependence that leaves them unable to leave their partners, or economic disadvantage that wrongly subordinates care to breadwinning. But this sort of equality should be secured for all regardless of marital status.

To put it another way: it is sometimes argued that marriage is necessary, because without marriage women are left vulnerable. In many jurisdictions that do recognize marriage it is true that a partnered woman who does not work outside the home is much more vulnerable if she is unmarried. In England and Wales, for example, if she were married she would be entitled to a share of the family property and income after divorce; if she is unmarried she is entitled to

---

[32] For discussion and critique of the situation in the UK see Mothers at home Matter at http://www.mothersathomematter.co.uk; the Coalition government required single parents on benefits to look for work from the point that their youngest child turned five, reduced from age seven, and Prime Minister David Cameron discussed his aim to reduce it still further. See 'David Cameron's welfare speech in full' in *The Telegraph* (25 June 2012) at http://www.telegraph.co.uk/news/politics/david-cameron/9354163/David-Camerons-welfare-speech-in-full.html.

[33] See, for example, the Labour Manifesto for Women 2015, which proposed to 'support women and men to better balance work and care' by increasing childcare provision, including providing wraparound care from 8am to 6pm, and allowing parents to transfer their unpaid leave to grandparents, but *not* by increasing welfare support for stay-at-home parents or requiring employers to allow flexible and part-time work. http://action.labour.org.uk/page/-/150414%20women%27s%20manifesto%20final.pdf.

[34] Williams, *Unbending Gender* p. 235.

nothing and is dependent on her partner's goodwill and the survival of the relationship. If ending the state recognition of marriage meant levelling down to the position of the unmarried in these societies, then it would be wrong to end the state recognition of marriage. The right thing to do, though, is to level *up*: to ensure that those protections that currently exist for married women and men are extended to *all* women and men who are left vulnerable by relationships.

The content and structure of marriage undoubtedly does make a difference to women's status. Lídia Farré analyses studies from many countries around the world. She shows that marital practices and structures, such as dowries, residence with the husband's family, polygamy or monogamy, and brother/sister paired marriages, make a significant difference to issues such as economic equality, women's education, and domestic violence.[35] So if marriage is recognized by the state, careful attention should certainly be given to ensuring that it is at least maximally-compatible with gender equality.

The proponents of the radical argument go further and suggest that marriage could be used to bring about a greater level of gender equality, one that brings about a revolution in family life or even moves beyond gender. But this argument is problematic for all egalitarians. It cannot work as a public reason for political liberals, because for them the gendered division of labour inside the family is a matter of reasonable disagreement. Rawls states that political liberals 'cannot propose that the equal division of labour in the family be simply mandated, or its absence in some way penalized at law for those who do not adopt it'[36] since the equal basic liberties require that people are free to choose an unequal division.[37] Tax breaks and symbolic privileging of marriage do constitute penalties for the unmarried, so the recognition of only radically egalitarian marriage is ruled out. Advocates of the radical argument who are feminist or comprehensively liberal may be unconcerned about the state promoting radical equality. But these theorists should not be satisfied with tying gender equality to marital status, as was the case with the moderate argument.

Gina Schouten offers an intriguing argument that the political liberal state ought to incentivize lifestyles containing comprehensive liberty and equality,

---

[35] Lídia Farré, 'The Role of Men in the Economic and Social Development of Women: Implications for Gender Equality' in *The World Bank Research Observer* 28(1) (2013).

[36] John Rawls, 'The Idea of Public Reason Revisited' in his *The Law of Peoples* (Cambridge, MA: Harvard University Press, 1999) p. 162.

[37] S. A. Lloyd proposes three different unequal divisions of household labour that may reasonably seem just from the participants' perspectives, and argues that Rawlsian political liberalism, with its commitment to neutrality and toleration, cannot prevent families from arranging themselves in such ways. S. A. Lloyd, 'Situating a Feminist Criticism of John Rawls's *Political Liberalism*' in *Loyola of Los Angeles Law Review* 28 (1994–5) p. 1340.

if without such incentives there will not be a critical mass of people living those lifestyles.[38] On her analysis, that critical mass is needed so as to keep the possibility of *changing* one's conception of the good genuinely open in people's minds, something that is a basic requirement of political liberal citizenship. This argument, though promising, does not provide grounds for incentivizing egalitarian relationships via marriage, since marriage is already adequately modelled and need not instantiate either comprehensive freedom or equality. Indeed, what Schouten's analysis calls for is precisely the modelling of those conceptions of the good that do not follow strong social institutions. Her argument endorses incentivizing the unusual, the bespoke, not the traditional and communal. So the state could, if her argument is correct, incentivize egalitarian relationships—but it should incentivize them across the board rather than only via marriage. Schouten suggests various policies that could work for a variety of non-marital relationships, including 'family leave initiatives, work time regulation, and substitute dependent care provisions'.[39]

It would be possible, then, to introduce radically egalitarian legislation, or protection for vulnerable care-givers, that did not apply only to married couples, and this marriage-blind option is vastly superior. Tying egalitarian regulation to marriage leaves inequality and vulnerability intact for the unmarried. Equality is better served by the default regulation of the marriage-free state.

So, the argument for gender equality meets at most two of the three criteria for a liberal defence of marriage. First, the concern to secure gender equality of the moderate sort is certainly a valid public reason, one that is compatible with equality and autonomy, and one that is weighty enough to override the non-neutrality of marriage. The more radical proposals will be convincing to many comprehensive liberals but go too far for political liberals to endorse (which is one reason that I am not a political liberal). Second, it is appropriate to use the state to secure gender equality, certainly of the moderate form, since this is a basic requirement of justice. But, third, state-recognized marriage is not the appropriate form of state action, since it leaves the unmarried behind even though gender inequality affects them too.

## 3.3 Marriage and Care

Fineman argues that the most pressing issues of gender inequality within the family are no longer those associated with conjugality but those associated with

---

[38] Gina Schouten, 'Citizenship, reciprocity, and the gendered division of labor' in *Politics, Philosophy & Economics* (2015).
[39] Schouten, 'Citizenship, reciprocity, and the gendered division of labor' p. 13.

the family more broadly: 'motherhood is the real "gender issue"'.[40] The gendered division of labour is most keenly felt with the onset of motherhood and other caring responsibilities, since these require sacrifices of resources and autonomy. These sacrifices are most usually made by women; when they are made by men they suffer the same disadvantage.[41] Since dependency is universal and inevitable, so too is caring. In other words, we cannot tackle the disadvantage associated with caring by trying to eliminate care and dependency: the liberal idea that the human condition is characterized by autonomy is a myth.[42] Fineman thus argues that what she calls the 'obsession with the marital tie' should be replaced with a focus on care, and recommends ending the state recognition of marriage.[43]

A number of feminist liberals endorse this focus on care. Some of them advocate the state recognition of relationships based on care. For Tamara Metz, the legitimate role of the state is to protect caring relationships, and she recommends replacing marriage with what she calls Intimate Care-Giving Union (ICGU) status.[44] ICGU status is not like marriage in that it is not based on conjugality, but it is like marriage in that it is based on the state recognition of a particular relationship status. I discuss this general strategy, and Metz's specific proposals, in more detail in Chapters 4 and 5.

In this chapter I focus on Elizabeth Brake's work, since she argues that the fact that caring is the legitimate interest of the state requires a reformulation of marriage rather than its abandonment. Her account is particularly interesting because it is a defence of what she calls 'minimal marriage' that is based on political liberalism. I endorse a great deal of Brake's account, including her thorough and powerful critique of traditional marriage and her diagnosis of the ways in which it violates political liberalism. Minimal marriage would be a great improvement on the status quo, and Brake and I agree on many specific policy issues. However, I disagree with her claim that state recognition of even minimal marriage is the best way of securing equality and autonomy, and that disagreement is the focus of the discussion that follows.

The 'central idea' of Brake's account 'is that individuals can have legal marital relationships with more than one person, reciprocally or asymmetrically, themselves determining the sex and number of parties, the type of relationship

---

[40] Fineman, 'Why Marriage?' p. 255.    [41] Fineman, 'Why Marriage?' p. 256.

[42] Martha Albertson Fineman, *The Autonomy Myth* (New York: The New Press, 2004).

[43] Fineman, 'Why Marriage?' p. 271. I discuss Fineman's own proposals in Chapter 4.

[44] Tamara Metz, *Untying the Knot: Marriage, the State, and the Case for their Divorce* (Princeton, NJ: Princeton University Press, 2010).

involved, and which rights and responsibilities to exchange with each'.[45] The only restriction on which relationships may count as marital relationships is that they must be *caring* relationships.[46]

Earlier in the book I defined state-recognized marriage as constructing a *bundle* of rights and duties and requiring people to *opt in* to marriage to receive that bundle. Minimal marriage dispenses with bundling[47] but maintains the opt-in requirement: rights and duties are allocated to people only if they marry. Third parties (such as employers or insurers) must provide benefits to all married people but not to unmarried people in otherwise identical relationships. Brake does not take a stance on what the minimal marriage rights should be since that depends on social context, but she suggests:

[T]he best candidates for such rights, in an ideal egalitarian society, would include eligibility for spousal immigration, employment and relocation assistance, and preferential hiring (currently offered to U.S. military and civil service spouses and by some private employers), residency (where relevant for in-state tuition, etc.), hospital and prison visiting rights, bereavement or spousal care leave, burial with one's spouse in a veterans' cemetery, spousal immunity from testifying, and state designation for the purpose of third parties offering other benefits.[48]

Minimal marriage therefore contrasts with the marriage-free state in that the former maintains a system whereby a significant number of rights and duties depend on whether a relationship has been designated as (in some sense) marital, a designation that requires both individual consent and state approbation.

Brake argues that political liberalism not only permits but also *requires* state recognition of minimal marriage: contractualization or abolition of marriage is inadequate.[49] She does so by arguing that care and caring relationships meet the Rawlsian definition of a primary good,[50] so that 'supporting caring relationships

---

[45] Brake, 'Minimal Marriage: What Political Liberalism Implies for Marriage Law' in *Ethics 120*, no. 1 (January 2010) p. 303; and Brake, *Minimizing Marriage* p. 157.

[46] Brake, 'Minimal Marriage' p. 305; and *Minimizing Marriage* p. 158. Other theorists have defended versions of marriage based on the importance of care, but Brake's account is particularly relevant since it is explicitly premised on political liberalism. Other defences of care-based forms of relationship regulation are found in Metz, *Untying the Knot*; Mary Lydon Shanley, *Just Marriage* (Oxford: Oxford University Press, 2004), Maxine Eichner, 'Marriage and the Elephant: The Liberal Democratic State's Regulation of Intimate Relationships Between Adults' in *Harvard Journal of Law and Gender* 30 (2007).

[47] Brake, *Minimizing Marriage* p. 161.

[48] Brake, *Minimizing Marriage* p. 161. She argues that an ideal egalitarian society would dispense with other aspects of marriage law, such as tying health care and income to marital status (pp. 162–3).

[49] Brake, *Minimizing Marriage* p. 162.

[50] John Rawls, *Political Liberalism* (New York: Columbia University Press, 1993) pp. 75–6.

is an important matter of justice . . . a law performing the functions of designating, recognizing, and supporting caring relationships is justifiable, even required'.[51]

One ambiguity is whether the relevant primary good is care, or caring relationships, or social recognition of those relationships. *Care* is clearly a primary good—after all, no one can survive childhood without receiving care, and adults periodically require care throughout their lives. *Caring relationships* also make sense as primary goods: while it is possible for children to survive if brought up in impersonal orphanages such childhoods are sub-optimal at best.[52] Moreover, as adults we gain enormous sustenance from caring relationships, and most conceptions of the good require at least some caring relationships. Brake offers a sustained defence of the importance of caring relationships, and I happily accept her arguments.[53] But caring relationships could be primary goods without *state recognition* of those relationships being a requirement of justice, so further argument is needed.

In general justice is concerned with social primary goods and the social bases of those goods, so it might be thought that state-recognized marriage is the social basis of the primary good of caring relationships. But Brake needs to show that state action is an appropriate way to secure the social good of caring relationships, *and* that the state should do this by recognizing a specific status rather than by securing piecemeal rights as in the marriage-free state. To do this, Brake suggests a test for prospective marriage entitlements: 'Can it be justified as essential to support a caring relationship? Is it normally needed, in current circumstances, to sustain such relationships? It is needed in special circumstances to allow day-to-day contact and relationship maintenance?'[54]

The first requirement, that a marriage right should be *essential* to support a caring relationship, will be hard to meet. People can certainly have the primary good of care and caring relationships without being married, for otherwise everyone who is currently unmarried would lack these primary goods, and therefore would lack the moral powers of citizens and be unable to frame, revise, and pursue a conception of the good. That would be implausible. So state recognition of relationships, whether in the form of traditional or minimal marriage, cannot be *essential* to secure the primary good of caring relationships, and it cannot be right to say that political liberalism *requires* such recognition.[55]

---

[51] Brake, 'Minimal Marriage' pp. 305–7.

[52] See Sara J. Morison, Elinor W. Ames and Kim Chisholm, 'The Development of Children Adopted from Romanian Orphanages' in *Merrill-Palmer Quarterly* 41(4) (October 1995).

[53] Brake, *Minimizing Marriage* p. 173ff.      [54] Brake, *Minimizing Marriage* p. 163.

[55] There are lots of things that the state could do to make it easier for people to get into caring relationships, but it cannot be a *requirement* of justice that the state provide things like subscriptions

What of the weaker claim, that state recognition might be the best way—or simply a permissible way—of securing a primary good? After all, care is such an important part of human life, and carers and caring relationships can so easily suffer vulnerability and inequality, that it might well be appropriate to support them with state action even if such support is not strictly necessary for their survival, and that is the point of Brake's second and third clauses.

Consider the sorts of social arrangements that are beneficial to caring relationships. They include a lack of legal restrictions on relationships, time in which to form them, and the freedom to stipulate things such as the identity of one's next-of-kin and who may visit one in hospital. Some such arrangements are not in the state's domain at all. For example, it is easier to sustain a caring relationship with a partner if that relationship is accepted and endorsed by one's family of origin. But even state recognition of controversial marriages (such as same-sex or inter-faith marriages) cannot ensure that they are endorsed or accepted by the families of the married couples.[56]

Nevertheless, Brake is right to suggest that state action may be the best practical way of supporting some aspects of caring relationships. Some social arrangements that are helpful to caring relationships are matters in which the state can make a significant difference. For example, the state could require hospitals to grant visitation rights to certain people, or employers to extend care-friendly benefits to employees. State action is the only way of ensuring universal provision of such benefits. Moreover, some social arrangements supporting caring relationships can be provided only by the state, such as immigration rights and the lack of legal restrictions on forming relationships.

Brake is right, then, that state action in support of caring relationships is permissible and sometimes necessary. But all the state-secured social arrangements necessary to securing the good of caring relationships could be protected by a regime of piecemeal rights that made no reference to marriage, as in the marriage-free state. I discuss the regulatory regime of the marriage-free state in

---

to dating sites, therapy to help resolve commitment issues, beauty treatments or gym memberships to increase attractiveness to potential partners. The most obvious way to avoid the implication that such things are requirements of justice is to stipulate that the social bases of the primary goods, the things whose distribution must be secured by justice, must be those things that are essential for realizing the good in question. Since marriage is not essential to caring relationships state recognition of it cannot be a requirement of justice. Of course, this does not rule out Brake's idea that things that are merely helpful to caring relationships could be endorsed by the state, such as emotional education in schools (*Minimizing Marriage* p. 184). A political liberal could endorse such policies if they met the test of public reason. But they would not be requirements of justice.

[56] This fact is also problematic for Hartley and Watson's argument, discussed in Section 3.2, that state-recognized marriage is a way of countering discrimination in private marriage.

detail in Chapter 5, but to give an outline: visitation rights in hospitals could be secured by rights to freedom of association and privacy. Generic anti-discrimination law could be applied to employers' provision of benefits. Rights to time off for caring relationships could be secured either by giving all employees rights to additional discretionary time off work, or by stipulating the sorts of activities that give rise to entitlements (those connected to care). The marriage-free state does not depend on any particular constellation of rights and duties; its key feature is that whatever rights and duties there are do not depend on a pre-registered state-recognized status.

Brake's use of the term 'minimal marriage' and her defence of it as a 'distinctive legal category'[57] indicate that she wants the state to recognize a specific status that people either have or lack. She envisages a form for prospective spouses, on which people 'tick off boxes to indicate the rights they chose to transfer to another person or persons'.[58] On this interpretation one would be allowed time off to care for a sick partner, for example, only if one had married that partner and acquired the relevant marital right. Brake does specify that 'individuals can have legal marital relationships with more than one person, reciprocally or asymmetrically, themselves determining the sex and number of parties, the type of relationship involved, and which rights and responsibilities to exchange with each'.[59] So individuals would be free, one supposes, to allocate 'caring for when sick' rights and responsibilities to one's partner, one's neighbour, one's child, and one's favourite aunt. But casting these responsibilities in terms of 'marriage' is not helpful.

There are several problems, and these help us to see the general problems with the opting-in requirement of state-recognized relationships. First, requiring people to marry in order to acquire rights leaves people vulnerable to unexpected events. What if one has not (yet) married one's partner when she becomes sick and in need of care? A generic right to a certain amount of time off to care for the sick would cover this situation, but a minimal marriage right would not. Second, if the exchange of rights and responsibilities can be asymmetrical and plural, why does it make sense to think of them in terms of marriage? Surely they are better conceptualized as rights belonging to an individual *qua* individual, rather than rights belonging to relationships. Indeed, there are many cases where calling an asymmetrical right a 'minimal marriage right' just sounds wrong. Consider

---

[57] Brake, 'Minimal Marriage' p. 308. Brake implies that the only alternative to marriage as a distinct legal category is the contractualization of marriage; I show in Part II of this book that this is not the case.

[58] Brake, *Minimizing Marriage* p. 163.    [59] Brake, 'Minimal Marriage' p. 303.

visitation rights, for example. I might quite sensibly want to be visited in hospital by my religious leader, my massage therapist, or my doula, without those people wanting to be visited by me in return. Such rights are best cast as rights to freedom of association and privacy than as rights of marriage. It would not seem right to describe myself as even minimally married to these people. But if visitation rights can be secured by neutral rights of freedom of association or some other basic liberty why not allow me to grant visitation rights to my partner and my family members on precisely the same grounds?

As previously noted, Brake's minimal marriage dispenses with the bundling aspect of state recognition since participants can choose to exchange only some of their marital rights. This feature makes minimal marriage more compatible with neutrality than other forms of marriage, and it is for this reason that Brake argues that minimal marriage is the most extensive form of marriage that can be justified within political liberalism.[60] I agree with Brake on that count: more-extensive-than-minimal marriage violates political liberalism, as I argued in Chapter 2. Yet three aspects of even minimal marriage remain non-political and thus problematic for political liberals: first, it is called 'marriage'; second, criteria are imposed on what may count as a marriage; and third, a distinction is made between marriage and non-marriage.

First, the name. Brake recommends, though does not insist,[61] that minimal marriage be called marriage. As she puts it: 'Nomenclature matters: political resistance to calling same-sex unions "marriages" is often an attempt to deny them full legitimacy.'[62] She is right that nomenclature matters, but I draw from this fact the opposite conclusion to Brake's. Marriage is a term that is sullied by its exclusionary and oppressive past. Keeping the term signifies continuity with that past: Brake's very idea that 'minimal marriage' signifies a needed *change* in marriage demonstrates that it remains, at heart, still marriage. And the term 'marriage' brings with it the deeply non-neutral idea of a form of relationship that has specific, unique value.[63] Brake recognizes this problem, and suggests various

---

[60] Brake argues: 'Public reason implies that a legal framework for adult relationships should not endorse an ideal of relationship depending on a comprehensive doctrine—but this is just what the monogamous ideal of marriage, gay or straight, is.' (Brake, 'Minimal Marriage' p. 320; see also p. 323.) See also Brake, *Minimizing Marriage* p. 167ff.

[61] Brake modified her position on nomenclature between 'Minimal Marriage' and *Minimizing Marriage*, becoming open to the possibility of replacing 'marriage' with an alternative term such as 'personal relationships'. See Brake, *Minimizing Marriage* p. 186.

[62] Brake, 'Minimal Marriage' p. 323; see also Brake, *Minimizing Marriage* p. 86.

[63] See Andrew F. March 'What Lies Beyond Same-Sex Marriage? Marriage, Reproductive Freedom and Future Persons in Liberal Public Justification' in *Journal of Applied Philosophy* 27(1) (2010) pp. 40–1.

solutions, but she notes that it remains somewhat intractable: 'On the one hand, to rectify past discrimination, the symbolism of legal marriage must be strong enough that recognizing the marital status of same-sex relationships and networks has a corrective effect. On the other hand, the symbolism should not be so strong that children or adults outside minimal marriages face stigma!'[64] Ending the state recognition of marriage scores much better on both counts.

Second, criteria for marriage. Brake herself would accept that even the term 'minimal marriage' denotes special value since not all relationships qualify. Brake stipulates that relationships can be recognized as minimal marriages only if they are caring and non-unilateral. Brake allows for minimal marriage rights to be exchanged asymmetrically, but the relationship itself must have a two-way element: parties must be 'known personally to one another, share history, interact regularly, and have detailed knowledge of one another'.[65] Given the range of rights that are to be categorized as marriage rights, this requirement seems overly restrictive: why should I not grant visitation rights or next-of-kin status to the adult child whom I see rarely and who tells me little about her life?

Moreover, while it is possible for individuals to sustain meaningful relationships with many people Brake insists there is a limit: Hugh Hefner cannot marry 'his top fifty Playmates', nor may 'a hundred cult members marry'.[66] Minimal marriage is a mechanism for supporting the primary good of caring relationships, not a libertarian free-for-all. But the problem with this otherwise sensible restriction is that it involves the state in continuing to make judgements about which relationships truly are caring ones. Brake accepts that 'should a surprisingly large number of people genuinely sustain caring relationships, there is no principled reason to deny them distributable benefits such as visiting rights'.[67] But if such relationships are to be distinguished from those such as Hefner's, the state will have to engage in assessing whether someone seeking marital rights has the status of caring relationship member or Playmate. It is hard to see how the political liberal state that Brake envisages could do this while respecting the dignity and privacy of citizens and remaining neutral between conceptions of the good.[68]

Third, by maintaining a hierarchy between minimal marriage and other relationships, Brake's policy maintains an inequality between married and unmarried people and their children. As well as being problematic in itself this inequality may actually make it harder for people to access the primary good of a

---

[64] Brake, *Minimizing Marriage* p. 187.       [65] Brake, 'Minimal Marriage' p. 310.

[66] Brake, 'Minimal Marriage' p. 310.       [67] Brake, 'Minimal Marriage' p. 310.

[68] Indeed, among the relatively few writers who confront the tension between state-recognized marriage and liberalism, the most common criticism of marriage is its violation of privacy. For one example see Metz, *Untying the Knot*.

caring relationship, if that relationship is not designated a marital one. Some people may not wish a particular caring relationship to become a state-recognized minimal marriage. People might have all sorts of reasons for not wishing their relationships to become state-recognized minimal marriages, such as a principled opposition to the very concept of marriage and its place in state policy, or simple uncertainty about whether a particular relationship is (yet) one they wish to commit to in this way. These caring relationships will not receive the state support that Brake insists is necessary.

Overall, state-recognized marriage is not supported by a concern for care. As with the argument from gender equality, at most two of the three criteria are satisfied. The first criterion is satisfied: although there are some conceptual complexities there are grounds for categorizing care and caring relationships as primary goods, important enough to override neutrality concerns, so that justice does require enabling them, public reason can endorse supporting them, and perfectionists should value them. We can also grant the second criterion: state action can legitimately be used in the service of care. Once again, though, the third criterion is not satisfied. Caring relationships do not require state-recognized marriage (as opposed to state action of some other sort) to survive or flourish, and supporting care by recognizing marriage has a number of problems.

## 3.4 Marriage and Society

In order to protect its status as such, a liberal society must have certain features. Most fundamentally it must include the conditions for creating citizens with a sense of justice. William Galston insists that this requirement justifies the liberal state not only in recognizing but also in promoting marriage. He argues that the very survival of liberal democracy depends on 'the character of its citizens and leaders', and appeals to empirical evidence to support his claim that '[t]he erosion of the two-parent family structure...threatens to generate a growing subset of the population that cannot discharge the basic responsibilities of citizenship in a liberal democracy'.[69] Married parents, he argues, are the best at bringing up children who are 'prepared—intellectually, physically, morally, and emotionally—to take their place as law-abiding and independent citizens'.[70] It follows for Galston that the liberal state has a legitimate interest in promoting

---

[69] William Galston, 'The Reinstitutionalization of Marriage: Political Theory and Public Policy' in David Popenoe, Jean Bethke Elshtain, and David Blankenhorn (eds), *Promises to Keep: Decline and Renewal of Marriage in America* (London: Rowman & Littlefield, 1996) pp. 272–3.
[70] William Galston, *Liberal Purposes* (Cambridge: Cambridge University Press, 1991) p. 285.

policies that encourage people to marry. On Galston's analysis the relevant policies must 'bolster marriage by increasing the practical advantages it offers and by reinforcing its moral standing'.[71] He thus suggests changes such as tax regimes that incentivize marriage, laws making it harder for couples with dependent children to divorce, and an 'intensive campaign' to promote marriage to both adult citizens and children in schools.[72]

Galston's account is interesting because it is a profoundly conservative policy programme justified on terms that are meant to appeal to liberals. However, the account cannot sustain the toleration essential to liberalism. Suppose it were true that liberal democracy depended for its survival on a certain sort of citizenry, and suppose that it were also true that this sort of citizenry depended on 'intensive' state promotion of a certain family structure. Such a society, one where intensive state promotion and recognition of heterosexual monogamy were required in order for the citizenry to have the basic competencies required for liberal democracy, would be a society which simply could not be just.

There must be limits on a liberal state. A state could not be liberal if it *coerced* individuals into marrying, for such coercion would itself violate justice. So a society which could maintain a competent citizenry only by coercing its members into marrying would be a society that simply could not be just.[73] Of course, even a liberal state will have to engage in some coercion in order to secure justice: laws may coercively require citizens to pay taxes and to refrain from various forms of criminal activity, for example. But coercively requiring marriage would be unjust since requiring citizens to participate in a particular family form would amount to requiring them to participate in a particular comprehensive doctrine, thus violating their equal basic liberties.[74] The 'intensive' state promotion of marriage that Galston calls for is at odds with the fundamental ideals of political liberalism,

---

[71]   Galston, 'The Reinstitutionalization of Marriage' p. 283.

[72]   Galston, 'The Reinstitutionalization of Marriage' p. 287.

[73]   Nancy Rosenblum makes a similar point when she points to 'Laurence Tribe's rhetorical question about the prohibition of polygamy in *Reynolds*: If monogamous marriage as a support of democracy was at stake, why not order the marriage of priests and nuns?' (Nancy L. Rosenblum, 'Democratic Sex: Reynolds v. U.S., Sexual Relations, and Community' in David M. Estlund and Martha C. Nussbaum (eds), *Sex, Preference, and Family* (Oxford: Oxford University Press, 1997) p. 67.)

[74]   Linda McClain offers a liberal feminist version of the argument from citizenship promotion in her *The Place of Families: Fostering Capacity, Equality, and Responsibility* (Cambridge, MA: Harvard University Press, 2006). The crux of her argument is that the liberal state 'has an important responsibility to carry out a formative project of fostering persons' capacities for democratic and personal self-government' (p. 15). However, while she defends marriage as an important part of family law, her arguments focus on the importance of '(f)amilies and other institutions of civil society' in general (p. 15). But of course neither marriage nor even committed couples exhaust the realm of family and so, just as with Galston's work, the connection between fostering citizenly capacities and the state recognition of marriage is rather weak.

and a society that needs such intensive promotion is surely one in which citizens lack a sense of justice and reject reasonable pluralism, and in which pluralism and toleration cannot exist. And if the need is not so pressing then, as David Estlund puts it, '[u]nless limitless improvement of citizens, as citizens, is required to avoid the collapse of political life altogether . . . then a liberal political philosophy will be led, on principle, to prefer something like privacy to most opportunities for making better citizens'.[75]

Another argument that marriage promotes social goods and contributes to the character of a liberal society comes from Macedo, who calls himself a liberal. He is best described as a perfectionist liberal or possibly a conservative (his views on marriage are very similar to those of Conservative former UK Prime Minister David Cameron quoted in Chapter 2).[76] Macedo endorses what he calls a 'judgmental liberalism', one that 'would defend a broad range of freedoms while insisting that people need not simply options but channels encouraging them to favour better over worse ways of life'.[77] State-recognized marriage should be part of this encouragement, for Macedo, since stable commitments are generally good for people. Stability does not always need promotion: in societies where stability is valued extremely highly, such as deeply religious societies, committed relationships can lead to oppression. But 'in the sex-riddled, divorce-prone culture of contemporary America, most of us do not err mainly on the side of excessively stable personal commitments'.[78] In Western societies, then, marriage can and should be promoted, because it is good for people regardless of sexuality. For Macedo, marriage is a traditional social form that can and should be adapted to include same-sex couples since its key features of monogamy and commitment are central to liberal democratic values.

The core of Macedo's defence of marriage is that it is a relationship form with distinct benefits to the marrying couple, their children, and society at large—although, as Macedo notes several times but does not fully take on board, the benefits to men are more significant than the benefits to women, with increased *divorce* actually being of considerable benefit to women.[79] These benefits come from commitment and stability: in marrying, a couple settle various aspects of their relationship by entering into a social form with a widely shared meaning

[75] David Estlund, 'Shaping and Sex' in Estlund and Nussbaum (eds), *Sex, Preference, and Family* pp. 161–2.

[76] Or perhaps, as Estlund suggests, Macedo is more communitarian. (Estlund, 'Shaping and Sex' p. 164.)

[77] Stephen Macedo, 'Sexuality and Liberty: Making Room for Nature and Tradition?' in Estlund and Nussbaum (eds), *Sex, Preference, and Family* p. 93.

[78] Macedo, 'Sexuality and Liberty' p. 94.

[79] Macedo, *Just Married* p. 21 and 112; 'Sexuality and Liberty' p. 94.

and strong social norms of appropriate behaviour; in entering into a *legal* marriage they bolster that commitment still further by making themselves liable to legal sanction if the commitment is broken. For Macedo, the state recognition of marriage is an important part of this process:

Individuals could still make commitments to each other without the law of marriage. They could still publicize their commitment to their friends and try to inform the world at large by posting about it on social media and in other ways. The law of marriage furnishes resources that individuals and private associations never could. It codifies a public understanding of what is for most people's life's single most important relationship. It offers a widely understood set of marital default rules, subject to the parties' revisions, which others have found useful and advantageous in the past.... Cohabiting is likely to involve only private commitments and undertakings.[80]

Although Macedo does refer to empirical research throughout the book, he does not give any evidence for the claim about cohabitation. He does claim that 'Marriage is the "committed relationship" par excellence',[81] which is also odd given that divorce is not particularly unusual, to put it mildly, and given that, as he himself notes later on, motherhood is far more committed than either marriage or fatherhood.[82]

It seems that, as with Galston, marriage is a proxy for what is really at stake, which is committed and stable relationships; but of course these are perfectly possible in cohabiting relationships, as the existence of long-term same-sex couples before the recognition of same-sex marriage demonstrates. As Macedo recognizes, 'stability in marriage is not an unconditional good: separation and divorce can serve everyone's interests in high-conflict marriages. Children and spouses benefit from stable, *healthy* marriages, in which open conflict is reasonably low and the long-term happiness of the spouses is advanced.'[83] Nothing would be lost if 'marriage' in the second sentence were replaced with 'relationships'.

Macedo notes that there is a significant class divide in marriage in America, with higher levels of education and income correlating with higher levels of marriage and stability. He does not consider whether this difference in itself might account for much of the benefit attributed to marriage. There is a considerable difference in cohabitation practised in a context of financial disadvantage, poor education, and relationship instability versus cohabitation as practised by educated, middle-class, professional couples. Research by Sharon Sassler and Amanda Miller found that working-class couples move into cohabitation more rapidly than middle-class couples, often for financial reasons rather than romantic

---

[80] Macedo, *Just Married* p. 95.   [81] Macedo, *Just Married* p. 92.
[82] Macedo, *Just Married* p. 110.   [83] Macedo, *Just Married* p. 40.

ones. Middle-class couples are more likely to view cohabitation as part of the history of a committed, lifelong relationship, so that for them cohabitation is the first step towards marriage; for working-class couples 'cohabitation may serve as more of an alternative to singlehood'.[84] The implication is that marriage may not be doing the work Macedo imputes to it: it is a means for some couples to *express* a commitment they have already made, rather than a means of making a commitment that would not otherwise exist. And there are, of course, many ways of expressing and making a commitment—not just posting about it on social media, as Macedo rather mockingly suggests, but by engaging in *practices* of commitment, such as buying a house together, or combining finances, or committing to jointly parent a child by planning a pregnancy, committing to an unplanned pregnancy, or adoption.

Another social dimension to marriage is race, particularly in the USA on which both Macedo and Galston focus. Katherine Franke directly addresses this issue:

> black women face a rather bleak 'marriage market' in which it is extremely difficult to find eligible men who are financially and otherwise attractive partners. First of all, there is a gross imbalance in the ratio of black women and men wanting and able to marry, in no small measure due to the number of black men in prison.... With so few marriageable African American men, African American women are making other choices about love and family.[85]

In some African American communities high rates of male imprisonment and violence, combined with lower life expectancy due to poor health, mean that 'many African American women come to feel that having a child, even without the father's involvement, will create a more permanent form of attachment than would holding out hopes for romantic love and marriage'.[86] Franke's account suggests that a focus on marriage as the pinnacle of stability and commitment is factually false and racially biased. It ignores the fact that marriage is not a reliable way for African American women to ensure stability, and it misses a range of alternative family forms that do provide stability and are more prevalent outside the white middle class. For African Americans the dominant stable family form is a female-headed single-parent family bolstered by enduring care networks with other female relatives: sisters, mothers, aunts, and grandmothers.

Macedo notes that married couples need not follow the marriage script, and that unmarried couples 'can do many of the things that married couples do, without marrying'.[87] Why, then, should the state 'encourage young people to

---

[84] Sharon Sassler and Amanda J. Miller, 'Class Differences in Cohabitation Practices' in *Family Relations* 60 (2011) p. 175.

[85] Franke, *Wedlocked* p. 87.    [86] Franke, *Wedlocked* p. 87.

[87] Macedo, *Just Married* p. 117.

recognize the benefits of marriage and commitment'[88] as opposed to just encouraging them to value *commitment*? Macedo is inconsistent about the extent of legitimate state action. On the one hand, he argues that polygamy should be decriminalized and that marriage 'does not require, and I doubt that it benefits from, any social stigma being attached to those who are single or couples who choose not to marry',[89] but Macedo makes no suggestions about how to avoid what Franke calls the 'offload[ing] of stigma from gay couples to their constitutive outside, African American families most prominently'.[90] For Macedo, concerns about marriage unfairly promoting a deeply controversial conception of the good can be dispersed by 'providing appropriate recognition and assistance to those in caring and caregiving relationships that are not marital'.[91] But he provides no model for how to do this, and even effusively endorses stigmatizing the unmarried: 'The failure to get married ought to raise eyebrows and occasion comment; marriage should be encouraged... I join [Jonathan] Rauch and others in thinking that the "channelling function" of marriage would do many gay males a lot of good.'[92] Once again, with emotion: 'monogamous marriage helps imprint the DNA of equal liberty onto the very fibre of family and sexual intimacy'.[93] There is some serious bait-and-switch going on here.

Macedo and Galston are certainly right to claim that stability and the creation of the conditions for a democratic citizenry are significant values, ones that can legitimately count in the balance of reasons and ones that may justify state action. We can also grant, for the sake of argument, that stable family life is part of this picture. That is to say, their arguments satisfy the first and second criteria for a liberal defence of marriage. However, neither theorist has satisfied the third criterion, of showing that state recognition of marriage is the best way to achieve them, or even that it is ever responsible for doing so when compared with the alternative of the marriage-free state.

## 3.5  Marriage and Children

Galston and Macedo both advocate marriage in part because they argue that it has salutary effects on children. Children's welfare is often cited as a reason for state promotion of marriage.[94] If state-recognized marriage is indeed beneficial to

---

[88] Macedo, *Just Married* p. 117.
[89] Macedo, *Just Married* p. 98.   [90] Franke, *Wedlocked* p. 206.
[91] Macedo, *Just Married* p. 208. Macedo does not specify what would count as 'appropriate recognition and assistance'.
[92] Macedo, *Just Married* p. 116.   [93] Macedo, *Just Married* p. 211.
[94] William A. Galston, 'Causes of Declining Well-Being Among U.S. Children' in Estlund and Nussbaum (eds), *Sex, Preference, and Family* p. 303.

children then it might be justifiable within liberalism. It is an inescapable requirement of justice that we must design laws that protect children, since children are incapable of protecting themselves and cannot give meaningful consent.[95] If state-recognized marriage were needed to protect children, then, it would be a legitimate policy for all liberals.

In order to justify state promotion of marriage on the grounds of child protection the liberal would have to show three things. First, she would have to determine the empirical facts about the effects of state-recognized marriage on children. Second, for specifically political liberal support she would have to show that any benefits to children could be described in neutral, political terms. Third, she would have to show that these benefits legitimately outweigh considerations of equality and freedom that would otherwise tell against endorsing marriage. But each of these tasks is problematic, as the next three sections show.

### 3.5.1 Empirical facts

It is beyond the scope of this book to settle the competing claims about the effects of marriage on children. But this limitation is not troubling for the question at hand, which is whether children's welfare justifies the state recognition of marriage, because *no evidence is available that bears on that question*. Galston and other advocates of marriage[96] cite evidence showing that children of married parents do better, on a number of indicators such as school performance and law-abidingness, than children with unmarried parents. Some of this evidence fails to isolate other salient factors, such as family income, levels of parental education, the effects of having two parents rather than one (regardless of whether the parents are married), the benefits to children of having a male as well as a female role model, and household stability. For example, Galston begins his remarks by lamenting the increasing number of children born 'outside of marriage' and claims that children are affected by family structure regardless of 'family income, parental education, and prior family history', yet much of the data he cites relates to the negative effects on children not of having *unmarried* parents but of having a *single* parent, a very *young* parent, or *divorced* parents.[97] Galston writes as if the only alternative to single parenthood, teen pregnancy, and divorce is marriage, but of course that is false. Macedo makes a similar mistake when he tries to defend the state recognition of marriage by arguing that 'evidence suggests that

---

[95] As Rawls states, 'the principles of justice impose constraints on the family on behalf of children who as society's future citizens have basic rights as such.' (Rawls, 'The Idea of Public Reason Revisited' p. 160.)

[96] For example, Maggie Gallagher, 'Re-creating Marriage' in Popenoe et al. (eds) *Promises to Keep*.

[97] Galston, 'Causes of Declining Well-Being Among U.S. Children' pp. 299–303.

marriage confers benefits on adults, *as compared with being single*, and on children, *as compared with being raised in a single-parent home*.[98] As the two clauses that I have italicized show, Macedo does not show that state-recognized marriage provides benefits as compared with unmarried but stable, committed, two-parent households.

Sara McLanahan also examines empirical research and concludes: 'What matters for children is not whether their parents are married when they are born, but whether their parents live together while the children are growing up.'[99] This evidence suggests that what is important to children's well-being is some combination of stability in family relationships and having one's own parents live together, not simply having married parents. For example, children of divorced parents are not benefited if their parents re-marry, so merely having a married couple at the head of the household is not what confers advantage.[100] Advocates of marriage for this reason thus need to recognize that the empirical evidence for marriage benefiting children is indeterminate, as Andrew Lister does when he tentatively suggests that such an idea is 'not implausible'.[101]

But the problem is not merely one of inadequate data. Even if additional research studies could be designed to isolate all these factors and simply compare the outcomes for children with married parents and those for children with unmarried but stably-partnered parents in similar socioeconomic circumstances, the outcome would not be conclusive for the question of whether the state should recognize marriage. For even such studies would not provide data on outcomes for children with unmarried parents *in a society where marriage does not exist as a state-recognized institution*.

To put this point another way: it is quite possible that it is better for children to have married parents if they live in a society in which marriage is recognized and promoted. In such a society there are a number of reasons why having unmarried parents might harm children. They might suffer from stigma, as was the case when such children were routinely referred to as 'bastards' or 'illegitimate'.

---

[98]    Macedo, *Just Married* p. 115. Emphases added.

[99]    Sara McLanahan, 'The Consequences of Single Motherhood' in Estlund and Nussbaum (eds), *Sex, Preference, and Family* p. 309.

[100]    McLanahan, 'The Consequences of Single Motherhood' p. 309.

[101]    Lister, *Public Reason and Political Community* p. 159. For further discussion of the inconclusiveness of the data on marriage and children's welfare see Brake, *Minimizing Marriage* pp. 146–51; Iris Marion Young, *Intersecting Voices: Dilemmas of Gender, Political Philosophy, and Policy* (Princeton, NJ: Princeton University Press, 1997) ch. 6; and Robin Fretwell Wilson, 'Evaluating Marriage: Does Marriage Matter to the Nurturing of Children?' in *San Diego Law Review* 42 (2005). For discussion of the inconclusiveness of the data on children's welfare and same-sex marriage see Macedo, *Just Married* pp. 66–8.

We should not complacently believe that this discrimination is over. Cynthia Bowman notes: 'Historically, illegitimate children were punished because their parents were unmarried. The children of opposite-sex cohabiting couples are disadvantaged in similar ways today.'[102] She points to a number of ways that the American legal system seriously discriminates against such children, including rights to inheritance, government benefits, and tort claims. Richard Storrow notes that 'discrimination and harassment against "illegitimate families" linger and thrive, whether in rules about who can marry and why, attitudes about who should be excluded from reproducing and adopting, perspectives on citizenship, and the fact that not all children receive the same entitlements'.[103] Other scholars agree that children of unmarried parents are currently subject to a range of legal and symbolic disadvantage, and that the move towards same-sex marriage does nothing whatever to undermine this inequality.[104] Moreover, stigmatization of illegitimacy further entrenches other forms of discrimination, such as racism, since single-parent families are more common in some groups than in others. For example, in the USA African Americans become scapegoats for 'irresponsible' illegitimacy.[105]

In a marriage regime, where marriage is recognized and promoted, there might be some characteristic of at least some parents who choose not to marry that in itself adversely affects their children. Perhaps they are disinclined to commit, or they disvalue stability, or they are unable to maintain secure relationships. I suggest these options as logical possibilities rather than likely hypotheses. However, none of these factors could be true of unmarried parents in a society which did not recognize marriage, for in such a society there would be no married parents to act as comparators. So, there would be no stigma resulting from being the child of unmarried parents, and the factors that might make people worse parents would not be correlated with marital status.

---

[102] Cynthia Grant Bowman, 'The New Illegitimacy: Children of Cohabiting Couples and Step-children' in *Journal of Gender, Social Policy, and the Law* 20(3) (2012) p. 437.

[103] Richard F. Storrow, '"The Phantom Children of the Republic": International Surrogacy and the New Illegitimacy' in *Journal of Gender, Social Policy, and the Law* 20(3) (2012) pp. 564–5.

[104] See, for example, Tanya Washington, 'The new battleground for same-sex couples is equal rights for their kids' in http://www.theconversation.com (7 October 2015); Nancy D. Polikoff, 'The New "Illegitimacy": Winning Backward in the Protection of the Children of Lesbian Couples' in *Journal of Gender, Social Policy, and the Law* 20(3) (2012); Sacha M. Coupet, 'Beyond "Eros": Relative Caregiving, "Agape" Parentage, and the Best Interests of Children' in *Journal of Gender, Social Policy, and the Law* 20(3) (2012); Julie Shapiro, 'Counting From One: Replacing the Marital Presumption with a Presumption of Sole Parentage' in *Journal of Gender, Social Policy, and the Law* 20(3) (2012).

[105] Melissa Murray, 'What's So New About the New Illegitimacy?' in *Journal of Gender, Social Policy, and the Law* 20(3) (2012).

Of course, a society without state-recognized marriage is not the same as a society without marriage. The marriage-free state is compatible with private marriage ceremonies, whether religious or secular. However, if marriage is not a state-recognized category then there are a number of ways in which stigma to the children of unmarried parents is lessened. First, and crucially for the political liberal, if the state does not recognize marriage then *the state does not participate* in any ranking of families or stigmatization of unmarried families. Indeed, the state might go further and take action against discrimination perpetrated by others.

Second, if marriage were not recognized by the state then one of two things might occur, either of which would lessen stigma to children of unmarried parents. Numbers of private marriages might fall, with only people with a genuine religious commitment choosing to engage in what would then become a purely religious ceremony. In this scenario the distinction between 'stable, decent, respectable' married parents and 'feckless, irresponsible' unmarried parents would change to a distinction between religious and non-religious parents, a distinction that does not carry the same connotations or implications for children.

Alternatively, numbers of private marriages might increase, with many people choosing to celebrate marriages of many varieties. Some people would engage in traditional religious heterosexual monogamous marriages, but others would be free to call themselves 'married' if they participated in arrangements that look nothing like either traditional marriage or even Brake's minimal marriage. Hefner would be perfectly at liberty to call himself married to all his playmates, and a person would be free to call herself married to her pet or her sister or her friend.[106] Private companies could offer ceremonies for all such arrangements, but of course no ceremony would be required—just as no ceremony is required for people to give themselves any other label that is not recognized by the state, such as 'friends'. If a marriage-free society were characterized by this sort of expansion of marriage then the stigmatization of the children of unmarried parents would be even more difficult, since 'married' would no longer be any sort of metaphor for 'stable, respectable, traditional' and so on.

An objector might argue that if children of married parents do better, in a society with state-recognized marriage, then justice requires not abolishing marriage but rather increasing the incentives and even pressures on people to get married. Rather than denying the benefits of marriage to all children, we should try to extend those benefits to as many children as possible. For example,

---

[106] Such a scenario also mitigates Hartley and Watson's worry that privatized marriage hands control of the meaning of marriage to heterosexist religions. See Hartley and Watson, 'Political Liberalism, Marriage and Family' p. 203ff.

Lister argues that the interests of children support the state recognition of marriage rather than of caring relationships because 'a status no longer tied to conjugality would also not bring to bear the force of social norms that reinforce commitment and responsibility'.[107]

There are several problems with Lister's position. First, it is difficult to distinguish correlation and causation, as he recognizes. In order for children to benefit from the social promotion of marriage it would have to be the case that becoming married gave people a new commitment to child-friendly values such as stability and secure relationships, and that is unlikely. It is at least as plausible that the people who choose to marry are those who already value stability and security. And, since Lister is not advocating making divorce more difficult, marriage is no guarantee of stability. Britney Spears and Jason Alexander were married for a total of 55 *hours* in 2004; Jack Evans and George Harris had cohabited for 54 *years* in 2015.[108] They married at that point because they already had a stable, committed relationship, not because they needed marriage to bring those virtues.[109]

Second, the idea that there is some necessary link between conjugality and stable parenting plays into the hands of the new natural lawyers, who argue that marriage is essentially procreative and thus should be confined to different-sex couples. Lister's comments bring to mind Margaret Somerville's arguments, as endorsed and recounted by Patrick Lee:

In every society we find the following type of relationship: an inherently procreative relationship between men and women, that includes a commitment to share their lives with each other, and if children come to be, to rear those children together.... Marriage is that type of community in which the personal community, and the bodily, sexual relationship, are *intrinsically* oriented to the twofold good of personal communion between the spouses, and bearing and raising of children.[110]

For writers such as Lee this necessary connection between conjugality and children's welfare means that children's welfare is best served 'if they are raised

---

[107] Lister, *Public Reason and Political Community* p. 159.

[108] See BBC News 'Britney's short marriage annulled' (6 January 2004); Diane Herbst, 'First Same-Sex Couple Marries in Dallas County After 50-Year Wait' in *Time* (26 June 2015).

[109] As Kimberley Yuracko puts it, 'Marriage does not transform the ill-equipped into good spouses and good parents. Instead, such individuals must be transformed before entering the institution in order to avoid degrading and destroying the institution itself. If...it is social norms, rather than marriage, doing the work that is benefiting children, then it makes sense to focus society's attention and resources on norms, not marriage.' Kimberley A. Yuracko, 'Does Marriage Make People Good or Do Good People Marry?' in *San Diego Law Review* 42 (2005) p. 893.

[110] Patrick Lee, 'Marriage, Procreation, and Same-Sex Unions' in *The Monist* 91(3/4) (2008) p. 422.

by their biological parents, who have formed a community dedicated to providing the most suitable environment for any children they may procreate'.[111] For him, same-sex couples fall short of this standard not only because they cannot be biological parents without reproductive assistance, but also because same-sex marriages are predicated on the relationship between the couple, not on the couple uniting as a procreative entity. As Lee puts it, same-sex marriage would 'affirm that marriage is essentially concerned only with sexual or romantic relationships between adults', leaving 'no principled reason why marriage should be long-lasting, or between two people, these requirements being logical consequences of marriage's orientation to children'.[112]

Lister rightly does not want to endorse the new natural lawyers' insistence on the link between procreation, marriage, and children's interests, or their rejection of same-sex marriage.[113] After all, as marriage defender Macedo points out, 'it seems clear that many heterosexual marriages are much less oriented toward the good of raising and nurturing children than are those homosexual couples raising children together'.[114] So why argue that the sort of stable and committed environment that children need should be tied to conjugality? Why not promote the connection between these values and *parenthood*, regardless of the relationship between the parents? We could even imagine a state ceremony for parents, a solemnization of their new status, combined with extensive legal or social norms about proper parental behaviour. This would be more in children's interests than the same things connected to marriage, because it would include *all* children's parents.

Third, there will always be some parents who are unmarried, voluntarily or involuntarily.[115] Even if all people want to be married and divorce is extremely difficult, events such as accidental pregnancy outside a committed relationship or the death of one parent cannot be prevented. The development of reproductive technologies such as sperm donation, egg donation, and surrogate motherhood

---

[111]  Lee, 'Marriage, Procreation' p. 424.       [112]  Lee, 'Marriage, Procreation' p. 432.

[113]  For discussion and critique of new natural law see Adèle Mercier, 'On the Nature of Marriage: Somerville on Same-Sex Marriage' and 'Mercier's reply to Lee' both in *The Monist* 91(3/4) (2008); John Corvino, 'Homosexuality and the PIB Argument' in *Ethics* 115(3) (2005); Lister, *Public Reason and Political Community*; Sadler, 'Public or Private Good?'; Macedo, *Just Married* ch. 2.

[114]  Macedo, *Just Married* p. 49.

[115]  Rates of childbirth within cohabitation rather than marriage have been steadily increasing in Europe in recent decades, but vary widely between countries. For example, over 40 per cent of births in Norway and Sweden, but only 9 per cent of births in Switzerland, occur within cohabitation. See Brienna Perelli-Harris and Nora Sánchez Gassen, 'How Similar are Cohabitation and Marriage? Legal Approaches to Cohabitation across Western Europe' in *Population and Development Review* 38(3) (2013) p. 436. See Chapter 1 for statistics of the numbers of children born out of wedlock; in Western liberal democracies the average proportion is between 40 per cent and 50 per cent.

further complicate the links between marriage and parenthood.[116] Thus there will always be children without married parents, and we need measures to ensure such children can obtain the goods available to the children of married parents. Encouraging marriage does nothing to help such children, and indeed adds stigma to any disadvantage.

The fairest way for the state to help children, then, is by refusing to distinguish between married and unmarried parents and focusing instead on helping all parents and all children.[117] In fact this point can be made even more strongly: if marriage benefits children, then supporting marriage benefits the already-advantaged.[118] In a state that recognizes marriage, justice for children requires directing additional, compensatory state support to the children of the unmarried, not providing perks to married parents. And full justice requires abolishing the entire system by which the state recognizes and entrenches that disadvantage.

A marriage-free state would not mean that the values of marriage that benefit children were lost. Parents who would be married in a marriage regime would still be parents in a marriage-free state, and there is no reason to think they would lose their commitment to values such as stability and enduring relationships. Indeed, if stability and security are valuable to children then there are good political reasons for the state to endorse those values directly for all *parents*, rather than indirectly via marriage.

## 3.5.2 Neutral descriptions

Political liberal defences of marriage must also satisfy a second difficult requirement: providing neutral descriptions of outcomes. Suppose it were shown empirically that children with married parents had certain advantages over those with unmarried parents: perhaps they felt more secure and were more optimistic about human relationships. But suppose it were also shown that children with unmarried parents did better on other measures: they were more resilient and were more likely to question unjust hierarchies.[119] It would be very difficult to

---

[116] For discussion see Nicholas Bala and Christine Ashbourne, 'The Widening Concept of "Parent" in Canada: Step-Parents, Same-Sex Partners, and Parents by Art' in *Journal of Gender, Social Policy, and the Law* 20(3) (2012); Susan Frelich Appleton, 'Illegitimacy and Sex, Old and New' in *Journal of Gender, Social Policy, and the Law* 20(3) (2012).

[117] See also Brake on this point, in 'Minimal Marriage' pp. 318–19.

[118] This point is also made by Laura S. Adams in 'Privileging the Privileged: Child Well-Being as a Justification for State Support of Marriage' and Yuracko, 'Does Marriage Make People Good?' both in *San Diego Law Review* 42 (2005).

[119] Iris Marion Young argues that 'single-parent families are better for children in some respects and not better in others,' and provides a variety of empirical data to support that claim, in her *Intersecting Voices* p. 118. Elise Robinson et al. argue that 'postdivorce families actually have goods to offer children that the sentimental family offers less well—among them, the sense that the

defend state-sponsored marriage by a neutral appeal to the interests of children in such circumstances. There is deep controversy about what can reasonably be said to be in children's interests.[120] A political liberal is committed to remaining neutral on questions such as whether children are better served by being obedient or adventurous, conformist or revolutionary, and so it will be very difficult for a political liberal to say that one family form such as marriage is best for children— let alone necessary for their needs to be met.

The problem of how to provide neutral descriptions for the effect of marriage on children is particularly pertinent in the work of the new natural lawyers, who base their defence of heterosexual-only marriage on its procreative aspect. Brook Sadler summarizes their view as follows:

The idea seems to run like this: If sex is to be non-exploitative, it must have a purpose other than mere pleasure. That purpose is procreation. To engage in procreative sex is to be responsible for the possible birth of and care for a child, a being of intrinsic worth and dignity. This is the most profound responsibility, for its object is a human life. Thus, to engage in sex without a commitment to caring for any child that results is to devalue human life. Marriage preserves that commitment, while preserving a morally defensible form of sexual congress.[121]

As Sadler notes, this view rests on deeply controversial views about the purpose and nature of sexual activity, as well as problematically implying that marriage is both necessary and sufficient for taking responsibility for securing the flourishing of children. And, as she puts it, 'an appreciation of human life and particularly of the lives of children can be recognized by means other than heterosexual marriage, such as better sex education, access to contraception, better education, enforcement of child support, improved quality and cost of childcare, safe public parks, guaranteed maternity or paternity leave, etc'.[122]

---

children's important relationships will continue no matter what the family looks like, affirmation of the child's sense of herself as an agent, the advantages of living in two worlds, and useful strategies about the families they will form when they themselves become adults'. (Elise L. E. Robinson et al., 'Fluid Families: The Role of Children in Custody Arrangements' in Hilde Lindemann Nelson, *Feminism and Families* (London: Routledge, 1997) p. 99.) One should not be too optimistic: divorce and family breakdown can clearly be deeply distressing for children, but then so too can life with married parents. The point is that there is no obvious way to adjudicate once and for all.

[120] An example of the controversies surrounding appeals to children's interests is found in Claudia Card, 'Against Marriage and Motherhood' in *Hypatia* 11(3) (1996). Card argues that not just traditional marriage but even motherhood, as currently socially conceived, acts against children's interests.

[121] Sadler, 'Public or Private Good?' p. 28.

[122] Sadler, 'Public or Private Good?' p. 28. See also Sadler, 'Re-thinking Civil Unions and Same-Sex Marriage'.

### 3.5.3 Children's interests versus other values

In general, the advocate of marriage for the sake of children needs an account of how to balance the interests of adults and children. Parents also have rights and interests, and it is legitimate for them to prioritize their own interests in certain ways, even while there are undoubtedly some ways in which children's interests override their parents' freedom.[123] Rawls offers characteristically vague advice on this issue, noting that 'the prohibition of abuse and neglect of children, and much else, will, as constraints, be a vital part of family law. But at some point society has to rely on the natural affection and goodwill of family members.'[124] Even the staunchest defenders of marriage cannot plausibly argue that it is *necessary* to prevent abuse and neglect; whether marriage is a crucial part of 'much else' is anyone's guess. But it is crucial to be clear about what is at stake. Promotion of marriage involves promotion of a particular conception of the good; even if child protection is the intention behind state recognition, non-neutral promotion is the inescapable means.

Moreover, state promotion of marriage has negative consequences for equality, given the patriarchal implications of traditional marriage and its equality-undermining effects for adults. Iris Marion Young notes that marriage usually involves an economic inequality between women and men, with women earning less than their husbands either because they do not work outside the home at all, or because they work part time, or because even when they work full time the gender pay gap leaves them worse off. It follows, for Young, that Galston's argument is based on a contradiction: marriage is needed so that children grow up to be independent, economically self-sufficient citizens, but that independence is won for boys and men at the expense of women and girls: 'Independence is a paragon virtue of liberal citizenship, but [for Galston] a mother's virtue entails dependence on a man.'[125] Marriage is only to be recommended from the perspective of a 'gender-neutral theory of family values',[126] one that ignores the reality of gender inequality and the ubiquity of dependence.

The inequality that marriage enacts between adults may negatively affect children, as Okin argues when pointing out that the family is a school of justice.[127] But marriage also *directly* undermines equality for children, by providing greater status, support and stability for the children of married parents.

---

[123] Harry Brighouse and Adam Swift, 'Parents' Rights and the Value of the Family' in *Ethics* 117 (October 2006).

[124] Rawls, 'The Idea of Public Reason Revisited' p. 160.

[125] Young, *Intersecting Voices* p. 122.     [126] Young, *Intersecting Voices* p. 123.

[127] Okin, *Justice, Gender, and the Family*.

A society that wishes to help children equally needs to do so via measures that do not give additional advantages to children who are, *ex hypothesis*, already advantaged.

## Conclusion

This chapter has considered five potential liberal reasons in favour of state-recognized marriage: gender equality, communication, care, social value, and children's interests. These arguments generally highlight legitimate public goods, though these are of varying importance. But in every case they fail to show that state-recognized marriage is a necessary and acceptable way of achieving the good in question. State recognition of marriage is therefore ruled out as at best bad policy and at worst injustice (depending on which form of liberalism and which sort of neutrality, if any, one endorses). Instead, liberals should endorse a marriage-free state, in which the state regulates those aspects of personal relationships in which it has a legitimate interest in a piecemeal fashion, without recognizing a particular relationship status such as marriage.

I do not claim to have refuted all possible liberal defences of state-recognized marriage. But I do claim to have demonstrated that any proposed defence must meet various robust objections. First, the benefits claimed for state-recognized marriage must be sufficiently weighty to counter-balance marriage's connections to inequality and non-neutrality. Second, it is important to distinguish the benefits of marriage from the benefits of stable, secure relationships. Third, it is important to remember that any benefits currently adhering to marriage do so in the context of state recognition: we do not know how things would change in a marriage-free state. Finally, even the most marriage-promoting society will always contain unmarried people and unmarried parents. Recognition of marriage will always leave such people and their children out. If marriage brings benefits, state recognition of marriage simply widens the inequality gap.

# PART II

# The Marriage-Free State

# 4

# The Limitations of Contract

We have seen that there are good reasons to end the state recognition of marriage. From a feminist and egalitarian perspective the abolition of state-recognized marriage would be a decisive break from the patriarchal and discriminatory associations of the institution. From a comprehensive liberal perspective state-recognized marriage is problematically restrictive, since it involves the state defining the terms of personal relationships and holding people to those terms. From a political liberal perspective state-recognized marriage violates state neutrality since it rests on deeply controversial values that are not acceptable to all reasonable conceptions of the good. As I argue throughout Part I, then, justice would be best served by the abolition of state-recognized marriage and the creation of what I call a marriage-free state.

But even in the marriage-free state the question of how to regulate personal relationships remains. Personal relationships still have to be regulated so as to protect vulnerable parties, including but not only children; so as to regulate disputes over such matters as joint property; so as to establish the rights and duties of third parties; and so as to appropriately direct state benefits and taxes. These benefits might include immigration rights, next-of-kinship status, inheritance tax relief, and so on. One issue that arises is precisely which benefits and responsibilities are legitimate for the state to impose on people in particular sorts of relationship. For example, an advocate of open borders will not support differential immigration rights and some egalitarians will not support any inheritance tax relief. These questions are important but will not be addressed here. Instead, I consider what legal form the regulation of personal relationships should take.

Many theorists defend relationship contracts. Some argue that enforceable relationship contracts should be available alongside existing or reformed state-recognized marriage, and available to either married or unmarried couples. So married couples might wish to draw up pre-nuptial contracts to set out financial arrangements in case of divorce, or unmarried couples might wish to draw up cohabitation contracts. Other theorists argue that relationship contracts are the best sort of legal regulation to *replace* marriage.[1] It is this latter question that concerns me in this chapter, although many of my arguments are also relevant to the former question. I argue that relationship contracts are much more problematic than they first appear, so that it is not appropriate to use them as the regulatory framework to replace state-recognized marriage. Instead the marriage-free state should implement a series of default directives setting out the rights and duties of parties engaging in various relationship practices. Some contractual deviation from these directives may be permitted, but to be permissible a deviation must not undermine the justice that the default directives are designed to secure. The form of regulation used in the marriage-free state is described in detail in Chapter 5.

Here the focus is contract. By 'contract' I mean that the legal duties and benefits that apply between partners are those that they have freely and formally agreed to, the content of which suits their precise circumstances and preferences.[2] The law does not specify what the content of the contract must be, so individuals have a great deal of freedom to develop a wide range of contractual agreements. The law does regulate contracts, by stipulating general requirements to which all contracts must adhere (for example, that contracting parties must be fully informed and freely consenting, and that certain egregious terms or contracts will not be allowed, such as contracts for slavery). The law also stipulates and provides the method by which contracts can be enforced. But these are general and limited restrictions, so that contract allows for significant diversity and freedom.

For my purposes, the alternative to contract is what I call 'directive'. By 'directive' I mean that the state dictates responsibilities and rights, in advance and for all relevant people. The usual contrast is between contract and status. But

---

[1] See, for example, Lenore J. Weitzman, *The Marriage Contract: Spouses, Lovers and the Law* (New York: The Free Press, 1981); Marjorie Maguire Shultz, 'Contractual Ordering of Marriage: A New Model for State Policy' *California Law Review* 70(2) (1982); Elizabeth A. Kingdom, 'Cohabitation Contracts: A Socialist-Feminist Issue' in *Journal of Law and Society* 15(1) (1988); Martha Albertson Fineman, *The Neutered Mother, The Sexual Family and Other Twentieth Century Tragedies* (New York: Routledge, 1995); Fineman, *The Autonomy Myth: A Theory of Dependency* (New Press, 2005); Fineman, 'The Meaning of Marriage' in Anita Bernstein (ed.), *Marriage Proposals: Questioning a Legal Status* (New York: New York University Press, 2006); Brook J. Sadler, 'Re-Thinking Civil Unions and Same-Sex Marriage' in *The Monist* 91(3/4) (2008).

[2] In this chapter I sometimes refer to the jurisprudence of legal scholars who have considered the limitations of contract law in dealing with intimate relationships. Often such scholars point to issues that are of fundamental relevance to my argument, such as the difficulties of enforcing contracts or the undesirability of doing so. However, this book is a work of normative political philosophy, not a work of jurisprudence. That is to say that I focus on the *normative* limitations of contract, not the legal limitations to upholding personal relationship contracts within any particular contract law tradition, as set by legislation, case law, and precedent. So the use of the term 'contract' in this chapter is not synonymous with 'contract law', classical or otherwise.

'status' implies precisely what I argue against: a category of approbation which one can apply to a person or relationship which sets them above and apart from those who lack that approbation. My meaning is closer to what lawyers refer to as 'public ordering'.[3]

The relationship between directive and choice is not straightforward. In some cases the directive approach will mean that regulations apply to people without their having any choice at all in the matter, if directive regulations apply between people who have no choice about their relationship to one another, such as siblings. However, directive regulation could also be used to stipulate duties in relationships that are entered into through choice, such as sexual partnerships. The existing legal regulation of marriage in liberal democracies is regulated by directive in this sense. When two people marry their relationship is governed by the laws of marriage of their state. The marrying couple have no choice about which of those laws to follow, particularly if pre-nuptial contracts are not enforced. Although the spouses do consent to marry, they need not consent to the various regulations that apply to them on marriage. If the laws of marriage change, so do their responsibilities.

## 4.1 The Appeal of Contract

On this characterization of directive, contract seems straightforwardly more appealing. A contract approach to personal relationships seems to answer all the concerns about traditional marriage raised by liberals, and to counter many of the concerns of feminists as well. For liberals, contracts allow an extremely wide sphere of personal freedom, as individuals may draw up contracts in any form they wish (subject only to general limitations on contracts, which can themselves be drawn up along liberal lines). Contracts avoid violating state neutrality since the state does not stipulate what forms of contracts may be drawn up: it does not say who may contract, or stipulate what sort of relationship the contracting parties must have. Feminist concerns about the position of women may be addressed by the fact that, simply by being different, relationship contracts break from the traditional patriarchal symbolism of marriage. Contracts also allow women to negotiate their position in the relationship in advance, and this may help them to secure adequate recompense and financial independence if they take on domestic and caring labour rather than labour paid outside the

---

[3] I discussed the sense in which status implies approbation in Chapter 2. For an example of the 'public ordering' terminology see Craig W. Christensen, 'Legal Ordering of Family Values: The Case of Gay and Lesbian Families' in *Cardozo Law Review* 18 (1996–7).

home. And contracts meet concerns about discrimination against same-sex couples, since they too can make contractual arrangements. Finally, contracts have the practical benefit of reducing the need for additional legislation. Courts are already experienced in enforcing contracts, and while some new legislation may be needed to stipulate what the limits of legal contracts are (particularly in cases concerning children) there is no need to draw up exhaustive and comprehensive legal definitions of marriage.

Individual choice is inherent in the contract model, meaning that both holistic and piecemeal contracts would be available to contracting partners. *Holistic* regulation of relationships involves creating a status, analogous to marriage, which confers upon people a bundle of legal rights and responsibilities. So contracts could be made that confer such a bundle on the contracting parties: detailing the various arrangements that would govern their lives together, possibly with interlinked conditions. For example, partners could choose to contract such that any breach of sexual fidelity incurs an increase in housework. Such contracts could institute wide-ranging partnerships similar to marriage, detailing obligations on everything from sexual fidelity to property to domicile. Unlike marriage, however, each relationship contract could be unique to the partners.

*Piecemeal* regulation, in contrast, rejects both *bundling* and *special status*: rights and duties are kept separate from one another, and no special status is conferred by the state. Piecemeal contracts would see individuals making a series of separate contracts about each area of their lives. Each contract could be with a different person, so that an individual could draw up a contract with her mother to govern their shared property, another with her co-parent to govern their childcare responsibilities, and another with her brother concerning her wishes if he were to have to act as her next-of-kin. Alternatively, there could be multiple contracts within one partnership. A partnership with multiple piecemeal contracts would keep regulation of each area separate, so that one partner's failure to comply with the contract concerning childcare, for example, would have no bearing on their contract concerning property ownership.

Contracts thus appear to bring a variety of desiderata: freedom, equality, neutrality, and diversity.[4] They allow for significant individual freedom: individuals have the freedom to contract in a holistic or a piecemeal fashion, the freedom to contract with whomever they please, and the freedom to design personalized contracts to suit their own priorities. Contracts break with traditional marriage and thus shed its inegalitarian symbolism, and allow partners to design progressive

---

[4] A detailed account of the advantages (and disadvantages) of contract is found in Jana B. Singer, 'The Privatization of Family Law' in *Wisconsin Law Review* 1443 (1992).

equitable relationships. Neutrality and diversity are fostered since the state neither lauds one form of relationship above others nor dictates how relationships must be ordered.

As a result several theorists have argued that existing models of marriage should be either supplemented or replaced with private contracts. One notable advocate of relationship contracts, Marjorie Maguire Shultz, writes that private relationship contracting best fulfils the principles 'woven into the fabric of today's intimate relationships: diversity, tolerance, privacy, choice, impermanence, individualism'.[5] To this end Shultz envisages a variety of possible contracts that partners might agree to, including a 'Domestic Services' contract that involves one partner paying the other a salary for housework; an 'Open Marriage' contract that permits the partners to have sexual relationships outside the partnership under certain conditions; a 'Domicile' contract that instigates rules to govern changes of domicile to further each partner's career; and a 'Homosexual Marriage' contract that replicates traditional heterosexual marriage.[6]

Another prominent advocate of private relationship contracts is Lenore Weitzman. Weitzman argues that relationship contracts have many benefits. According to her, contracts help couples to clarify their expectations, to resolve problems and disagreements before they become insurmountable. Moreover, contracts are useful throughout the duration of the relationship as they provide a standard to refer back to. This guidance and security makes it easier for couples to stick to their promises and goals, such as egalitarian goals, without falling into a routine that does not suit their normative commitments. And a contract 'provides the parties with the security that stems from predictability'.[7] Contract also allows couples 'to formulate an agreement that conforms to everyday reality' rather than being restricted by the model offered by marriage. Contract 'aids couples who wish to establish an egalitarian relationship' and 'affords couples the freedom and privacy to order their personal relationships as they wish'. And contract allows those who are unmarried, by choice or by legal prohibition, 'to formalize their relationship'.[8] Weitzman also argues that relationship contracts have societal benefits: they accommodate diversity, they are a quick method of enacting social change, and they are more likely to serve 'the state's goal of supporting stability in marriage and other family relationships'.[9]

[5] Shultz, 'Contractual Ordering of Marriage' p. 245.
[6] Shultz, 'Contractual Ordering of Marriage' pp. 219–23.
[7] Weitzman, *The Marriage Contract* pp. 232–7.
[8] Weitzman, *The Marriage Contract* pp. 227–8.
[9] Weitzman, *The Marriage Contract* pp. 238–9.

A third major figure in the relationship contract debate is Martha Fineman. Fineman advocates the abolition of marriage as legal category and argues that 'the interactions of female and male sexual affiliates' should instead:

be governed by the same rules that regulate other interactions in our society—specifically those of contract and property, as well as tort and criminal law...[T]his proposal is actually not very farfetched. We already encourage antenuptual agreements that are contractual deviations from state-imposed marriage consequences....My proposal would merely mandate that such bargaining occur *prior* to the termination of the relationship, ideally before the couple became too 'serious'.[10]

As will become clear later in the chapter this version of Fineman's proposals takes orthodox or classical contract law as the model for relationships, although she does suggest that the assumptions of contract law may need to be rethought. Fineman's proposals retain a strong role for the state, but her state directives would be centred around the Mother–Child Dyad. This phrase is meant to capture the vital role of care, as exemplified by motherhood, since dependency is an inevitable and recurring part of everyone's lives. While the caring activities undertaken in the family deserve recompense and support, and vulnerable adults should be protected, Fineman argues that relationships between non-dependent adults should be left to those adults. For Fineman the prohibition of relationship contracts treats women as inherently unequal, and so recognition of gender equality requires treating relationships contractually: 'abolishing legal marriage and the special rules associated with it would mean that we are taking gender equality seriously. If people want their relationships to have consequences, they should bargain for them.'[11]

Relationship contracts have therefore been advocated by various feminist theorists as promoting both equality and liberty. However, in what follows I argue that the contract model does not straightforwardly promote either value.

## 4.2 Contract and Equality

Relationship contracts appear to enhance equality since everyone is able to make a contract, including same-sex couples and those in non-sexual relationships, and since contracts can structure relationships in an egalitarian way. Consider both in turn.

First, it is an important benefit of contracts that they allow people who are excluded from marriage, or who choose not to marry, to gain legal security for

---

[10] Fineman, *The Neutered Mother* pp. 228–9.
[11] Fineman, 'The Meaning of Marriage' pp. 57–8; chapter 5 of *The Autonomy Myth* is similar.

their relationship. Weitzman is right to argue that contracts can be a crucial mechanism for couples to regain control over their own affairs and seek legal and social recognition for an alternative partnership *against the background of marriage as a state-recognized institution*. But in a marriage-free state there is no need for a couple to make a contract in order to escape the implications of an outmoded institution. Contracts are also not needed to secure fair treatment of those who cannot marry (such as same-sex couples): if there is no marriage then no one can be unfairly denied access to it. The model of regulation in the marriage-free state, detailed in Chapter 5, does a better job of securing equality between relationships since it encompasses all relationships, whether contractual or not.[12]

Second, while contracts *allow* couples to regulate their relationship along egalitarian lines that best fit the desires of each member and facilitate diversity, they also allow couples to formulate contracts that conform to a norm, entrench hierarchy, or are not equally desired by both. Thus many feminists have criticized the contract tradition for its links to patriarchy and its concealment of inequality.[13] The landmark feminist criticism of contract is Carole Pateman's *The Sexual Contract*, which argues that the contract approach as a whole is founded on an unequal 'sexual contract' subordinating women to men. On Pateman's account intimate contracts, including marriage, become 'universal prostitution',[14] a claim that made particular sense when rape was not recognized as a crime within marriage. Indeed, the unwillingness to enforce 'meretricious' contracts for sexual services still underpins some courts' reluctance to enforce private relationship contracts.

---

[12] As Jana Singer writes, 'the privatization of family law is most likely to increase opportunities for individual control where the most salient barriers to that control have been barriers set up by the state. The state's traditional ordering of marriage and its refusal to recognize consensual alternatives to marriage may be one such example. Where, by contrast, the efforts of individuals to control their lives have been thwarted primarily by private concentrations of power, or by power inequalities within the family, the link between privatization and control becomes considerably more problematic. At best, a shift from public to private ordering in these areas is likely to enhance the control of some family members at the expense of others.' ('The Privatization of Family Law' p. 1537.)

[13] See Carole Pateman, *The Sexual Contract* (London: Polity Press, 1988); K. O'Donovan, *Sexual Divisons in Law* (London: Weidenfeld and Nicolson, 1985); M. Neave, 'Private Ordering in Family Law—Will Women Benefit?' in M. Thornton (ed.), *Public and Private: Feminist Legal Debates* (Melbourne: Oxford University Press, 1995); P. Goodrich, 'Gender and Contracts' in A. Bottomley (ed.), *Feminist Perspectives on the Foundational Subjects of Law* (London: Cavendish, 1996); M. J. Frug, 'Re-reading Contracts: A Feminist Analysis of a Contracts Casebook' in *American University Law Review* 34 (1985); Patricia A. Tidwell and Peter Linzer, 'The Flesh-Colored Band Aid: Contracts, Feminism, Dialogue, and Norms' *Houston Law Review* 28 (1991); Martha Minow and Mary Lyndon Shanley, 'Relational Rights and Responsibilities: Revisioning the Family in Liberal Political Theory and Law' in *Hypatia* 11(1) (1996); Mary Lydon Shanley, *Just Marriage* (Oxford: Oxford University Press, 2004).

[14] Pateman, *The Sexual Contract* p. 184.

The contract model relies on equality between the contracting partners, but if the parties are unequal then individuals can face pressure to agree to unfair contracts—just as women have always faced considerable pressure to agree to the profound inequality of traditional marriage.[15] Outside traditional marriage partners could face romantic pressure, 'If you really loved me you'd choose the Permanent Commitment Contract'; cultural pressure, 'A good member of our religion would choose a Male Head of Household Contract'; or manipulative pressure, 'If you don't sign this Unequal Property Contract I'll leave you and the children'. As David McLellan puts it, 'In a society where power is systematically distributed asymmetrically, contract is likely simply to reinforce such an asymmetry.'[16] The problem of unjust contracts is exacerbated if those contracts concern third parties, most obviously children.

Contracts may not bring about equality and justice, then. This is not surprising: since one of the fundamental advantages of contracts is that they maximize diversity and individual liberty, they let in inequality. In general terms, contracts can violate justice by violating freedom or equality, either by the parties not being free and equal at the moment of contract, or by their agreeing terms that leave them unfree, or unequal, or both. The dominant political liberal response is to argue that inequality should be permitted by the state if individuals have chosen that inequality, where freedom of exit is taken as the proxy for choice.[17] Comprehensive liberals and feminists are rightly sceptical of such arguments, pointing out that there are limitations to 'free' choice and that choice should not be used to excuse injustice.[18] It is beyond the scope of this book to provide an exhaustive account of justice in contracts. It is worth noting here, however, that relationship contracts provide their own special concerns.

The first possible general injustice in contracts is that the contracting parties may not be in an equal position when they enter into the contract. Existing contract law in liberal societies typically contains provisions to guard against the most egregious instances of contracts founded on inequality but these may not be sufficient for personal relationship contracts. Amy Wax argues that women are systematically disadvantaged in marriage bargaining as a result of inequalities in

---

[15] Notable historical critics of traditional marriage were discussed in Chapter 1.

[16] David McLellan, 'Contract Marriage—The Way Forward or Dead End?' in *Journal of Law and Society* 23(2) (June 1996). See also Singer, 'The Privatization of Family Law' pp. 1540ff; Maxine Eichner, *The Supportive State* (Oxford: Oxford University Press, 2010) p. 102.

[17] See, for example, Martha Nussbaum, *Sex and Social Justice* (Oxford: Oxford University Press, 1999); Brian Barry, *Culture and Equality* (Cambridge: Polity Press, 2001); Chandran Kukathas, *The Liberal Archipelago: A Theory of Diversity and Freedom* (Oxford: Oxford University Press, 2003).

[18] I argue for this point extensively in Clare Chambers, *Sex, Culture, and Justice: The Limits of Choice* (University Park: Penn State University Press, 2008).

the labour and marriage markets. This systematic disadvantage would be exacerbated by regulating relationships via contract.[19]

The second potential area of injustice, that the contracts themselves might instantiate unequal or excessively freedom-limiting terms, is also even more potent in the relationship case. There are a number of reasons why people might be inclined to agree to unjust relationship contracts. Entering into a relationship contract will typically be done at a time of optimism, even a time of heady romance. This romance can cloud people's views: it is hard to think of one's partner as a potential adversary at precisely the time one is about to make a binding contract with them. As Ruthann Robson and S. E. Valentine put it, 'the myth of equality may never be more powerful than at the inception of coupledom, the very time at which a relationship contract would be drafted. Thus, from a pragmatic perspective, the contract solution is flawed because it depends on the existence of real, perceived, continuing, and absolute parity.'[20]

Even if people are cognitively able to put themselves in a self-interested, pessimistic mindset when drawing up a relationship contract there are social norms against such thinking, as well as strong social and religious norms about good husbandly and wifely behaviour. These norms limit individuals' freedom of choice and make unequal contracts more likely than they would be in the business context.

Finally, it can be difficult for contracting partners to envisage how their lives will change and how they will feel after major life events. Several studies show, for example, that even committed egalitarian couples find it very difficult to sustain a non-gendered division of labour after having children, and many people find that their preferences about matters such as work–life balance change profoundly on becoming parents.[21] Traditional contract law requires presentation, spelling out every eventuality in advance, so that all disputes that arise can be referred back to

---

[19] Amy Wax, 'Bargaining in the Shadow of Marriage: Is there a future for egalitarian marriage?' in *Virginia Law Review* 84(4) (May 1998). Although *Against Marriage* considers how personal relationships should be ideally regulated, it would be naïve and complacent to assume that such regulation would take place against a background of generic gender justice. For the realization of full gender equality is remote. As theorists such as Susan Moller Okin have shown, establishing gender justice requires policies more radical than even those required to realize more general liberal theories of justice such as those of John Rawls and Ronald Dworkin, and neither Rawlsian nor Dworkinian justice look politically imminent. So it is essential to consider the possibility that relationship contracts will take place against a background of structural gender inequality. Pateman argues that the structural inequalities between men and women undermine the use of contract, not only for marriage but in general, in *The Sexual Contract*.

[20] Ruthann Robson and S. E. Valentine, 'Lov(h)ers: Lesbians as Intimate Partners and Lesbian Legal Theory' in *Temple Law Review* 63 (1990) p. 524.

[21] See, for example, Pepper Schwartz, *Love Between Equals: How Peer Marriage Really Works* (New York: The Free Press, 1994); Ira Mark Ellman, '"Contract Thinking" was *Marvin's* fatal flaw'

the intentions of the parties at the moment of making the contract. But this process does not occur in intimate relationships in the same way as it might in a business deal, as John Wightman describes:

> Where the parties intend to share their lives, they abstain from presentation not so much because it is not practically feasible (although it isn't), but because it is not part of the relationship that they will individuate 'performances' which are then done in return for each other. This difference is reflected in the fact that there may well be inhibitions on attempting to spell out a deal.[22]

Ira Ellman points out that 'couples do not in fact think of their relationships in contract terms' and asks, rhetorically, 'Do we want courts to think broadly about the rules that yield a fair dissolution of an unmarried couple's relationship or do we want to limit courts to searching the parties' conduct for evidence that at some point in the past they agreed upon terms that should now govern their mutual obligations?'[23] Fairness and contract do not always coincide.

It is fairly well-accepted, then, that the contract approach is problematic for egalitarians. Indeed, considerations of equality lead Fineman, a prominent advocate of relationship contracts, to include 'ameliorating doctrines' so as to protect 'the economically weaker party'.[24] Nonetheless, she argues that contracts can be used to govern many aspects of relationships, including sexual aspects.[25] In part this is because Fineman holds the general view that contracts are liberty-promoting. In the remainder of the chapter I argue that even this aspect of relationship contracts must be questioned.

## 4.3 Contract and Liberty

Contracts are generally thought to uphold liberty since individuals can contract on their own terms. Couples are not limited to the regulatory form of marriage, and legal relationships are not limited to couples. They can structure their relationship in a wide variety of ways and can also choose to keep their relationship non-contractual. Thus contracts appear to foster liberty both by allowing diversity and by freeing couples from the straitjacket of state-defined marriage.

in *Notre Dame Law Review* 76 (2000–1) p. 1369; Melvin A. Eisenberg, 'The Limits of Cognition and the Limits of Contract' *Stanford Law Review* 47 (1995) pp. 251–8.

[22] John Wightman, 'Intimate Relationships, Relational Contract Theory, and the Reach of Contract' in *Feminist Legal Studies* 8 (2000) p. 108.

[23] Ellman, 'Contract Thinking' pp. 1367 and 1368.

[24] Fineman, 'The Meaning of Marriage' p. 58.

[25] Fineman, 'The Meaning of Marriage' p. 61.

This goal is what Fineman has in mind when she imagines a contract-based regime in which 'Women and men would operate outside of the confines of marriage, transacting and interacting without the fetters of legalities they did not voluntarily choose.'[26] And it causes minimal marriage advocate Elizabeth Brake to declare 'liberty requires that terms of adult relationships be chosen contractually'.[27]

However, the contract approach to regulating personal relationships does not mean that the state keeps out of relationships altogether. The state plays a vital role in regulating relationships, even if relationship contracts are allowed, for two main reasons. First, default directives are still needed. Second, contracts require state enforcement. In what follows I discuss both aspects of state involvement and show that the necessary role of the state in a contract regime actually undermines the appeal of such a regime.

## 4.4  Default Directives in a Contract Regime

As previously noted, even a marriage-free state requires legal regulation of intimate relationships since such relationships involve matters that cannot be left anarchic. This need for state regulation means that contract cannot be the only mechanism by which intimate relationships are regulated. As well as the problem of what to do if couples sign contracts that are manifestly unfair or hierarchical, the state also faces the problem of what to do if people do not draw up a contract to regulate some area of their relationship in which there are high stakes.[28] For example, a couple might buy a house, have children or require a next-of-kin to make decisions without having drawn up a contract to govern those eventualities. In such cases the state must take some position if a dispute or need for action arises. In the absence of a contract, this requires directives. In a marriage regime these default directives are found in forms of law that are neither marriage-specific nor contractual, such as property law and family law pertaining to children. The contract model does not, therefore, mean leaving individuals immune from state interference. It means allowing individuals to deviate in some way from the directives that the state cannot avoid putting in place.

[26] Fineman, *The Neutered Mother* p. 229.
[27] Elizabeth Brake, *Minimizing Marriage: Marriage, Morality and the Law* (Oxford: Oxford University Press, 2012) p. 149.
[28] Fineman recognizes the need for default directives or what she calls 'ameliorating doctrines'. See her 'Why Marriage?' p. 262.

State directives in a contract regime are of two types. First, the state needs default directives for those cases where regulation is needed but no contract has been made. Second, the state needs principles and limits of contract law, setting out what makes a valid contract and the recourse for breach.[29]

Thus the question 'should personal relationships be organized according to contract?' is not equivalent to the question 'should individuals have the freedom to organize their relationships as they see fit?' even though much of the appeal of a contract approach comes from this idea of maximal personal autonomy in relationships. But as well as providing the general limits of contract already described, the state will have to provide default regulations for use in circumstances where no contract exists but where regulation or intervention is needed: for example, in disputes over child custody, child support, or joint property.

A contract regime is also in need of state directives since contract alone does not impose obligations on third parties. Relationships need support from third parties, be they businesses, employers, or the state itself. For example, a relationship contract on its own does not compel a US health insurance provider to extend coverage to a policyholder's contractual partner, nor does a contract on its own compel the state to grant immigration rights to the contractual partner of a citizen. The state must therefore put directives in place to determine which obligations a relationship imposes on third parties.[30]

The same is true of third parties who have *rights* that are affected yet not provided for in a relationship contract. Children are the obvious example. If two parents contract with each other, or a parent contracts with a non-parent, the interests of the child are affected and must be protected. Providing this protection may mean overriding the contractual terms.

---

[29] The first sort of directive, default rules for non-contractors, might seem more extensive than the second, but in practice the directives involved in regulating contracts can be extensive. As Shultz writes, 'To argue that marriage ought to be governed to a greater degree by private choices about behavior and obligation is not to recommend the abandonment of public policy considerations. Important public policies already permeate contract law. If marriage contracts were legally recognized, special policies would be developed to meet the particular needs of this subject area as they have been in other areas of contract law. Thus, even while conceding greater private governance of marriage, the law might choose to retain public policy barriers that might, for example, render invalid contracts such as the Homosexual or Open Marriage examples.' (Shultz, 'Contractual Ordering of Marriage' p. 304.)

[30] See Christensen, 'Legal Ordering of Family Values'; Mary Lyndon Shanley, 'The State of Marriage and the State in Marriage' in Anita Bernstein (ed.), *Marriage Proposals: Questioning a Legal Status* (New York: New York University Press, 2006); Martha Albertson Fineman, 'The Meaning of Marriage' in Anita Bernstein (ed.), *Marriage Proposals: Questioning a Legal Status* (New York: New York University Press, 2006) p. 58.

To see the role of state directives more clearly, consider the following aspects of personal relationships:

1. Those which need regulation because they involve non-consenting third parties, for example children, employers, or businesses.

2. Those which the state has a legitimate interest in regulating, because they concern matters of justice or because they are matters which need to be determinate in law. For example, property distribution is both a matter of justice and something about which the law must provide a determinate answer in cases of dispute. Next-of-kinship arrangements, to take another example, also require legal determinacy.

3. Those which the state has no interest in regulating, other than as part of the general state function of regulating agreements. For example, the state has no interest in regulating who mows my lawn *unless* I enter into a legally-binding agreement attributing this responsibility to someone, in which case the state has a legitimate interest in regulating my contract simply *qua* contract.

The first and second areas will need to be settled by state directive even if we take a contract approach to personal relationships: the need for regulation is such that there will need to be default rules for those without contracts. The state cannot refuse to rule on a question of who is responsible for looking after a child, or who owns a house in which more than one person has invested, simply because there is no contract in place. Moreover, the areas in which the state needs to provide default rules even under a contract approach are often, by that very logic, the most important areas of personal relationships. So even under a contract approach the state will inevitably make directives about fundamental, and possibly controversial, aspects of partnerships. It cannot be a benefit of contract, then, that it avoids state directives on these areas.[31]

Instead, the advocate of contract needs to show that the state ought to allow deviation from the default directives via the contract mechanism. She also needs to show that the state should allow contracts on aspects of relationships not governed by default laws. By definition, under the directive approach the state can refuse to rule on questions of type 3. If two partners dispute whose turn it is to mow the lawn they do not, under the directive approach, have recourse to a

---

[31] As Singer notes, the need for state directives on matters such as these should not be a source of regret. There is a crucial role for state involvement in family life, since it allows not only for protection of individuals within families but also for the promotion of basic justice. See 'The Privatization of Family Law' Part IV.

court to settle the dispute. Advocates of contract need to show that courts can legitimately be called upon to regulate such disputes if the two parties have chosen to draw up a relationship contract governing them. This highlights the second way in which contracts involve the state: enforcement.

## 4.5 Contract and Enforcement

The question of whether to allow personal relationships to be regulated by contract is therefore a question about legal enforcement. The case for relationship contracts is a case for allowing individuals to make *legally enforceable* agreements about their relationships, even on matters in which the state would otherwise have no interest. As Shultz asks, framing the question in terms of marriage, 'would it be desirable for the state to decline to prescribe marital conduct and values, leaving those matters to private choice, while *at the same time* accepting the role of enforcer and dispute resolver regarding obligations privately chosen?'[32] On a contract approach the state appears to step away from personal relationships, leaving their structure to individuals, but at the same time it embroils itself firmly at the heart of such relationships, gaining *new* powers to intervene, enforce, and punish on any matter at all on which the parties have chosen to contract. There is no necessary correlation, then, between a libertarian minimal state and the immunity of the private sphere.[33]

Both personal choice *and* enforcement are needed for a regime to be described as contractual. If the state enforces rules about personal relationships but allows for no private choice about how relationships are governed then it is clear that state uses a directive model. But a state that allows for great diversity in personal relationships but which refuses to enforce any agreements between partners is also using a directive model, not a contractual model. Such a state is simply using directives that are few in number or libertarian in character. For example, a state that says 'all disputes in personal relationships are to be solved by the private negotiations of the parties involved' is using a directive model, even though it is

---

[32] Shultz, 'Contractual Ordering of Marriage' p. 213, emphasis added.

[33] As Christensen puts it, 'As a starting position, ideological proponents of private ordering are favorably disposed towards the state's legal abstention from nonmarital family affairs.... Such libertarianism works well enough so long as family members are willing to honor their agreements or to sensibly modify terms in light of evolving circumstance. As in traditional families, it is when relationships deteriorate irreparably (or end by death), that the state's legal intervention may be required.' (Christensen, 'Legal Ordering of Family Values' p. 1326.) Now of course state intervention to enforce contracts has a different flavour from state intervention to enforce directives, in that the former need not imply that the state approves of the contract which is being enforced. Yet enforce it it does.

one that allows for unlimited diversity within relationships. It is a directive regime since it states an inescapable rule for all relationships (that they are entirely privately regulated), and since it refuses to allow state enforcement of private arrangements.

This example emphasizes that there is no direct link between liberty and state inaction, and between liberty and the choice of contract versus directive. The directive regime of non-interference just envisaged is in no way equivalent to one maximizing individual liberty (at least not equal liberty), since it is compatible with traditional patriarchal views of marriage that allowed husbands to rape and attack their wives without fear of legal penalty. And we can envisage other directive regimes that actively manage personal relationships so as to secure maximum equal liberty for both parties. On the other hand, we can imagine contracts that both maximize individual liberty (by setting out very few restrictions on how the partners may act) or those that curtail it significantly (for example, a contract that imposes a great many restrictions on daily action and allows for enormously punitive punishments if the contract is breached or if one party seeks to dissolve the partnership).[34] So the choice between directive and contract is not a choice between liberty and constraint: the liberty inherent in either regime depends entirely on the content of the directives or the contracts.

The matter at stake, then, is not whether to maximize personal liberty. Instead the dispute is whether individuals should be able to devise their own forms of legal obligation. The defining feature of the contract approach is that it allows for private ordering of personal relationships via *legally enforceable* agreements.

Return to Weitzman's advantages of relationship contracts. Many of these refer to the way that the *process of drawing up a contract* can strengthen a relationship: by clarifying expectations and providing a standard against which the couple can measure their own behaviour. These significant advantages could be secured without the ensuing discussion resulting in a contract, or without any formal written document that the couple might agree on being legally enforceable. They are advantages of full, frank, and formal discussion in a relationship, not advantages of a particular legal regime. Any acceptable, just state must of course permit or even encourage such discussion: there could be no freedom of personal relationships without the freedom for partners to debate the terms of their relationship and come to agreements about how it will be organized. In questioning the value of relationship contracts, then, I am in no way questioning

---

[34] Here I set to one side the complicated question of whether a contract can properly be said to restrict individual liberty if it is entered into freely. I discuss this question at length in my *Sex, Culture, and Justice*, particularly in chapter 7.

the value of formal discussion and agreement between partners about their relationship. The question is whether the *legal regulation* of relationships should be contractual, and thus whether the agreements that may well be invaluable to a secure relationship should be *legally enforceable.*

A legally enforceable relationship contract, then, will either create legally enforceable duties where none previously existed, in cases such as the lawn-mowing example, or it will create legally enforceable duties that differ from the default directives. Different issues are raised in each case.

Consider first whether individuals should be free to enter into contracts that deviate from the default directives. As discussed above, even under a contract regime there are aspects of personal relationships in which the law will have to provide regulation where there is no contract. These aspects are inevitably among the most important: they concern matters like shared property, caring responsibilities, and child custody.[35] Their importance means that they are crucial to the wellbeing of the partners and others affected by them, and so it is likely that some people will want arrangements different from any mandated by the state.

This issue is similar in structure to that of whether married couples, in a regime of state-recognized marriage, should be allowed to enter into legally enforceable contracts alongside their marriage. These contracts would impose legal duties on the marrying couple that were either over and above those imposed by marriage law (for example, if the couple contracted about responsibility for housework) or that modified the duties imposed by marriage law (for example, a pre-nuptial contract designed to prevent a divorce court from imposing its own financial settlement). Pre-nuptial contracts are now common in the USA, but until recently American courts usually refused to enforce such contracts, for several reasons.[36] Where contracts are designed to override marriage law then the public policy concerns that underpin that law naturally tell against allowing deviation, whether those concerns be liberal commitments to liberty and equality or communitarian or religious commitments to particular marital forms.

Even where contracts merely add to existing law, courts have been reluctant to enforce them. The reasons for this reluctance fall into two categories. The first set of reasons concerns the way that courts have interpreted contract law. According to orthodox, classical contract law a contract can exist only where there is a bargain, an exchange of benefits, and this model does not easily fit intimate relationships—particularly where there are also legal prohibitions to 'meretricious'

---

[35] As noted above, the default directives on these cases may be found in other branches of law, such as property law.

[36] Shultz, 'Contractual Ordering of Marriage' p. 232ff.

contractual exchange of sexual services.[37] The reasons in the second category are normative. They include 'a fear of disrupting domestic harmony, sometimes with a suggestion that such enforcement should not be necessary in a successful marriage' and concerns about 'the institutional competence of courts to deal with the issues that arise between spouses'.[38]

Shultz argues that these reasons do not withstand scrutiny, and I agree that the public policy concerns that prevent contracts deviating from marriage law are insufficient normative grounds for forbidding private contracts in a society which recognizes marriage. For, as we saw in Part I, there are no adequate public policy reasons for egalitarians, be they liberals or feminists, to support the existing institution of marriage. If the institution as it stands is unjust then there are good reasons for allowing partners to deviate from it via their own contracts. But, when thinking about the marriage-free state, we assume that the default regulations will themselves be just. Therefore, allowing people to make contracts that deviate from the default directives means allowing them to make contracts that deviate from *just* directives.

Earlier I outlined the ways that contracts can violate egalitarian justice. A just state would not permit relationship contracts that were unjust in those ways. But the state might permit deviations from the default directives if those deviations were themselves compatible with justice.[39] If all deviations from the default must be just then the only reason to prevent contracts would be that there is a specific good that is attained by having universal directives that apply to everyone: a fixed set of duties that everyone shares and that no one can change. This argument is essentially communitarian rather than liberal, appealing to the value of shared understandings and traditions, and both liberals and feminists are rightly sceptical of such appeals.[40] So there is good reason to allow deviations from the default

---

[37] See Christensen, 'Legal Ordering of Family Values'; John Wightman, 'Intimate Relationships'. Alternative interpretations of contract law exist which do not have these limitations, most notably Ian Macneil's Relational Contract Theory set out in works such as his 'Contracts: Adjustment of Long-Term Economic Relations Under Classical, Neoclassical, and Relational Contract Law' in *Northwestern University Law Review* 72 (1977). Relational contract theory is discussed later in this chapter.

[38] Shultz, 'Contractual Ordering of Marriage' p. 235.

[39] One reason to allow contracts as a supplement to default directives is as a mechanism for a couple to achieve greater certainty in cases where the default directive allows for the exercise of judicial discretion. I am grateful to Jo Miles for this observation.

[40] See Susan Moller Okin, *Justice, Gender, and the Family* (New York: Basic Books, 1989) and 'Is Multiculturalism Bad for Women?' in Susan Moller Okin, Joshua Cohen, Matthew Howard, and Martha Nussbaum (eds), *Is Multiculturalism Bad for Women?* (Princeton, NJ: Princeton University Press, 1999); Brian Barry, *Culture and Equality*; John Rawls, *Political Liberalism* (New York: Columbia University Press, 1993).

where those deviations are themselves compatible with egalitarian justice.[41] Indeed, Fineman associates US courts' increasing willingness to enforce pre-nuptial agreements with the increasing acceptance of gender equality.[42] Another way of describing this situation is that there could be a variety of available directives from which parties may choose, with a default applying if no choice has been made. After all, if only just agreements are to be allowed then the state will have to stipulate which agreements are just. Stability and secure expectations would be best served if the state made such stipulations in advance where possible, so that partners knew from the outset whether their agreements were enforceable.

But the most distinctive aspect of the contract approach is that it allows for partners to make contracts creating new duties in areas where there are no default directives. A traditional marriage vow creates a number of duties between two people. For example, traditional Christian vows stipulate that the spouses should have certain feelings for each other: they must love, honour, or cherish each other. They commit the spouses to do certain things and to refrain from others: to provide emotional and financial support, to share property, and to refrain from committing adultery. Traditional Christian vows also include conditions for the permanence of the agreement: the marriage should last in sickness and in health, for better or worse, for richer or poorer, and until death. Under a traditional marital regime, though, these duties are enforceable only in the sense that failure to live up to them is in some cases grounds for divorce. Are these the sorts of duties that could be managed via contract? Should individuals be able to make such agreements, and to make them legally binding?

An argument in favour of relationship contracts of this sort is made by Elizabeth Scott and Robert Scott.[43] They argue that freedom entails the freedom to commit. It is a mistake, they argue, to think of such contracts as inimical to freedom; on the contrary, autonomy is enhanced if people are able to make binding commitments, because such commitments allow access to greater goods than can be achieved without them. These greater goods could be personal, such as when an individual finds personal fulfilment in committing herself to live a certain sort of valuable life. Or they could be goods that can only be achieved in partnership with another person. Commitments to relationship contracts enable

---

[41]  Of course, a great deal more needs to be said about what sorts of relationships are just and thus what sorts of deviations count as being compatible with justice. I am not able to say more about that here, but have done so with respect to Rawlsian justice in my '"The Family as a Basic Institution": A Feminist Analysis of the Basic Structure as Subject' in Ruth Abbey (ed.), *Feminist Interpretations of Rawls* (University Park: Penn State University Press, 2013).

[42]  Fineman, *The Autonomy Myth* p. 125ff.

[43]  Elizabeth S. Scott and Robert J. Scott, 'Marriage as Relational Contract' in *Virginia Law Review* 84(7) (October 1998) pp. 1246–7.

the contracting partners to reap the benefits of cooperation without the risks of defection. The security of a permanent commitment allows people to make investments that they would otherwise be wary of making, since the costs of defection would be high. These could be financial investments, such as purchasing a house together; emotional investments, such as having a child together; or investments that allow for specialization and the division of labour, such as giving up paid employment in favour of domestic and caring responsibilities.[44]

Undoubtedly these are among the many benefits of being in a committed relationship. But we must ask not 'are committed relationships beneficial?' but 'is justice best served by *legal enforcement* of relationship contracts?' It is worth noting that the decision to enforce a relationship contract will almost always entail the choice to end the relationship, for surely few if any relationships would survive a legal case. Legal enforcement will therefore mean the end of the relationship, and this in itself will be a barrier to its use in those cases where the wronged party wants to continue the relationship.

There are two main methods for enforcing contracts: specific performance and compensation. Both are complex and problematic in the relationship context.

### 4.5.1 Specific performance

As Shultz notes, 'public enforcement of private bargains . . . is partial at best', since many people do not seek redress, and since in most cases courts order compensation rather than specific performance. Specific performance is a legal term indicating that the court requires the defaulting party actually to perform that aspect of the contract on which she has defaulted. So if specific performance were required of an employment contract then a doctor who had refused to perform an operation would be compelled actually to perform that operation. In another context, a building company that had provided workmanship below the standard agreed in the contract with the client would be required not to waive the fee or pay compensation but to re-do the job.

There are various reasons why specific performance in cases such as these might be inappropriate, most obviously that such failures reduce the wronged party's faith in the work of the violating party (who would want to be operated on by an unwilling surgeon)? These generic problems of enforcement apply particularly to relationship contracts. Specific enforcement may be possible in cases where couples have contracted on matters such as property division upon separation, and other matters on which the state must provide default directives.

---

[44] For discussion of these issues see Antony W. Dnes and Robert Rowthorn (eds) in *The Law and Economics of Marriage & Divorce* (Cambridge: Cambridge University Press, 2002).

But specific performance looks particularly unlikely if couples move beyond these subject matters and contract on matters in which the state would otherwise be uninterested. Many aspects of the traditional marriage contract are too vague to be enforced: it is not clear what they require, and their requirements are likely to differ from couple to couple.[45] How could a court tell whether one partner had failed in her responsibility to 'cherish' the other? And it is not possible to force someone to love another, and quite possibly honouring, cherishing, and even straightforward caring are also necessarily voluntary.

Even where a contract is clear and compliance can be objectively assessed, it is still difficult to envisage legal enforcement. For example, Elizabeth Kingdom advocates relationship contracts and imagines one with 'a clause to the effect that the partners take turns over relocating in order to take advantage of job opportunities, even if it involved financial loss'.[46] Specific enforcement of this clause would be impossible. It would be a profound violation of individual liberty to coerce one partner into compliance, since that would entail coercing her to resign from her job, coercing her to leave her home (both the physical property and the geographical location), and coercing her to live somewhere where she did not want to live. This level of coercion is generally reserved for cases where people need to be punished for egregious criminality; making such coercion simply what the relationship contract entailed would be a stunning violation of liberty. Moreover, the idea of such enforcement is virtually nonsensical, for a loving relationship could surely not survive if one partner were legally coerced in this way.

Contract-type negotiations about matters such as relocation are very difficult in an intimate relationship. This is partly because negotiations conflict with the strong norm that such relationships should not be conducted in a self-interested, maximizing manner. And it is partly because personal relationships and personal preferences develop and evolve and yet are supposed to remain voluntary and enjoyable for both parties, exacerbating problems of presentiation referred to above. In a one-off economic contract it does not matter too much if one party comes to wish they had not agreed to a particular clause: it does not undermine my mortgage contract if I wish, one year after signing it, that I had not agreed to be tied in for five years. I simply have to grin and bear it. But significant grinning and bearing it, particularly over major issues such as location, is not

---

[45] For discussion see Ira Mark Ellman and Sharon Lohr, 'Marriage as Contract, Opportunistic Violence, and Other Bad Arguments for Fault Divorce' in *University of Illinois Law Review* (1997) pp. 744–6.

[46] Elizabeth Kingdom, 'Cohabitation Contracts and the Democratization of Personal Relations' p. 19.

compatible with the happiness and affection that a personal relationship is supposed to foster.

The defender of relationship contracts might respond that the purpose of the contract is simply for the parties to set their expectations at the beginning of the relationship, and that it is valuable for people to be able to negotiate and agree on matters such as this. It is clear that the state should permit these sorts of non-legal agreements, in the sense that it should permit people to discuss the terms of their relationships and to come to agreements about matters such as relocation and career priority; it is barely possible even to imagine a well-functioning relationship where such discussions and agreements did not take place. But what distinguishes the contract approach is the claim that these agreements should be legally enforceable.

### 4.5.2 Compensation

If specific performance is rarely plausible as a legal remedy then enforceability in a relationship contract context must mean the ability to impose a sanction in the case of an objectively-identifiable breach.[47] The most likely candidate for a sanction in the relationship contract context is compensatory fault-based alimony. Imagine, for example, that one party failed to meet their contractual commitment to monogamy and had an affair. An enforceable relationship contract might mean that the non-adulterous party would be entitled to compensatory payments from the adulterous one. Or, in the case suggested by Kingdom, the partner whose turn it was to relocate but who refused to do so could be compelled to compensate the other partner.[48] This approach, in the marriage context, is advocated by Margaret Brinig and Steven Crafton, who argue that divorce *without* fault-based alimony renders the marriage contract unenforceable and encourages 'opportunistic behavior' by encouraging default on the

---

[47] This is also true for other contracts. If an employee breaches her contract of employment by refusing to perform her contracted duties, the employer will not be able to use the courts to force her actually to perform those duties. Its rights are limited to the right to terminate the contract, and possibly to extract a financial penalty if it has suffered losses.

[48] Note that the wronged party is unlikely to feel happy with the situation: monetary compensation is unlikely to compensate. Financial compensation seems to be the wrong sort of thing. Unlike in a commercial contract, where the ultimate objective for both parties is financial gain broadly construed, personal relationships are not pursued with that objective. The very wording of the clause imagined by Kingdom highlights this: the parties agree to take turns to relocate 'even if it involve[s] financial loss'. If the wronged party prefers that, in accordance with their relationship contract, the partnership persists but relocates to the new location, whereas the wronging party prefers that the partnership persists in the existing location, it is somewhat unsatisfying that the only legal recourse is that the partnership should break up, that the two parties should live in separate locations, but that one partner should pay the other some money.

terms of the contract. Brinig and Crafton thus advocate the retention of no-fault divorce but the institution of fault-based alimony.[49]

The equivalent position for a contract-based regime in the marriage-free state would be that couples would not have to demonstrate fault in order to halt their contractual obligations, but that breach of contract would be compensable. The amount of money could be agreed in advance, but in order to be an effective sanction, as Brinig and Crafton advocate, it would need to be fairly considerable. Alternatively, if the compensatory payment were justified in corrective justice terms, and if the breach were such that separation occurred, the payment would have to compensate the wronged individual for the investments she had made into the relationship, and these too could be considerable. They might include direct financial investment into joint property, emotional investment into the relationship, career sacrifices to enhance the career of the other party or to take on domestic and caring work, and sacrifices in future romantic prospects. In order to be a sufficient disincentive for breach, such payments might also be significant disincentives against contracting in the first place—a result that would displease most advocates of relationship contracts.

Fault-based compensatory payments for breaches of the relationship contract face two main problems: problems concerning equality and distributive justice, and problems concerning third parties, particularly children. The problem with children is easy to see. Many partnerships include dependent children. Arrangements made for dissolving those partnerships will have to be in the interests of the children, possibly even their best interests. These considerations could easily conflict with any fault-based alimony claims. If the partner who has breached the relationship contract and is therefore liable to pay compensation will also have even partial custody of the children then any loss she suffers through having to pay compensation is also an unjust loss to her children.

The second problem relates to issues of distributive justice: need, equality and dependence. If alimony is awarded according to fault, then the partner who has to pay compensation could be left considerably worse off than the wronged partner, and possibly even in a condition of need. This might particularly harm women, since they are more likely to take on caring responsibilities rather than paid employment within a relationship, and so if they are left having to pay compensation to their partners for breach of relationship contract (for example by having an affair) they could easily be left with little or no financial support. So fault-based alimony could result in a woman who

[49] Margaret F. Brinig and Steven M. Crafton, 'Marriage and Opportunism' in *Journal of Legal Studies* 23(2) (June 1994).

has sacrificed her career and devoted many years to her family, leaving her with no independent source of income and a severely compromised position in both the labour and the relationship markets, having to pay compensation to a wealthy professional man who has undamaged career and relationship prospects because she has had an affair or does not wish to relocate, away from friends and family, to follow his career. This is not a position that feminists or egalitarians should support.

Of course, all compensation payments may leave the person receiving the compensation better off than the person paying it, so this cannot be a general objection to compensation. The specific problem in the relationship contract case is that personal relationships involve people combining the most intimate aspects of their lives, and engaging in practices such as sexual fidelity and cohabitation that must be fully consensual if they are to be compatible with justice. Imposing a financial penalty on someone who wishes to stop such practices is deeply problematic, since that penalty or its threat undermines the consent. For example, Ellman and Lohr raise the horrifying fact that in some states in the USA a spouse cannot receive alimony *at all* if she has committed adultery, meaning that 'In those states a violent husband could physically abuse his adulterous wife mercilessly, without triggering any consequences insofar as his alimony obligations were concerned.'[50] Now, a contract regime is preferable to a profoundly unjust directive regime such as this, since it at least allows some couples to draw up more tolerable agreements. But of course a contract regime also allows couples to draw up agreements that replicate or exacerbate such injustice, such that an abused woman could be left unable to leave her abusive partner if some other, more minor, fault of hers would leave her destitute if the relationship were to be dissolved and its contract enforced.

Moreover, the problems of children and inequality are not independent. A partner who has been the primary carer of children is likely to be best placed to retain custody of them on separation. So if the partner who needs to pay fault-based alimony does not work outside the home, or works part-time in order to prioritise caring responsibilities, then she is *both* more likely to be left in need as a result of the payments she must make *and* more likely to be responsible for the care of children. Fault-based alimony will thus have extremely deleterious consequences for stay-at-home parents and their children.

One response to this problem is to say that the state should be responsible for those in financial need, not their ex-partners. Just because two people used to be in a relationship it does not follow that they should have permanent

---

[50] Ellman and Lohr, 'Marriage as Contract' pp. 747–8.

responsibility for each other's ongoing financial support. On this response a stay-at-home partner who is left in a position of need as a result of having to pay fault-based alimony should still have to pay that alimony, but should be eligible for support from the state. This solution has some appeal since it reflects the idea that a relationship should not permanently define a person's financial status. However, the solution actually satisfies neither the advocate nor the critic of fault-based alimony. It does not satisfy the advocate of fault-based alimony since it lessens the motivation to comply with the contract in the first place: if the state bails out a partner who is made needy because she has to pay compensation for having breached a contract, then the contract is not a workable sanction. It does not satisfy the critic of fault-based alimony, someone who finds the idea of financial penalty for relationship failings distasteful, since it merely shifts the financial burden to the state. If it offends egalitarian sensibilities that a stay-at-home mother should have to pay her wealthy professional partner compensation for an affair, it surely offends still further to think that taxpayers in general should have to provide that compensation.[51]

Finally, note that it will be very difficult for courts to identify fault in a sufficiently precise manner to allocate compensation. As Ellman and Lohr point out, allegations of fault are likely to be made by both sides. Interpreting and ruling on them requires a detailed and nuanced understanding of the relationship as a whole—an understanding that is impossible to acquire without yet more investigation into the most intimate aspects of a relationship. And experience of judges' behaviour, and of human behaviour in general, suggests that rulings on such cases may reflect judges' explicit or implicit bias as much as they reflect an accurate interpretation of fact and contract.[52]

There are various problems, then, with allowing individuals to regulate their relationships via enforceable contracts. Some sorts of contracts cannot realistically be legally enforced at all, since it is nonsensical to think of a legal obligation to love or to care for another. Other aspects of relationship contracts are more determinate but are unlikely candidates for specific performance. The question of enforcement therefore becomes one about the appropriateness of compensation in the case of breach, and it is here that contracts between

---

[51] A related but inverse consideration applies to the alternative remedy of community service considered by Elizabeth F. Emens in her 'Monogamy's Law: Compulsory Monogamy and Polyamorous Existence' in *New York University Review of Law and Social Change* 29 (2004). While this may act as a deterrent or punishment of breach it does not act as compensation for the wronged party. It also implicates the state or the community, as beneficiary of the remedy, as endorsing the initial contract. Depending on the content of the contract this may fall outside the public interest, even if only as a breach of neutrality.

[52] Ellman and Lohr, 'Marriage as Contract' p. 735.

those in a personal relationship may be more problematic to enforce than those between strangers.

## 4.6   Relational Contract Theory

Relational contract theory (RCT), developed by Ian Macneil and others, draws attention to the limits of orthodox contract law in dealing with arrangements that are ongoing and trust-based, rather than discrete and purely based on wealth-maximization.[53] Traditional contract law works best for one-off contracts. But many contracts, both commercial contracts and *a fortiori* relationship contracts, take place in the context of an ongoing relationship and recurring transactions.[54] In these contexts the parties have an interest in maintaining the relationship, not just in enforcing the particular terms of the contract; and the parties' obligations and legitimate expectations are laid out in informal and context-sensitive norms as well as in explicit contractual terms.[55]

RCT has gained significant support in the jurisprudence of contract law, and several scholars have argued for its particular applicability to family law.[56] Some courts have also employed an RCT approach in deciding cases in which unmarried couples separate and assets must be divided. The landmark case in the USA is *Marvin v Marvin*, in which the California Supreme Court found that non-marital relationship contracts could be enforced, whether written or not, as long as their existence could be demonstrated to the court.[57] What this approach means is that courts must look not only for explicit, formal, written contracts between parties, but also for 'relational' contracts: implicit, evolving, unwritten agreements based on the realities and everyday functioning of a particular relationship. So, in deciding how to divide the equity in a house, a court might look not only at the name on the deeds but also at who has actually been paying the bills, or whether one of the parties provides unpaid domestic services to the household as a whole. To take another example, in deciding whether to grant custody of a child to a person who is not a legally-recognized parent (for example,

---

[53] Macneil, 'Contracts: Adjustment of Long-Term Economic Relations'; Christensen, 'Legal Ordering of Family Values'.

[54] Eisenberg goes further, stating boldly 'Every aspect of [classical contract law] was incorrect.' However, he is also critical of relational contract theory. Melvin A. Eisenberg, 'Why There Is No Law of Relational Contracts' in *Northwestern University Law Review* 94 (1999–2000) p. 808.

[55] Wightman, 'Intimate Relationships'.

[56] See, for example, Christensen, 'Legal Ordering of Family Values'; Kellye Y. Testy, 'An Unlikely Resurrection' in *Northwestern University Law Review* 90 (1995); Scott and Scott, 'Marriage as Relational Contract'; Tidwell and Linzer, 'The Flesh-Colored Band Aid'.

[57] *Marvin v Marvin* 18 Cal.3d 660 (1976). For a critique see Ellman, 'Contract Thinking'.

the non-biological parent in a same-sex couple who has not legally adopted the child), a court using an RCT approach would look not just at the legal facts of biological parenthood or adoptive status, but also at who actually engages in the everyday activity of parenting.[58]

The example of parenting demonstrates one of the strengths of this approach: it is able to deal with families as they really are, not as the state imagines they should be. So relational contract theory can be a truly inclusive approach to personal relationships. The particular issue of parenthood, be it biological, legal, or functional, raises issues too complex to deal with here. But the functional approach has the potential to work well in adult relationships. One of the benefits of such an approach is that it helps to remove the vulnerability that is suffered by partners who, whether by their own volition or by the reluctance of their more powerful partners, are neither married nor have a relationship contract.

However, a relational contract theory approach is not without problems. Christensen points out that, since it does not rely on simply enforcing a formal, written contract, RCT requires a court to delve into the realities, actual assumptions, and everyday actions of the partners. This inquiry is possibly a violation of privacy and certainly takes contract away from its libertarian roots.[59]

Moreover, Robson and Valentine point out that an attempt to discern an implied contract can lead to results that are surprising to the parties:

Because of a judge's power to find an implied contract—even if the couple has not expressly documented their promises and agreements—contract principles may enter a...relationship unexpectedly. In jurisdictions that follow *Marvin v. Marvin* and effectuate the 'intent' of the parties, 'conduct may give rise to an implied contract completely at odds with the intent of one or more of the parties; or unanticipated equitable relief may be granted contrary to expectation. Thus, both parties may be surprised by the consequences of verbal statements and nonverbal acts.'[60]

So relational contract theory lacks the determinacy of both traditional contracts, where determinacy is provided by the explicit terms of the contract to which both parties have formally agreed, and state directives, where determinacy is provided by explicit laws that are defined in advance and which apply to all couples in functionally-similar relationships.

An RCT approach attempts to capture the advantages of both contract and directive. It attempts to mirror the beneficial aspects of the directive approach by

---

[58]  See Christensen, 'Legal Ordering of Family Values'.

[59]  Christensen, 'Legal Ordering of Family Values' p. 1338.

[60]  Robson and Valentine, 'Lov(h)ers: Lesbians as Intimate Partners' p. 522, quoting H. Curry and D. Clifford, *A Legal Guide for Lesbian and Gay Couples: A NOLO Press Self-Help Law Book* §8 (1989).

involving the courts in making judgments about fairness in relationships. And it attempts to mirror the advantages of the contract approach by tailoring judgments to individual couples and their circumstances, rather than imposing a one-size-fits-all model. But this hybrid also replicates the disadvantages of both forms of relationship regulation. RCT replicates traditional contract's potential for inequality since it requires courts to make judgments with reference not to universal principles of justice but to an implied contract between the parties—a contract which might itself be unjust. And RCT replicates the potential that the directive approach has for state rulings that are heavy-handed and unwanted by either party. The regulation employed in the marriage-free state is a better alternative.

## Conclusion

Relationship contracts have been advocated as a means of protecting both equality and liberty. In this chapter I explored familiar egalitarian critiques of contract, and showed how these critiques are particularly applicable to relationship contracts. I then argued that contracts are not as beneficial to liberty as is often supposed. A contractual regime for regulating relationships does not keep the state out of family life, since default regulations are still needed and since a contract regime requires state enforcement. Moreover, these aspects of the state's involvement should make even non-libertarians wary of relationship contracts. It is hard to see how the state could meaningfully enforce relationship contracts without requiring specific performance, which would be a profound violation of liberty, or compensatory fault-based alimony, which would be a profound violation of equality.

Instead, the marriage-free state needs an alternative model of regulation, one that is based on neither contract nor status. The details of regulation in the marriage-free state are the subject of the next chapter.

# 5

# Regulating Relationships in the Marriage-Free State

This book advocates the abolition of state-recognized marriage and the institution of the marriage-free state. The marriage-free state is contrasted with a marriage regime, in which marriage not only exists as a social institution but is also legally recognized and directly regulated by the state. A marriage regime recognizes marriage by applying a *bundle* of rights and duties to married people *because* they are married.[1] The italics highlight the two parts of the claim. In a marriage regime, a society with state-recognized marriage, the members of a marrying couple thereby acquire a *bundle* of rights and duties that they did not previously have. These rights vary from one regime to another. They may include tax breaks, next-of-kinship rights, rights and duties of financial support, parental rights, and so on.[2] A significant portion of the rights and duties of marriage pertain to divorce: typically, a marriage regime will regulate divorce much more extensively than separation of unmarried couples. In a marriage regime, the bundle of rights and duties is given to the couple *because* they are married, not because they have

---

[1] This idea of state recognition does not exhaust the ways in which a state might take an interest in marriage. A state may also take an interest in marriage by defining and setting limits on it: stating who may and may not enter into a marriage and which procedures must be followed for a relationship to become a marriage. The next chapter sets out the ways that the marriage-free state takes an interest in private marriages.

Another important way the state might interact with marriage is by registering and enquiring about its existence, for example on official forms. The marriage-free state will not do this other than for the purpose of monitoring the prevalence of private marriage, or applying such regulations to private marriage as may be required by justice (such as a prohibition on marrying children).

[2] There are significant differences in family law across Western democracies, including significant variation in the differences between the legal rights of married and unmarried couples. In English and Welsh law, for example, married and unmarried couples are treated differently in matters of financial maintenance during the relationship; citizenship status; division of household goods, assets and debts on the dissolution of the relationship; alimony; inheritance rights and tax; and rights to a survivor's pension on the death of one partner. For more details, and for comparison between the legal position in various European countries, see Brienna Perelli-Harris and Nora Sánchez Gassen, 'How Similar are Cohabitation and Marriage? Legal Approaches to Cohabitation across Western Europe' in *Population and Development Review* 38(3) (2013).

chosen each right in turn (for they have not), and not because there is some other feature of their relationship that merits them (for non-married couples living in identical circumstances will lack some or all of these rights).

Abolishing state-recognized marriage and creating the marriage-free state would mean that the state would no longer provide a bundle of rights and duties to people because they are married. It would not mean making it illegal for people to participate in the symbolic institution of marriage or to call themselves married. Without state-recognized marriage people could still engage in private religious or secular ceremonies of marriage, but these would have no legal status.

The marriage-free state still needs to regulate personal relationships. Regulation is still needed to protect the vulnerable, to secure justice, to provide legal determinacy, to settle third-party rights and duties, and to appropriately direct state taxation and provision. It is a basic assumption of this book that, if well-designed, regulation is beneficial to those who are regulated. That is to say, I reject the libertarian principle that state regulation is an evil to be avoided wherever possible. A lack of regulation does not secure freedom and equality; it merely leaves untouched whatever patterns of power and hierarchy exist in civil society. The domain of personal relationships is a domain of inequality, oppression, and vulnerability as much as it is a domain of care, respect, and support. Regulation is needed to secure freedom and equality for all. I therefore consider the situation of being excluded from the purview of just regulation to be one of disadvantage.

Some argue that personal relationships should be regulated on a contractual basis.[3] As I argued in the previous chapter the contractual model has various problems, and contracts cannot be the paradigmatic form of regulation, although they may play a role. Even if relationship contracts are permitted, there still must be a regulatory framework for personal relationships. Such regulation is required for several reasons. Even if contracts are allowed, the state must set limits on contracts that would be unjust for the contracting parties (such as contracts amounting to slavery) or for third parties such as children. The state must also provide guidance for disputes that arise between people in personal relationships who have not made a contract. Regulation is also needed to protect legitimate state interests and to provide clarity on matters that must be determinate in law. So relationship contracts cannot replace marriage. There must still be a regulatory

---

[3] Advocates of regulating relationships on a contractual basis include Marjorie M. Shultz, 'Contractual Ordering of Marriage: A New Model for State Policy' in *California Law Review* 70 (1982); Lenore J. Weitzman, *The Marriage Contract: Spouses, Lovers and the Law* (London: Free Press, 1983); Martha Albertson Fineman, 'The Meaning of Marriage' in Anita Bernstein (ed.), *Marriage Proposals: Questioning a Legal Status* (New York: New York University Press, 2006).

framework, what I call a series of state directives,[4] applying to personal relationships.

In this chapter I set out my proposals for regulating relationships in the marriage-free state. The marriage-free state is informed by the two key values of equality and freedom. Equality is of paramount importance: the marriage-free state aims above all to secure equality between citizens. The sorts of equality that are most relevant to the regulation of relationships are equality between the parties in a relationship, equality between those in a relationship and those not in a relationship, equality between children regardless of their parents' relationship status, and gender and sexual equality.

The second key value of the marriage-free state is freedom or autonomy. Traditional marriage is deficient in its protection of liberty, since legal regulation of relationships is tied to one specific, traditional and value-laden relationship form. Contract is often proposed as a liberty-enhancing alternative to marriage, but contract is deficient in its protection of equality, and the need for default directives means that it does not straightforwardly enhance liberty either. The marriage-free state provides room for diversity of relationships since it offers no blueprint for personal relationships and does not confine regulation to any particular relationship model.

Regulation in the marriage-free state has three features, each of which is addressed in turn in this chapter. First, regulation of relationships is *piecemeal not holistic*. Second, relationships are defined by *practice not status*. Third, liberty is secured, without compromising equality, by *opting out not opting in*.

## 5.1  Piecemeal not Holistic

It is useful to distinguish two general models for the state regulation of relationships: holistic and piecemeal. Marriage is a holistic form of regulation. In contrast, the marriage-free state uses piecemeal regulation.

*Holistic* regulation of relationships involves creating a status, such as marriage or an analogous alternative, which brings with it a bundle of legal rights and responsibilities. Both existing marriage and civil unions are examples of holistic regulation. When entering into these relationships, individuals take on a bundle of rights and responsibilities covering multiple areas of life. On a holistic model of

---

[4] Alternative terms used by others include 'public ordering' (as a contrast to the private ordering of contracts) or 'ascription' (as contrasted with both private law and self-ascription or registration). See, for example, Craig W. Christensen, 'Legal Ordering of Family Values: The Case of Gay and Lesbian Families' in *Cardozo Law Review* 18 (1996–7); Law Commission of Canada, *Beyond Conjugality: Recognizing and Supporting Close Personal Adult Relationships* (2001).

marriage reform the state continues to award some people a bundle of special rights and duties. It simply awards that bundle on the basis of a status other than marriage.

Civil unions are the most familiar alternative to marriage on the holistic model, but they are not the only one. Several progressive thinkers have proposed new holistic statuses to replace marriage. Some advocate versions of civil unions that differ in some way from the existing legislative models.[5] Other theorists advocate completely new statuses, usually replacing the marital focus on adult sexual partnership with an emphasis on care. For example, Tamara Metz proposes disestablishing marriage and replacing it with a state-recognized Intimate Care-Giving Union (ICGU) status, one that could apply to any relationship of intimate care-giving.[6]

All of these alternative holistic models improve on the state recognition of traditional marriage by breaking from the patriarchal, exclusionary, and controversial meaning of that institution. In other words, each is to be preferred to marriage symbolically. Their practical advantages depend on their particularities. In England and Wales, civil partnerships afford the partners (who must be same-sex) much the same legal rights as are afforded to married spouses (who can be different- or same-sex). So these civil partnerships are neither better nor worse than marriage in terms of the practical support they provide to personal relationships.

Metz proposes a more radical alternative status which, unlike marriage, 'would be expressly tailored to protecting intimate care in its various forms'.[7] She makes the convincing case that care-giving is a better basis for public policy than marriage since care is a more fundamental activity: a primary good essential to human flourishing that nevertheless brings with it risks and vulnerabilities. For Metz, state recognition and protection of care-giving status therefore protects the vulnerable and allows all to access vital human goods. ICGU status thus has a different basis from marriage, but its holistic form is the same. As Metz puts it, 'In many ways, an ICGU status would look like marital status today. It would afford legal recognition from which would flow various legal presumptions. . . . It is as a

---

[5] See, for example, Richard H. Thaler and Cass R. Sunstein, *Nudge: Improving Decisions about Health, Wealth and Happiness* (New Haven, CT: Yale University Press, 2008) and Andrew F. March, 'What Lies Beyond Same-Sex Marriage? Marriage, Reproductive Freedom and Future Persons in Liberal Public Justification' in *Journal of Applied Philosophy* 27(1) (2010).

[6] Tamara Metz, *Untying the Knot: Marriage, the State, and the Case for their Divorce* (Princeton, NJ: Princeton University Press, 2010).

[7] Metz, *Untying the Knot* p. 135.

status in particular—that is, a bundle of rights and responsibilities—that the ICGU would benefit care.'[8]

I endorse the claim that care-giving is crucial and worthy of state protection. However, holistic regulation is not the best replacement for state-recognized marriage. Holistic regulation involves a *bundle* of rights and duties. Holistic approaches thus tend to assume that all the most important functions of life are met within one core relationship. This is the model behind civil unions. Many people, such as most married people, do centralize activities such as intimate coupledom, childrearing, property-sharing, next-of-kinship, and inheritance. For such people, the bundling feature of holistic regulation is unproblematic, even convenient. But the state should recognize that many individuals' arrangements are more wide-ranging.[9] Separated couples with children may continue to co-parent but share no other relationship. Others maintain a nuclear family unit but also share property or care with an elderly parent or sibling. Bundling caring activity into one privileged status does not capture the complexity and diversity of real lives.

A holistic bundled status involves the state in making value-judgements about better and worse ways of life and in marking one type of relationship out as the most fundamental.[10] This makes holistic regulation problematic for political liberals, and for anyone (comprehensive liberals, feminists) who rejects that particular relationship model. Indeed, as Metz herself notes, special expressive status akin to the symbolic significance of marriage might become attached to ICGU status, and the conferral of such status does involve the state in 'acting in a way that reflects particular political commitments'.[11] As discussed in Part I, privileging a particular relationship format or using it as the default social form can also entrench other forms of disadvantage. For example, African Americans often form female-headed single-parent households bolstered by supportive care

---

[8] Metz, *Untying the Knot* pp. 134, 138.

[9] According to the UK Office of National Statistics, in 2014 there were 2 million lone parents with dependent children (91% of which were women) and just under 7.5 million households containing only one person. There were also 313,000 households containing two or more families and these, along with cohabiting couple families, are the fastest growing household and family type in the UK. Only 63% of children live in a family headed by a married couple. 23% of children live in lone parent families and 11% of children live in families headed by opposite sex cohabiting couples. See Office of National Statistics, 'Families and Households, 2014' at http://www.ons.gov.uk/ons/rel/family-demography/families-and-households/2014/families-and-households-in-the-uk–2014.html.

[10] Metz explicitly acknowledges that '[b]oth marriages and ICGU status reflect value judgements' in *Untying the Knot* p. 148. Her argument is that ICGU status is preferable since care-giving is a legitimate area of state interest. Brake argues that political liberals should endorse minimal marriage since care is a primary good; I addressed her account in Chapter 3.

[11] Metz, *Untying the Knot* p. 148.

networks between female relatives, rather than two-person care unions, and African-American children are just as likely to live with a single mother who has *never* been married as they are to live with married parents. The majority of African-American children—66 per cent—do *not* live with married parents.[12]

Instead I propose *piecemeal* regulation, which rejects bundling. Piecemeal regulation involves the state regulating the different practices or activities of a relationship separately. By 'relationship practices' I mean an activity or area of life which is carried out in a personal relationship. So relationship practices include things such as property ownership, financial interdependence, emotional interdependence, care, parenting, cohabitation, next-of-kinship, and sexual intimacy. Under piecemeal regulation there is no assumption that all relationship practices coincide in one relationship. Thus there would be separate regulations for property ownership and division, child custody, immigration, and so on.

Not all relationship practices need regulation, or particularly extensive regulation, but the practices just listed are all candidates for regulation. Sex is regulated by laws requiring consent and, perhaps, limiting what can be consented to (for example, laws prohibiting extreme BDSM[13]). Emotional interdependence is largely unregulated in liberal societies, although the UK Serious Crime Act 2015 created a new offence of coercive control in intimate and family relationships. Care may be regulated by state provision of payments or respite for those with caring responsibilities. Cohabitation is regulated very differently in different jurisdictions, and is often one of the most pressing areas of legal vulnerability for the unmarried. Property, finances, and parenting are routinely tightly regulated.

In the marriage-free state, regulations pertaining to each of these relationship practices would stand separately, recognizing that individuals form relationships with different people for different functions. Piecemeal regulation thus starts by working out what justice requires in any given area of human life, and secures that requirement for everyone.

---

[12] According to The United States Census Bureau, in 2015 the same proportion—34%—of black children live with a never-married single mother as live with married parents. This is in stark contrast with the situation for white children, of which 71% live with married parents and only 7% live with a never-married single mother. Among Hispanic children, 60% live with married parents and 13% live with a never-married single mother. Despite this racial variation in family forms, the gendered nature of lone parenting is standard across the races, with only between 1% and 2% of children living with a never-married lone father. See the United States Census Bureau, 'America's Families and Living Arrangements: 2015: Children: Table C3' at https://census.gov/topics/families. html.

[13] 'BDSM' stands for bondage and discipline, dominance and submission, and sadism and masochism.

The content of each and every one of the ideal piecemeal regulations is beyond the scope of this book. After all, my argument is that there should not be a separate category of marital or relationship law, but rather that each area of law should be considered separately or piecemeal. So separate arguments are needed both to identify each area of state interest and to specify what the just regulations should be. Such arguments would proceed as follows. For each proposed area of state regulation we ask first whether, and second why, the state has a legitimate interest in that regulation. The answers to these questions indicate the content of that regulation. Crucially, the arguments are separate for each proposed area of regulation.

The Law Commission of Canada report *Beyond Conjugality* proposes a form of regulation that has similarities to the marriage-free state.[14] It envisages a four-step process of lawmaking:

**Question 1**: Does the law pursue a legitimate policy objective?
- If not, the law ought to be repealed or fundamentally reconsidered.

**Question 2**: If the law's objectives are sound, do relationships matter? Are the relationships that are included important or relevant to the law's objectives?
- If not, revise the law to consider the individual and to remove the unnecessary relational reference.

**Question 3**: If relationships do matter, could the law allow individuals to choose which of their own close personal relationships they want to be subject to the law?
- If so, revise the law to permit self-definition of relevant relationships.

**Question 4**: If relationships do matter, and public policy requires that the law delineate the relevant relationships to which it applies, can the law be revised to more accurately capture the relevant range of relationships?
- If so, revise the law to include the appropriate mix of functional definitions and formal kinds of relationship status.[15]

Question 3 of this four-step process reflects the fact that the Law Commission of Canada prioritizes self-ascription through a process of registration, which is problematic since it retains the requirement to opt in so as to receive legal protection (what happens if one partner refuses to register another as a legitimate

---

[14] Similarities between the marriage-free state and the proposals of *Beyond Conjugality* are: an awareness of the need to consider non-conjugal relationships since a regulatory focus on conjugality limits autonomy; a practice-based approach to recognizing relationships; a focus on equality and autonomy; and a piecemeal approach to considering legislation. Differences include the fact that *Beyond Conjugality* prioritizes relationship registration over what I call directives and it calls ascription; and that it advocates retaining marriage, albeit for populist or democratic reasons rather than objective normative ones.

[15] Law Commission of Canada, *Beyond Conjugality* p. 30.

recipient of protection or rights?). Thus Question 4 recognizes that relationship functions sometimes need to be identified externally, and the four-step process as a whole is one way of thinking about the process of piecemeal lawmaking in the marriage-free state.

Another advocate of piecemeal regulation is Elizabeth Brake, whose idea of 'minimal marriage' was discussed in Chapter 3. Minimal marriage is a non-bundled, piecemeal regulation based on care-giving.[16] It means that the state 'can set no principled restrictions on the sex or number of spouses and the nature and purpose of their relationships, except that they be caring relationships'.[17] For example, under Brake's scheme each individual can be 'minimally married' to more than one person at a time, assigning different rights (which Brake calls 'minimal marriage rights') to different people.[18] This piecemeal aspect of Brake's account is valuable and important. She is right to highlight the fact that people can develop significant relationships (for her, this means caring relationships) and engage in significant relationship practices with more than one person at once. Minimal marriage, as a form of piecemeal regulation, enables the law to take proper account of the fact that someone might share property with a sibling, live with an elderly parent, co-parent with a former partner, and be financially dependent on a current partner, for example.

Piecemeal regulation has many advantages, then. It is more flexible, allowing a variety of ways of life to receive appropriate state attention. It can meet the needs of caring relationships but does not assume that all caring relationships are attached to other forms of intimacy or that people have only one sort of caring relationship. It avoids non-neutral bundling: the state does not have to make any pronouncements or assumptions about the sorts of relationship practices that should go together. Marriage, and alternative holistic regulations, assumes that activities such as economic interdependence, emotional commitment, parenting, and shared residence not only do but should coincide. Piecemeal regulation allows the law to engage with relationships as they really are, without imposing a one-size-fits-all model that is increasingly out of step with real lives.

---

[16] Elizabeth Brake, *Minimizing Marriage: Marriage, Morality, and the Law* (Oxford: Oxford University Press, 2012). In earlier work I described Brake's approach as an example of holistic regulation. That description was based on using the label 'holistic regulation' to refer to both bundling and status-based regulation. Distinguishing status-based regulation from the bundling aspect of holistic regulation, as I do here, reveals that Brake's approach is an example of the former but not the latter. See Clare Chambers, 'The Marriage-Free State' in *Proceedings of the Aristotelian Society* 113(2) (2013) p. 135.

[17] Brake, *Minimizing Marriage* p. 158.    [18] Brake, *Minimizing Marriage* p. 303.

## 5.2  Practice not Status

The second feature of the marriage-free state is that relationships are defined according to their practices, not according to their status. The focus on practice not status is related to the distinction between piecemeal and holistic regulation, but the two are distinct. Whether regulation is holistic or piecemeal is a matter of *scope*: are a variety of different regulations bundled together, or are different areas of law considered separately? Whether regulation proceeds via practice or status is a matter of *justification*: does a particular regulation apply because a relationship has some acquired status, or because a relationship has some practice-based character? The various alternatives are shown in the following table.

|  |  | *Scope of regulation* |  |  |
|---|---|---|---|---|
|  |  | **Holistic** | **Piecemeal** | |
| *Justification of regulation* | **Status** | Marriage, Civil union, Metz's ICGU status | Law Commission of Canada's *Beyond Conjugality* | Brake's minimal marriage |
| | **Practice** | Common-law marriage (mythical in the UK), Marriage between slaves in the USA | | The marriage-free state |

Traditional marriage is a form of holistic, status-based regulation. One must register in order to be married, and once one is married one acquires a bundle of rights and duties. Civil union and ICGU status also fall into that category. Brake's minimal marriage is piecemeal, status-based regulation. One must register to be minimally married, but that registration could bring with it just some specific minimal marriage rights and duties.

Practice-based regulation can also be either holistic or piecemeal. Common-law marriage, if it were not a myth,[19] would be an example of holistic practice-based regulation: a couple would become common-law married by virtue of performing certain practices rather than as the result of acquiring a status, and would then

---

[19]  A survey conducted by the UK charity OnePlusOne in 2013 found that 58% of all respondents were not aware that common law marriage is not a recognized status and 47% of people aged 18–34 believed that cohabitation entails the same legal rights as marriage. See OnePlusOne, 'Nearly half of UK citizens believe in the common law marriage myth' at http://www.oneplusone.org.uk/2013/02/05/nearly-half-of-uk-citizens-believe-in-the-common-law-marriage-myth/. Marriage by cohabitation and repute did exist in Scotland until 2006 but has not existed as a legal category in England and Wales since The Marriage Act of 1753.

acquire the bundle of rights and duties of marriage. A holistic practice-based approach was also used for regulating African-American families during and immediately after the American War of Independence. Many slaves signed up to fight for the Union, thereby gaining freedom for themselves and their families, but since slaves were not legal persons they were not allowed to enter legal marriages and so there was no formal way of identifying who counted as eligible for freedom. 'Wives' of free soldiers were therefore identified by testimony about the nature of the relationship. Marriage was used as an imposed proxy for what Katherine Franke describes as 'the variety of slave relationships, which included "taking up," living together, and marriage. The community recognized these relationships as permanent, monogamous, and sacred without requiring formal legal sanction.'[20]

The marriage-free state, in contrast, uses piecemeal practice-based regulation. In the marriage-free state, the state does not concern itself with defining or identifying A Relationship at all (be it marriage, civil union, or anything else). It asks not 'are these people in A Relationship with each other?' but rather 'are these people engaged in a relationship practice that places them in need of state regulation?' So the rights and duties of piecemeal directives are attained not by adopting some special relationship status such as marriage, but rather simply by standing in the relevant practice-based relationship to someone.

The Law Commission of Canada advocates piecemeal regulation, sometimes based on practice and sometimes on status. Its preference is for status-based regulation. It recognizes that a commitment to equality and autonomy requires moving away from marriage and conjugality as the basis for regulating relationships, and 'relying less on whether people are living in particular kinds of relationships'.[21] It therefore argues strongly for piecemeal regulation. Its preferred method is that citizens should 'choose which of their close personal relationships they want to be subject to the particular law'.[22] In order for their preferences to count, and to avoid abuse of the system (such as someone claiming caring leave on false pretences), people should register their personal relationships

---

[20] Katherine Franke, *Wedlocked: The Perils of Marriage Equality—How African Americans and Gays Mistakenly Thought the Right to Marry Would Set Them Free* (New York: New York University Press, 2015) p. 75. Franke further describes how this imposition of legal marriage had disastrous consequences for many former slaves, who were subsequently viciously prosecuted for adultery and bigamy—acts that many were unaware were illegal, and which would, in any case, be condoned when committed by white people.

[21] Law Commission of Canada, *Beyond Conjugality* p. xii.

[22] Law Commission of Canada, *Beyond Conjugality* p. xii.

in advance. Registering a relationship thus 'offer[s] the opportunity for public declarations of commitment that will be respected by government'.[23]

However, the Law Commission of Canada recognizes that self-designation is not always suitable, and in those cases it advocates practice-based regulation.[24] The Commission thus treats practice-based legislation as a second-best to status-based registration. But practice-based regulation actually has several advantages over status-based regulation.

The practice-based approach allows state regulation and protection to take place on a more inclusive basis, without leaving some people vulnerable. Regulation via status, whether holistic or piecemeal, excludes those whose relationships do not have the relevant status. People who have not, or not yet, chosen to acquire the status of minimal marriage, ICGU, or civil union are left unprotected—*even if they are in relationships that are functionally identical to those who have acquired such status.*

The Law Commission of England and Wales offers a compelling example to explain what is wrong with this situation, in the context of English and Welsh marriage law:

Take the position of cohabitants who have children and have been living together for a long time. The mother stays at home to look after the children and has no real prospects of re-entering the job market at a level that would enable her to afford the child-care that her absence from home would require.... In order to obtain any long-term economic security in case of the relationship ending, she would first have to persuade [her partner] that he should take steps to protect her position. It might well be that he is quite happy with the status quo, which favours him.

Even if she were able to overcome this initial hurdle and persuade her partner that something should be done, they would then have to decide what steps were appropriate. It might be thought that the obvious answer is that they should marry. But research suggests... that many cohabitants think it wrong to marry purely for legal or financial reasons. The alternative would be for them to declare an express trust over their home or enter into a contract for her benefit. However, such arrangements may be complex and require legal advice. The couple may simply conclude that the issue is not sufficiently pressing to take any further, and that they have other spending priorities.[25]

The outcome is that if the couple separate the woman is left without the financial protection afforded to divorcing spouses, despite the fact that the relationship is functionally identical to many marriages.

---

[23] Law Commission of Canada, *Beyond Conjugality* p. xii.

[24] Law Commission of Canada, *Beyond Conjugality* pp. xii–xiii.

[25] The Law Commission of England and Wales, *Cohabitation: The Financial Consequences of Relationship Breakdown.* LAW COM No 307 (2007) p. 33.

The same problems occur with any proposed status. There must be a difference in law between those with that status and those without that status, for otherwise the status is purely symbolic and affording it is outside the state's purview. But then legal protection is denied to those who are engaged in personal relationships but have not acquired the protected status. And lacking the protected status may not be a matter of choice. For example, one partner may wish to acquire the protected status but the other may be unwilling (a situation that works in favour of the already-powerful), or their relationship may not meet the requirements of the status, or they may have failed to realize the importance of acquiring the status, or they may simply not have got round to acquiring the status yet. A practice-based approach helps to remove the vulnerability that is suffered by people in relationships that are not ratified by status.

The problem with status-based regulation, then, is that it requires individuals to acquire a particular status in order to access protections. Instead, the state should set a regulatory framework that stipulates the non-voluntary, default rights and duties that apply to everyone who performs any relationship practice that merits regulation: anyone who is the primary carer of a child, any people who share in purchasing their main home, and so on. Alternative statuses such as minimal marriage or ICGU status create differences between relationships with and without those statuses, even if there is no functional difference between them.

Practice-based regulation may seem to invoke problems of privacy, but these are avoided if the regulation is piecemeal rather than holistic. One issue for the state regulation of relationships is that the state needs to know to whom the regulations apply. On a holistic approach this means that the state needs to know who counts as being in A Relationship, and for some this requirement conjures up a nightmare scenario of state intrusion into the minutiae of intimate relationships.

Status-based regulation such as marriage solves this problem neatly by requiring a formal process of registration. The Law Commission of Canada suggests that relationship registration could be extended to non-conjugal relationships too. As they note, registration has the benefit of not compromising privacy since, unless a registration is contested (such as if one spouse seeks to annul a marriage), the state need know nothing about the internal workings of a relationship.[26] But as we have seen, the problem with registration is what to do about unregistered relationships. An unregistered relationship might meet all the criteria for, and engage in all the practices of, registered relationships: it might be functionally identical. But if regulation is tied to registration then unregistered relationships will not receive the protection of regulation. If both partners

---

[26] Law Commission of Canada, *Beyond Conjugality* p. xvi.

actively reject registration this might be unproblematic (a scenario that is discussed in the next section), but a relationship might be unregistered because one partner wants to deny the other rights, or because neither partner is fully aware of the importance of registration, or because the partners have simply not got round to registering their relationship before some significant event occurs, such as one partner suffering an incapacitating accident or dying.

To see this problem, consider two models of partnership registration in Europe: Dutch registered partnerships and French *Pacte Civil de Solidarité* (Civil Solidarity Pact) or *Pacs*. Both suffer from the problem of unregistered relationships. The French *Pacs* system retains differences between married and unmarried couples. Brienna Perelli-Harris and Nora Sánchez Gassen argue that *Pacs* 'was clearly a by-product of the initiative to provide legal status to same-sex couples.... On balance, the French government continues to emphasize the difference between marriage and *Pacs* by considering marriage the superior institution.'[27] As a result, *Pacsé* couples have fewer rights and duties than married ones. Unregistered cohabiting couples do not have any specific legal duties and rights towards each other, and do not have tax advantages. They do have social and welfare rights equivalent to marriage.[28]

The Netherlands has greater equality: the legal position of registered partners and married couples is the same in almost all policy areas,[29] with registered partnership regarded as being distinctive for sociological rather than juridical reasons.[30] But a significant number of Dutch cohabitees, around half, are not registered as such and thus do not receive legal protection. Perelli-Harris and Sánchez Gassen note that some cohabitees may be deliberately unregistered, wanting to avoid regulation, but that others:

may be unaware of the benefits of registering their partnerships, both for themselves and their children, or they simply may not bother to register their partnerships.... Thus, the Dutch example shows that even though a country may implement a system for registering cohabitation with the goal of providing protection to all families, a significant proportion of families can still remain outside of the law.[31]

---

[27] Perelli-Harris and Sánchez Gassen, 'How Similar are Cohabitation and Marriage?' p. 459.

[28] Laurence Francoz Terminal, 'Registered Partnership as an alternative to Marriage—France' presented at *The Future of Registered Partnerships Durham-Cambridge Conference* (University of Cambridge, 10–11 July 2015) pp. 1 and 7.

[29] Perelli-Harris and Sánchez Gassen, 'How Similar are Cohabitation and Marriage? pp. 458–9.

[30] Lynn De Schrijver, 'Registered Partnerships as an *Alternative* to Marriage: The Netherlands' presented at *The Future of Registered Partnerships*.

[31] Perelli-Harris and Sánchez Gassen, 'How Similar are Cohabitation and Marriage?' p. 459.

Lynn De Schrijver thus argues that the system should be reformed so that registered partnership is a true legal alternative to marriage, or that there should be legal consequences for *all* cohabitees.

The piecemeal practice-based approach avoids the problem of unregistered relationships without invoking a nightmarish privacy-threatening scenario. The state does not need to know a great range of details about people's private lives so as to determine whether they meet the criteria of being in A Relationship. It simply needs to know whether some particular relationship practice applies. In some cases this will be a matter of objective fact: are the people parents? Or, are they both named on the deeds of a property? Or, does one have caring responsibilities for the other? Liberal states already have procedures for determining facts so as to allocate welfare payments, to rule on the custody of children, and to identify property rights. In other cases it will be a matter of self-designation: who does this person want to count as her next of kin? Or, who does this person choose to sponsor for immigration? In some cases courts may need to investigate the nature of a relationship, but in most cases a practice-based approach means that the investigation is limited to a particular relationship practice rather than the nature of a relationship as a whole.

Another way of putting this point is to say that practice-based regulation must be piecemeal. Holistic practice-based regulation would avoid vulnerability for those in unregistered relationships. But there are disadvantages. We have already seen that holistic regulation in general cannot adequately deal with diversity, thus limiting autonomy and undermining state neutrality. And holistic practice-based regulation faces a specific problem, as the Law Commission of Canada notes:

the attributes of relationships that are relevant to state policies shift depending on the nature of the policy at issue.... For example, economic dependence or interdependence is the most important relational attribute for the purposes of a law that seeks to respond to the economic consequences of the breakdown of a relationship. Emotional intimacy is the most important relational attribute to be considered by a law that seeks to protect the value of trust and candour in intimate relationships. Relational definitions that do not focus on the relevant factual attributes of relationships will miss their mark, excluding some relationships that ought to be included, and including some relationships that ought to be excluded. Thus, carefully tailoring relational definitions to the objectives of particular laws will eliminate inequalities and enable laws to accomplish their objectives more effectively.[32]

For some people, emotional intimacy accompanies economic interdependence, and also accompanies other relevant practices such as shared residence, care for each other, care for third parties, and co-parenthood. Regulation according to

---

[32] Law Commission of Canada, *Beyond Conjugality* pp. 35–6.

marriage or an alternative holistic status assumes that all relationships are like this, or should be, and thus attributes all legal recognition and protection to those who are in the paradigmatic relationship form. It therefore becomes very important to consider whether people are in this paradigmatic relationship form or not, because a great deal follows from the answer. But this is *not* true of the piecemeal practice-based approach used in the marriage-free state. It is not necessary to know whether people are in A Relationship in general. It is only necessary to know whether people are engaged in some relationship practice, and only then if it has already been determined that that relationship practice is an appropriate criterion on which to base regulation.

The Law Commission of Canada gives a number of similar examples. Rather than restricting emergency 'caregiving leave' to a specified list of qualifying family relationships, employees could designate their own list of people to whom they might have to provide care, or care-giving leave could be capped at a maximum number of days. A real-life example is the University of Cambridge's excellent career break scheme, which allows employees to work greatly reduced hours for up to two years to cover domestic or caring responsibilities. The scheme places no stipulations on the type of relationship that must exist between the staff member and the person being cared for: the regulations refer to children, partners, family members, elderly dependent relatives, or 'other unforeseen situations of a domestic kind'.[33] To take another example, rather than restricting immigration sponsorship to certain sorts of relationships (such as spouses or children) individuals could be permitted to sponsor up a to a certain number of people to immigrate, or immigration sponsorship could be tied to a formal financial commitment and a self-designated emotional interdependence.[34] Tax arrangements that privilege marriage could 'apply to all persons who are living together in economically interdependent relationships'.[35]

This idea of practice-based regulation echoes the insight of relational contract theory (RCT), a leading but problematic jurisprudential approach to contract law. According to RCT what matters is not merely whether an explicit contract or status has been attained, but also how everyday life is patterned and whether legitimate expectations have arisen. Some courts have used RCT to decide property disputes between separating unmarried couples, such as in the landmark California Supreme Court case *Marvin v Marvin*. There the Court found that even

---

[33] University of Cambridge, 'Flexible working arrangements—career break scheme' in *Cambridge University Reporter* (15 December 1999).

[34] Law Commission of Canada, *Beyond Conjugality* pp. 41–6.

[35] Law Commission of Canada, *Beyond Conjugality* p. 89.

*unwritten* relationship 'contracts' could be enforced.[36] To enforce an unwritten agreement a court looks for a 'relational' contract: an implicit, evolving agreement based on the everyday workings of the relationship.[37]

As discussed in Chapter 4, however, the RCT approach is problematic because it leaves a couple in the dark about how the courts might interpret their relationship. In using RCT, the court looks for implicit agreements, understandings that the court presumes underlie observed behaviour. But of course observed behaviour can be accounted for by any number of underlying understandings. Does one partner do all the housework, for example, because she feels that this is a fair exchange for her partner's financial contribution to the household, or because she adheres to traditional gender roles and believes it is her job as a woman, or because she enjoys it and prefers to do it all herself, or because she has found from bitter experience that her partner simply refuses to pull his weight? The answer might not be clear merely from observing the distribution of household labour. It might not even be clear to the partners themselves. The result is that under RCT 'conduct may give rise to an implied contract completely at odds with the intent of one or more of the parties; or unanticipated equitable relief may be granted contrary to expectation. Thus, both parties may be surprised by the consequences of verbal statements and nonverbal acts.'[38]

The marriage-free state does not suffer from this problem. Instead the piecemeal directives state clearly which relationship practices give rise to which rights and duties. For example, a piecemeal directive might be of the following form:

> A person acquires full or partial ownership of a residential property by: being named on the lease; or residing in the property and contributing financially to that property for a year or more without a formal tenancy or lodger's agreement; or by residing in the property and providing unpaid domestic services to the household for a year or more. Ownership is assessed according to the proportion that each has contributed to maintaining the property. Unpaid domestic services are assessed as an hourly contribution equivalent to the hourly wage of the other owner's paid work.

The point of this example directive is not the justice or otherwise of its content, but rather its form. Such a directive is responsive to the realities of each particular

---

[36] *Marvin v Marvin* 18 Cal.3d 660 (1976). For a critique see Ira Mark Ellman, '"Contract Thinking" was Marvin's fatal flaw' in *Notre Dame Law Review* 76 (2000–1).

[37] See Christensen, 'Legal Ordering of Family Values'.

[38] H. Curry and D. Clifford, *A Legal Guide for Lesbian and Gay Couples: A NOLO Press Self-Help Law Book* §8 (1989).

relationship but is determinate in advance and is formulated with egalitarian justice in mind.

Or, consider the Swedish Cohabitation Act of 2003:

> Two people, regardless of sex, become 'cohabitees' when they live together on a permanent basis, and as a couple, and as a joint household (sharing chores and expenses), and are neither married nor in a Registered Partnership. If the cohabiting relationship ends (by marriage, separation, or death) either cohabitee can request a division of the cohabitees' joint home and household goods according to the rules set out by the Act.[39]

The Swedish regime is more restrictive than the form of regulation imagined for the marriage-free state since it stipulates that cohabitees must live 'as a couple' and thus is designed to exclude siblings and friends. Nevertheless, since regulation of this sort has been law since the passage of its closely-related predecessor, the Cohabitees Joint Act 1987, it demonstrates that piecemeal practice-based regulation can work.

A number of other countries have made similar moves towards regulating unregistered cohabitation, but with conditions attached on the nature of the cohabiting relationship. For example, the Family Law (Scotland) Act 2006 provides consequences for Scottish cohabitees who are 'living together as if they are civil partners'.[40] France is beginning to regulate unregistered cohabitation via case law, but once again with substantive normative restrictions that will not apply to many cohabiting couples: 'Monogamy, as well as the stable and continuous character of the relationship, must be established in order to prove cohabitation.'[41] New Zealand has regulations for both civil unions and *de facto* relationships (cohabitants), but both apply only to couple relationships. But New Zealand uses a practice-based approach similar to that of the marriage-free state. The existence of a *de facto* relationship is determined by a Court, if the parties dispute it, so that this question 'is a question of fact not law'.[42]

A few jurisdictions are exceptions to the rule that regulation of cohabitation is generally restricted to couple relationships. In Iceland the legal status of cohabitation is 'very uncertain' but the criterion for counting as cohabitees is merely

---

[39] This paragraph is my own summary; for detail see Maarit Jänterä-Jareborg, Margareta Brattström, and LisaMarie Eriksson, 'National Report: Sweden' (Commission on European Family Law, 2015) at http://ceflonline.net/wp-content/uploads/Sweden-IR.pdf.

[40] Kenneth McK. Norrie, 'Scotland' presented at *The Future of Registered Partnerships*.

[41] Terminal, 'Registered Partnership as an alternative to Marriage—France'.

[42] Margaret Briggs and Emma Peart, 'The Future of Registered Partnerships: New Zealand' presented at *The Future of Registered Partnerships*.

living at the same address for a certain period of time.[43] More formal arrangements are found in Belgium, which has a three-tier legal regime. Marriage has the most significant legal consequences, followed by a system of registered partnerships known as 'legal cohabitation', and last comes *de facto* partners or cohabitants. There is a much smaller leap in terms of legal consequences from *de facto* partners to legal cohabitation than there is from legal cohabitation to marriage. Legal cohabitation does require registration—it is a matter of status rather than practice—but it is significantly similar to the marriage-free state in that it is not restricted to sexual couples but can also apply to 'close relatives or friends'.[44]

In the marriage-free state there would not be different tiers of *status* for which one could register. Instead, different *practices* would trigger different levels of regulation. In terms of cohabitation, certain regulations might apply to those who have lived together for a certain period of time, but then additional regulations would apply to those who co-parent, and different regulations would apply to those who are financially dependent on each other, for example by having one partner act as breadwinner and the other act as unpaid domestic worker. In this way different cohabiting couples would be subject to different regulations, but that would be as the result of the differing practices of their relationship rather than as the result of having registered for a different status.

The marriage-free state need not rule out couples registering as fulfilling a particular practice, if such registration had practical benefits for the effective operation of law. For example, perhaps people could register that they were living together, or were financially dependent on each other. But the key feature of the marriage-free state is that any such registration should be neither necessary nor sufficient for regulation to apply. As is the case in New Zealand, the question of whether some particular regulation should apply to a relationship should be a matter of fact rather than prior registration. This aspect of the marriage-free state is also similar to the situation in some parts of Australia, which apply the same legal consequences to registered partnerships and *de facto* relationships, so that registration merely serves as a way of simplifying the process of accessing regulation which would apply even without it.[45]

---

[43] David Thór Björgvinsson, 'Registered Partnerships—Marriage: Iceland' presented at *The Future of Registered Partnerships*.

[44] Geoffrey Willems, 'Belgium—Legal cohabitation' presented at *The Future of Registered Partnerships*.

[45] Steve Martin, 'Australia' presented at *The Future of Registered Partnerships*. The relevant parts of Australia are the Australian Capital Territory, Queensland, Tasmania, Victoria, and New South Wales. In Tasmania regulation applies to caring relationships between family members as well as to couples.

Another way of describing the practice-based approach of the marriage-free state is the thought experiment outlined in the Introduction. Consider what you think the ideal regulations should be for those who are *not* married in the current, marriage regime. How should the state regulate duties and disputes between unmarried parents? Who should count as a parent? How should the state divide property between unmarried people who purchase it together and wish to separate? What rights, if any, should be given to somebody whose contribution to a household is mainly through domestic work rather than finances? Who should count as someone's next of kin? Should rights and duties in these cases be dependent on contract or some other voluntary agreement, or should they be automatic? If automatic, at what point should they apply?

Perhaps you disagree with the clause in the example directive given above that counts unpaid domestic labour as a financial contribution to the ownership of a property. Perhaps you advocate restricting property-ownership to those named on the lease. Perhaps you prefer an alternative method of protecting domestic workers from vulnerability, such as wages for housework. Whatever your position is on these and similar questions, the way to think about the marriage-free state is that the laws that should ideally apply to unmarried people in a regime of state-recognized marriage are those that should apply to *everybody* in the marriage-free state. The marriage-free state does not ask legislators to do anything—to invade any privacy, to make any assumptions, to consider any variables—that they do not already have to do when regulating the unmarried. The marriage-free state simply asks that legislators do in fact consider the unmarried, that they design regulations that secure equality and freedom, and that those regulations apply to all.

Consider, for example, immigration rights for partners. The question of whether this is a legitimate area of state legislation will meet with different answers. Advocates of open borders will argue that the state should not control immigration at all, so there is no justification for any relationship-based immigration rights. Others will argue that states do have a legitimate interest in controlling immigration, in which case an argument must be provided as to what sorts of immigration should be allowed and what that implies for the rights of immigrants to bring others with them. Depending on the outcome of that argument we might be left with a defence of immigration only for solitary economically-necessary workers, or with a defence of allowing all immigrants to bring a certain number of people of their choice with them (regardless of the relationships between them), or any number of other possibilities. The point is that no relationship status such as marriage settles these arguments in advance.

Or, consider the example of inheritance tax. Current UK law awards a privilege to spouses and civil partners that is not awarded to others, in the form of an exemption from inheritance tax for transfers between partners. Citizens in general are not allowed to nominate a person who is exempt from inheritance tax; they can opt in to the exemption only by marrying or entering a civil partnership. Inheritance tax exemptions might not be justified at all. But if they are justified this cannot be because married people are somehow more in need or more deserving of exemptions than others.[46] Exemptions might be justified on the grounds that if one cohabitant dies it is unfair to require the other cohabitant to leave their home in order to raise the money to pay tax on the inherited portion of the home. If this is the justification then the tax exemption should be awarded to all people who inherit a portion of their primary residence. Alternatively, an exemption from inheritance tax might be justified on the grounds that it is good public policy to allow people one tax-free heir (perhaps because doing so encourages saving and hard work, since people know that what they save will pass to their nearest and dearest rather than to the Treasury). If this is the justification for the policy then *all* people should be allowed to nominate one tax-free heir of their choice, for the incentive will work regardless of whether that heir is a spouse, child, or friend.

## 5.3  Opting out not Opting in

One potential objection to the marriage-free state is that it undermines liberty. A regime of state-recognized marriage allows people to choose whether to marry, and one reason people choose *not* to marry is to avoid the consequent legal regulations. So it might seem illiberal for the marriage-free state to impose regulation on people who may not want their relationships to be subject to it.

Should it be possible to form a relationship without incurring extensive legal duties? The answer to this question depends on the relationship practice in question. Some relationships, such as parenthood, rightly bring duties that cannot be avoided except in the most extreme circumstances. Other relationships, or relationship practices, seem more suitable for variation. I do not take a stand here on what those areas of legitimate diversity might be, or even if there are any; in general an autonomy-promoting state should regulate only when

---

[46] Doubtless some defend exemptions for married people as an incentive to marry. Such arguments fail on two counts: first, there is no legitimate state interest in incentivizing people to marry (as opposed to incentivizing stable relationships, or care, or some other good); and second, few proponents of this argument would actually want people to marry purely for the money.

there is a pressing need to do so. But *if* there are areas of relationships that need regulation but in which there can be legitimate diversity then the right approach is to allow people to *opt out* of the default regulations (which must be designed with justice in mind), rather than to leave people unprotected unless they *opt in* to some privileged status.[47]

Opting out would be a matter of drawing up a contract or trust expressly setting out how the relationship deviates from the default. The law would stipulate when opting out is possible, and any limits that might apply. So the legal complexity and expense described by the Law Commission of England and Wales would fall on those wanting to escape the protection offered in law, not on those wishing to be protected.[48]

In some cases, justice might permit deviation from a given directive, since there might be areas which must be determinate in law (and thus deserving of a directive) and yet in which considerable diversity is compatible with justice. In such cases deviation should be allowed, within set parameters, but any deviation should be via the format of traditional written contract, not via imputed relational contracts. In other words, vulnerable parties should enjoy the full protection of the law as set out in the piecemeal directive, unless they have explicitly and formally agreed to a different distribution, enforcement of which is forthcoming only if compatible with justice. For example, the hypothetical property-division directive might be supplanted with the following:

> Deviation from this directive is permitted by explicit contract, but any such contract must be compatible with the following requirements: any children of the contracting parties must be left no worse off than they would have been without the deviation; and neither party can be left with a share smaller than 20 per cent of the property or that which they would have received without the deviation, whichever is the smaller.

Again, I make no claims about whether this precise regulation is correct in content. Formulating each piecemeal directive is a considerable task in itself.

---

[47] Opting out of the legal consequences of cohabitation is permitted in countries such as Sweden, Croatia, New Zealand, and Slovenia. As Jens M. Scherpe writes, 'There is no good reason to assume that the couple have decided to avoid the consequences of cohabitation at the same time as taking the negative decision regarding marriage (or same-sex equivalent). In fact, making such an assumption could in some respects also be seen as infringing the autonomy rights of the parties.' See Jens M. Scherpe, 'The Nordic Countries in the Vanguard of European Family Law' in *Scandinavian Studies in Law* 50 (2007) p. 277.

[48] As John Stuart Mill argues, 'laws and institutions require to be adapted, not to good men, but to bad'. John Stuart Mill, *The Subjection of Women* in *On Liberty and The Subjection of Women* (Ware: Wordsworth Editions Ltd, 1996) p. 149.

I aim simply to demonstrate the form that regulation might take, and to illustrate how a regime of piecemeal directives with the possibility of limited deviation by traditional contract could work. And once again there is evidence from actual jurisdictions that opt-out mechanisms can work. The Swedish Cohabitation Act of 2003, which applies to all cohabiting couples regardless of whether they have registered, allows for cohabitees to make a formal cohabitation agreement, stating that they do not wish their joint property to be regulated by the Act.[49]

The Law Commission of Canada, which uses the term 'ascription' rather than directives for non-contractual regulation, recognizes that opting out can secure liberty, but draws attention to the need for publicity. It notes:

Governments use ascription to prevent the risks of exploitation inherent in a contractual model by imposing (ascribing) a set of obligations on people in conjugal relationships that are presumed to correspond to the expectations of the majority of people involved in such relationships. While ascription may help to prevent exploitation, it is a blunt policy tool, treating all conjugal relationships alike. It infringes on autonomy, as people are not always aware they may opt out of certain provisions. While appropriate for conjugal relationships in some instances, it would be inappropriate for non-conjugal relationships.[50]

The Commission is right to draw attention to the need for publicity. But it is wrong to suggest that ascription violates liberty, such that opting in to regulation via a registry of relationships is necessary. This suggestion is wrong for four reasons.

First, the problem that ascription treats all conjugal relationships alike is avoided if the ascription is piecemeal rather than holistic. Relationships are treated alike only insofar as they contain the same practices.

Second, even if the opportunity of opting out were not widely understood it would not follow that ascriptive directives infringe on autonomy. If the directives are well-crafted then they should enhance autonomy, not restrict it, since they should be designed with autonomy and equality clearly in mind.

Third, a lack of publicity applies just as strongly to marriage. When I first started working on marriage I wanted a quick guide to the legal implications of marriage in England and Wales. I looked on the UK Government website, expecting to find a simple summary aimed at couples considering marriage, setting out the legal consequences of their decision. The UK Government provides guides of this sort for many other areas of legislation. No such guide for marriage existed. Simple guides do exist explaining who may marry, and how to marry, but there is no account of the legal implications of marriage provided by

[49] Jänterä-Jareborg, Brattström, and Eriksson, 'National Report: Sweden' pp. 42–3.
[50] Law Commission of Canada, *Beyond Conjugality* p. xvi.

the government.[51] Since then, I have talked to many family lawyers who have very different views about the legal importance of the institution. Some have urged me to marry for my own protection; others insist that marriage has little significance in contemporary English and Welsh law. Claire Fenton-Glynn, an academic specialist in family law, told me that she tells all her students that the only way to understand divorce law in England and Wales is to read as many cases as possible. There are no principles that can be clearly set out. And so it would be wrong to suggest that most marrying couples enter the institution with a clear sense of its legal implications.

Fourth, the Commission gives no argument as to why conjugality marks the appropriate domain of ascription. Parenthood is an obvious example of a personal relationship that merits ascriptive regulation—not just in the area of parent–child relationships, which fall outside of the remit of the Commission's report, but also in the need to regulate the relationship between parents, with respect to how they share or divide matters like maintenance, custody, access, and decision-making.

Maxine Eichner writes that 'eliminating a civil route for formalizing relationships would ... be a mistake' since:

this formalization helps to identify the intent of its members and their own understandings with respect to the intended primacy and permanency of the relationship. In entering into a marriage, participants indicate their assent to a specific formal status that comes with a set of enforceable legal rights and responsibilities. And surely such understandings should be relevant in determining the default rules that apply to that particular relationship. For example, a commitment to a permanent relationship should be pertinent to the state's determination of whether and how long income should be redistributed between parties who have separated.[52]

But what Eichner misses is that the intent and understandings of a couple can be expressed by opting out of default directives, not just by opting in to a status such as marriage which, after all, offers considerably less scope for personalization. She also misses the fact that intent and understandings can change over time, rather than being isolated in one moment of entering into a marriage. She fails to note that understandings can be expressed by actions within the relationship, such as buying a house together or having a child. And her approach does not take adequate account of the fact that one person's intent and understandings might be incompatible with justice and fairness, either to the other partner within the relationship or to third parties such as children.

---

[51] Citizens Advice, a charity, does provide a useful guide 'Living together and marriage: legal differences' at https://www.citizensadvice.org.uk/relationships/living-together-marriage-and-civil-partnership/living-together-and-marriage-legal-differences/.

[52] Maxine Eichner, *The Supportive State* (Oxford: Oxford University Press, 2010) p. 103.

The approach of the marriage-free state, using piecemeal directives with the possibility of limited contractual deviation, avoids the problems of both a contractual approach and of marriage or marriage-like holistic regulation. The lack of a special status means that no one relationship format is singled out for state approbation, and no one is left without legal protection because they (or their parents) lack the relevant status. The possibility of contractual deviation via opting out protects liberty, and means that people are still able to make clear and consensual statements about their relationship.

## 5.4  Objections, Clarifications, Applications

In this final section I consider objections to the regulatory approach of the marriage-free state.

### 5.4.1  The place for holistic thinking

The first objection is that my proposals go too far in ruling out holistic thinking. Although not all personal or caring relationships include various relationship functions in a holistic way, many do. Many people live in marriage or marriage-like relationships, combining sexual and emotional intimacy, financial interdependence, property ownership, cohabitation, and parenting. So the existence of holistic relationships may mean that there is a role for holistic thinking. Even if the default regulations are piecemeal rather than holistic, this objection runs, there is a role for people to opt out of those default regulations in a holistic way.

Holistic opt-outs could take various forms. People might draw up their own holistic opt-out contracts. These could be holistic merely in the sense of combining a variety of opt-outs in one document, with separate clauses for each. Or they could be holistic in a more intertwined way, combining various relationship practices. For example, a couple in a traditional marriage-like relationship with a gendered division of labour might wish to draw up an opt-out contract with something like the following clause:

> Mr Smith will be the sole breadwinner. Mrs Smith will do all housework, and will undertake all the childcare while Mr Smith is at work. Mr Smith will pay the entirety of the mortgage and all household bills. Mrs Smith will be the joint and equal owner of all household assets as long as she remains a full-time housewife and stay-at-home mother.

This contract is holistic in the sense that Mrs Smith's ownership of the house, a financial matter, is dependent not on her financial situation but on her undertaking full-time caring and domestic work. It therefore violates the principle of piecemeal regulation that relationship practices should be considered separately. But, so the objection runs, holistic contracts like these might be justified on grounds of both autonomy and fairness. The Smiths might want such an arrangement and have come to that decision after full information and rational decision-making, so forbidding it would violate their autonomy. Moreover, if Mr and Mrs Smith were forced to make a series of piecemeal contracts to regulate their agreement, unfairness could result. Piecemeal contracts would involve one financial contract saying 'Mr Smith will be responsible for all financial contributions to the household but Mr and Mrs Smith will own everything in equal shares' and another saying 'Mrs Smith is responsible for all housework, and all childcare while Mr Smith is at work.' Each piecemeal contract looks unfair in isolation. If would be unfair if Mrs Smith were to acquire an equal stake in property to which she makes no financial contribution, unless that equal stake is justified by her domestic and caring work. Similarly, it would be unfair if Mrs Smith were obliged to be fully responsible for housework, unless that responsibility is compensated for financially.

I have various responses to this objection. The first response is to point out that the main problem with the bundling of holistic regulation is that it involves *the state* in making pronouncements about the normal or proper form of relationships. Holistic regulation, when performed by the state, imposes one model of relationships on everybody, despite the fact that many relationships do not fit that model and despite the fact that doing so violates equality. The same worries do not apply when the holistic regulation is imposed by the parties to the relationship upon themselves. It is not necessary, therefore, for the marriage-free state to forbid all holistic opt-outs.

The second response is to say that, while holism is not a sufficient reason to forbid an opt-out, the necessary limits to opt-outs may include limits on certain sorts of holistic arrangements. For example, while a co-parenting contract between non-cohabitants might contain provision for both maintenance payments and contact with the child, it would be wrong to make contact conditional on payment since that would harm the child. Any penalty for non-payment should therefore take another form. It would also be wrong for a contract to connect sexual and financial practices, for example by imposing a financial penalty for refusing sex, since that would violate requirements of sexual consent.

### 5.4.2 The relevance of commitment

A feature of the practice-based approach to regulation is that people do not have to engage in a specific or conscious act of commitment for their relationship to become subject to regulation. One feature of marriage is that it involves the couple in making a formal, legal commitment to each other. If they understand nothing else about the law of marriage, a marrying couple surely understand this. This conscious commitment, so this objection goes, is a legitimate basis of legal discrimination. Thus Sweden, for example, maintains general neutrality between marriage and cohabitation, but retains some differences between the two 'because the level of commitment in a cohabiting relationship is regarded as lower than in marriage'.[53]

On the other side of the commitment coin is dissolution. Some people might want clarity as to when a relationship is finished. Status-based regulation gives clarity by providing formal divorce or de-registration. Things are not so clear with practice-based regulation, and for some this may be an objection to the marriage-free state.

It is a central feature of the marriage-free state that the state does not involve itself in defining, or stipulating the conditions of, A Relationship. A great many important relationships form, persist, and dissolve without depending on this sort of state recognition. Some vital relationships, such as friendships, are not defined or acknowledged by the state at all. The state takes no consideration of any commitment to friendship that friends make, nor does it offer any method for declaring a friendship over. Other relationships, like parenthood, are assigned by a mixture of practice- and status-based regulation. In the UK the woman who performs the function of gestating and giving birth to a child is automatically its initial legal mother (practice); a legal father is a man who is married to a legal mother at the time of conception (status) or a man whose claim to be the father is endorsed by the birth mother (practice); an adoptive parent is given that status after a process of formal application and evaluation (status). But the state makes no legal distinction between those parents who have made some sort of formal commitment to parenthood and those who have not. Adoptive parents, who have made the most explicit, informed and formal commitment to their role, have just the same parental rights and duties as those who become legal parents by accident.

There are some relationship practices which are appropriately defined by commitment or formal agreement, and for which there should be procedures for formal dissolution. Shared property ownership, inheritance, and next-of-kinship may be examples. But it is not the role of the marriage-free state to say when two people are or are not in an important relationship to each other, beyond saying what counts as performing a particular relationship practice.

---

[53] Perelli-Harris and Sánchez Gassen, 'How Similar are Cohabitation and Marriage?' p. 460.

After all, many important relationship practices continue once emotional inter-dependence has ceased, a factor that explains why more than half of Dutch civil partnerships are entered into by divorcing couples: couples who no longer wish to be married but whose lives are still intertwined and who still require legal protection.[54]

### 5.4.3 The need for international recognition

One final problem remains. Even if all is well and good within the marriage-free state itself, other states are not marriage-free. Many states use marital status when determining people's rights to migrate, and even casual travellers may find that it is necessary to be married in order to gain rights such as hospital visitation or to be treated as a next-of-kin.

Reliance on marriage to regulate rights is unjust in general. In an ideal world all states would be marriage-free. Before that time the marriage-free state must take steps to ensure that its citizens are not disadvantaged when travelling. One interim solution might be for the marriage-free state to have a system of relationship registration that served no purpose other than to provide a certificate to be used abroad. In order to be consistent with the ideals of the marriage-free state this certificate would be issued by post or electronically, with no formal ceremony or solemnization. Conditions for obtaining it should be as minimal as is consistent with securing the necessary international recognition. It should bring no legal status or rights within the marriage-free state itself, and citizens would not be asked about it by any state department or official other than those directly involved in issuing it (so it should not be used as a proxy for any other sort of relationship function or agreement). And its official title should not be ceremonial, ideally referring to the certificate rather than to the people who are named on it.

## Conclusion

This chapter has described the regulation of relationships in the marriage-free state. Such regulation has three key features. First, it proceeds on a piecemeal basis. The state does not dictate or assume that there is only one significant sort of relationship, or that significant relationship practices are combined in one rela-tionship. Instead, relationship practices are regulated separately. Second, relation-ships are regulated according to their practices. The state does not discriminate

---

[54]  Perelli-Harris and Sánchez Gassen, 'How Similar are Cohabitation and Marriage?' p. 459.

between functionally-identical relationships according to whether or not those in them have acquired a particular status. Third, the state secures liberty by allowing opt-outs from default regulations. Those opt-outs may involve drawing up holistic contracts. However, all opt-outs are subject to limitations based on considerations of justice and equality.

# 6

# Marriage in the Marriage-Free State

Ending state-recognized marriage does not mean ending marriage altogether. In the marriage-free state citizens can still take part in religious or secular marriage ceremonies and practices. This is why the marriage-free *state* is not a marriage-free *society*. It does not follow, however, that the state should take no interest at all in such ceremonies and the marriages they enact, since such marriages may result from, or perpetuate, oppression and inequality.

As I have discussed throughout the book, theorists who advocate the end of state-recognized marriage tend to argue for one of two things to replace it: either a regime based on relationship contracts, or a regime based on an alternative status such as civil union. I have rejected both. Both contract and status regimes face the problem of what to do with people who have not opted in to the relevant status or signed a contract, and so there will need to be defaults to ensure that such people are not left unprotected. But if there is to be default legislation then we should focus on that. If the default regulation is adequate to the task of securing justice for the unmarried then it should be adequate to secure justice for everyone, and we should allow room for contractual deviation only within the bounds of justice.

Libertarians and conservatives of a certain sort might unite in endorsing my proposals as set out so far, since both might agree that matters of marriage can best be left to private citizens or groups. Conservatives might like the idea of religions having complete control over the meaning and content of their marriages; libertarians might like the idea of the state staying out of individuals' choices. However, it would be a mistake for libertarians and conservatives to support the marriage-free state for these reasons. The marriage-free state is based on the values of liberty *and* equality and these, especially equality, require the state to take an interest in the content of private marriages.

The arguments in this chapter are straightforwardly egalitarian, and will be most appealing to feminist and comprehensive liberals. Some of the arguments to come may be incompatible with political liberalism. Insofar as they are incompatible they demonstrate where I part company with the political liberal approach.

It is not necessary to endorse the arguments of this chapter in order to endorse the general idea of the marriage-free state. One could have a marriage-free state and leave private marriages unregulated. But this book presents an *egalitarian* defence of the marriage-free state, and this chapter indicates how the commitment to equality plays out.

In this chapter I use the term 'private marriage' to refer to a marriage, be it religious or secular, that is performed and practised in a marriage-free state. There are three broad ways in which private marriage might be problematic from the point of view of equality.

First, private marriage might be *over-inclusive*. If the state does not determine what counts as a legitimate marriage there is nothing to stop potentially troubling marriages, which may include polygamous marriages, incestuous marriages, and forced marriages.

Second, private marriage might be *under-inclusive*. Without state regulation, private groups might restrict access to marriage in a way that is discriminatory. For example, a religion or group might refuse to marry same-sex couples or different-race couples.

Third, private marriage might be *internally inegalitarian*. In the marriage-free state the law that applies to married people will be the same as that which applies to unmarried people. But a marrying institution, such as a religion, might normatively impose unequal standards within marriage. Typically these will include gendered norms for spouses, such as a gendered division of labour or unequal norms of dress or sexual behaviour. Religions might also set gender-unequal conditions for securing a religious divorce.

Some of these concerns apply only if the private marriage is endorsed by some group or authority. The concern of under-inclusivity is like this. For example, it is not a violation of justice if an individual marriage is between two people of the same race, or if a particular person is only willing to enter into a marriage with somebody of a certain sex. What might be of concern is if some group, such as a religion, were only willing to conduct marriages between people of a certain race or sexuality.

Other troubling marriages will be troubling regardless of whether they are endorsed by a group. The concern of over-inclusivity is of this type. If incestuous or polygamous marriages are wrong, for example, then there is some feature of the marriages themselves that makes them wrong. Group endorsement of such marriages would then be wrong because it would constitute endorsement of wrong action. Similar marriages that were not endorsed by any group would be wrong nonetheless.

We also need to consider whether different issues arise in the context of religions and other groups. May religions impose restrictions on their marriages that other groups may not? For example, many people find it acceptable for the Catholic Church to refuse to marry same-sex couples. If this is right (a position which I will interrogate shortly) would it also be acceptable for the National Trust or the Humanist Society or a party planning company to make the same refusal?

It should already be clear that the issues at stake here are too multiple and complex to be dealt with adequately in one chapter, and that many of them have implications far beyond marriage. I offer a map of the terrain and some starting arguments rather than a fully-settled position.

## 6.1 Over-inclusivity: Polygamy, Incest, Forced Marriage

One of the main moral panics around the extension of marriage to same-sex couples has been the idea that there is a slippery slope towards the acceptance of other, purportedly-immoral, relationships between consenting adults such as polygamy and adult incest.[1] As discussed in Chapter 1, some theorists argue that there is an unavoidable slide down the slope. Others argue that the descent can be stopped after same-sex marriage but before endorsing immorality. Still others argue that the slippery slope is to be embraced not feared since there is nothing wrong with recognizing other types of relationship, so that the slippery slope is better described as an exhilarating flume ride.[2]

The marriage-free state invites this discussion since it leaves marriage to private groups and religions, some of which might want to conduct marriage ceremonies that would not be permitted under a regime of state-recognized marriage. Indeed, we might think that there are grounds for greater permissiveness in a marriage-free state, since the label of marriage has no legal implications. After all, the state sets no limits on what may count as a friendship, or what ceremonies of friendship may be conducted, or between whom friendships may be solemnized, because the status of friendship has no legal implications. I can declare with impunity that I am friends with my dog, or with 5,000 people, or with people I have never met, or with members of my immediate family, or with children under the age of consent. So why not marriage?

To be sure, any state must set limits on *behaviour*. I can declare that a child is my friend but that does not mean that I can take her somewhere without her

---

[1] There are, of course, perfectly adequate other-regarding reasons for preventing or regulating purportedly-immoral relationships with non-consenting adults and those incapable of consent such as children.

[2] I owe this locution to Martin McIvor.

parents' permission, or physically hurt her, or make decisions about her life. So, given that restrictions such as these will inevitably be in place, should the marriage-free state make any additional restrictions on what may count as a private marriage? Should it be acceptable for an adult to marry a child, as long as he does not rape or kidnap her? Should it be acceptable for a brother and a sister to engage in a private marriage as long as they do not procreate (with the attendant genetic risks)? Can someone marry her pet, as long as she does not violate laws against animal cruelty?

We must consider these issues on a case-by-case basis, with an awareness of what the social meaning of marriage currently is and of what sorts of marriage have historically or currently been problematic. At least in the early stages of the marriage-free state the social meaning of marriage remains salient,[3] and it would be irresponsible for the state to turn a blind eye to private marriages that have a high likelihood of containing oppressive behaviour. Child marriage, for example, is too closely associated with existing relationships of coercion, rape, and gendered oppression for the state to permit it. Marriage still contains the social meaning of a sexual relationship, one that is permanent and monogamous and often hierarchical, so child protection requires the continued ban on marriage ceremonies for children. Obviously if an act is sufficiently harmful as to merit illegality then it should merit illegality when condoned as part of a private marriage as well. So if paedophilia is justly prohibited, then paedophiliac marriage should be too. If children are below the age of sexual consent and legal autonomy then they should not be married. In a possible future world, where marriage neither involves a sexual relationship nor restricts autonomy, there might be nothing wrong with child marriage. Marriage in such a world would bear little resemblance to the concept today, so this is pure speculation. But we are not in that world. In a closer version of the marriage-free state, one in which marriage still retains the social meanings it has today, child marriage should be impermissible.

Forced marriage should remain illegal even if marriage has no legal status. Much of the harm in forced marriage in a marriage regime comes not from the state recognition in and of itself, but from behaviours associated with forced marriage such as rape, kidnapping, and child abuse. These things are and should be illegal whether or not they attach to marriage. Nevertheless, there could be additional harm in a community insisting that a couple is married when one or both do not consent to that label, and applying community standards of marital

---

[3] The crucial and complex question of the longevity of the meaning of institutions was discussed in Chapter 1.

behaviour such as joint living, fidelity, and so on, with sanctions for non-compliance. In the marriage-free state forced marriage of this kind would be illegal in much the same way as other sorts of harassment: unwanted attention, manipulation, and coercion. Again, the question must be contextual: what would forced marriage mean in any given context, and would it involve significant harm or restriction of those subject to the forcing? The prevention of harm to others, to those who are non-consenting, is such an established tenet of all liberal and feminist thought that it needs little further defence here.

In contrast we can imagine many private marriages that would not be risky and would not merit prohibition. There would be no need to regulate or ban bizarre marriages such as someone marrying their car, or a marriage between 10,000 people who have met only on the internet and propose to continue with that same mode of interaction. Such marriages would stretch the concept of marriage, applying it to situations where it does not currently fit. The marriage-free state has no interest in preserving or defining the meaning of marriage, so it should not intervene to say that these are not 'real' marriages. Intervention should be restricted to cases where it is needed to prevent harm.

Incest and polygamy are more difficult areas to assess, as long as they concern only consenting adults, and this leads many theorists to endorse them. For some theorists, such as Ronald Den Otter, polygamous marriage should be recognized by the state.[4] Den Otter argues in favour of plural marriage in the US context on straightforward anti-discrimination grounds: mirroring the basic egalitarian argument for same-sex marriage, he writes that the values of state neutrality and equality mean that 'as long as states continue to license monogamous marriages—different sex or same sex—they must provide the option of different kinds of plural marriages to fulfil the constitutional mandate of non-discriminatory treatment'.[5] For him, this argument also applies to incestuous relationships between consenting adults.[6] Den Otter's defence rests on the claim that any harms associated with polygamy, such as gender inequality, are insufficient to override autonomy of marital choice.

---

[4] Other egalitarian supporters of polygamy, polyamory, and plural relationships include Elizabeth Brake, *Minimizing Marriage: Marriage, Morality, and the Law* (Oxford: Oxford University Press, 2012); Andrew F. March, 'Is there a Right to Polygamy? Marriage, Equality and Subsidizing Families in Liberal Public Justification' in *Journal of Moral Philosophy* 8(2) (2011); David Chambers, 'Polygamy and Same-Sex Marriage' in *Hofstra Law* Review 26(1) (1997); and Sarah Song, *Justice, Gender, and the Politics of Multiculturalism* (Cambridge: Cambridge University Press, 2007).

[5] Ronald C. Den Otter, *In Defense of Plural Marriage* (Cambridge: Cambridge University Press, 2015) p. 5.

[6] Den Otter, *In Defense of Plural Marriage* p. 10.

Stephen Macedo vehemently rejects the idea that support for same-sex marriage entails support for polygamous marriage. For him, there is a clear line between the two, since same-sex marriage can and should instantiate the values of equal liberty and stable commitment, whereas polygamous marriage is associated with internal gender inequality, a lack of reciprocity, an unequal distribution of spouses with attendant social ills, and a general degrading of the character of marriage.[7] Macedo thus launches a sustained attack against polygamy. Many of his arguments are compelling. Nevertheless, there is a significant difference between the question of whether the *state* should recognize certain sorts of marriages and the question of whether it should prevent *private groups* from offering such recognition in the marriage-free state. Even Macedo does not want polygamous relationships to be illegal. His concern is that the state should not endorse those relationships. He allows that polygamous relationships can exist without inequality and oppression, so that polygamy should not be demonized and non-abusive polygamous families should not be separated.[8]

It is right to distinguish the question of what the state should allow from what it should recognize, and I see no reason for the marriage-free state to criminalize all private polygamous marriages—just as it should not criminalize sex before marriage, casual sex, or serial monogamy. However, many of the most oppressive polygamous relationships are not based on legal recognition. For example, Macedo rightly condemns the oppressive, secluded forms of polygamy such as those practised by 'creepy cult leaders like Warren Jeffs',[9] in which children are pressured into marrying and subjected to various forms of abuse. But merely refusing to recognize such arrangements as marriages does nothing to stop them.

Indeed, Macedo emphasizes an important point against permissiveness. As he points out, allowing incest for adults has implications for children since it would affect general norms that permeate into childhood. He therefore argues that the blanket ban on adult incestuous relationships should remain, because 'we could not accept the propriety of brother–sister or child–parent sexual relations among particular people at any stage of life without revising and relaxing the very strong general prohibition on sexual relations among immediate family members',[10] something that would be very dangerous for children. This is an important consideration that, if true in any given social context, may well be overwhelming.

---

[7] Stephen Macedo, *Just Married: Same-Sex Couples, Monogamy, and the Future of Marriage* (Princeton, NJ: Princeton University Press, 2015) pp. 162–5.
[8] Macedo, *Just Married* pp. 146 and 185.    [9] Macedo, *Just Married* p. 159.
[10] Macedo, *Just Married* p. 195.

The marriage-free state should be laissez-faire about the term 'marriage'. It should set no limits on who may call themselves married other than those that are needed to prevent or limit harm, such as the requirement that all concerned are consenting adults. But this does not mean that the marriage-free state should be laissez-faire about what goes on within marriages, or about the terms that private religious or secular groups set upon marriage. Macedo is both too moralistic and not moralistic enough. He is too moralistic in his claims about monogamous marriage being a uniquely valuable form of relationship, but he is not moralistic enough insofar as his argument stops with withholding recognition. If polygamous marriages are as dangerous as Macedo says they are, the state should go beyond a refusal of recognition. What is needed is a systematic account of when polygamous practices are harmful and unjust and when they are not, together with a solution for preventing or minimizing harm and injustice.[11] The marriage-free state should interfere in the oppressive marital norms set by private groups or institutions, as I discuss in Section 6.3 below.

## 6.2  Under-inclusivity: Heterosexism, Racism

It is an essential part of all of the six major world religions that, as Don Browning, Christian Green, and John Witte Jr put it, 'persons are not free to marry just anyone'[12] and 'an ample roll of sexual sins or crimes'[13] is kept. A number of theorists advocate privatizing marriage because it allows churches to define marriages as they see fit, and these theorists are usually happy about the possibility of under-inclusivity. The marriage-free state seems to be beneficial for religions because it allows them to define marriage however they wish without falling foul of state legislation, and so it seems like a way of enabling issues such as same-sex marriage to be resolved in a compromise fashion. On this libertarian model same-sex couples would be subject to just the same *legal* regulation as different-sex couples, with no special state approbation given to any kind of relationship; but *religions* would not have to endorse same-sex relationships at all, and certainly would not have to endorse them as being on a par with traditional marital relationships.

---

[11] For the argument that polygamy violates equality see Thom Brooks, 'The Problem with Polygamy' in *Philosophical Topics* 37(2) (2009). For a discussion of different varieties of polygamy and their compatibility with equality see Greg Strauss, 'Is Polygamy Inherently Unequal?' in *Ethics* 122(3) (2012).

[12] Don S. Browning, M. Christian Green, and John Witte Jr, *Sex, Marriage and Family in World Religions* (New York: Columbia University Press, 2006) p. xxiii. The six religions in question are Judaism, Islam, Christianity, Confucianism, Hinduism, and Buddhism.

[13] Browning et al., *Sex, Marriage and Family in World Religions* p. xxv.

Thus Richard Thaler and Cass Sunstein endorse a situation in which 'Marriages would be strictly private matters, performed by religious and other private organizations. Within broad limits, marriage-granting organizations would be free to choose whatever rules they like for a marriage conducted under their auspices. So, for example, a church could decide that it would marry only members of that church, and a scuba diving club could decide that it would restrict its ceremonies to certified divers.'[14] Thaler and Sunstein recognize that under-inclusivity is problematic when performed by the state, but they do not find it problematic when religions do it. 'Our basic claim,' they write, 'is that state-run marriage makes it impossible to protect the freedom of religious organizations to proceed as they see fit while also safeguarding the freedom of couples to make the commitments they seek without being treated as second-class citizens by the state.'[15]

Similarly, Lawrence Torcello endorses what he calls the Marriage Privatization Model, according to which the state recognizes only civil unions and 'any comprehensive tradition may endorse a particular understanding of marriage. For instance, a Roman Catholic tradition may wish to limit marriage to a covenant between a man and a woman. This is completely consistent within the dictates of that tradition.'[16] He further emphasizes religious freedom when he writes 'This does not mean that any Catholic priest or any other representative of a comprehensive tradition would ever be obligated to wed a particular couple, unless he saw it as appropriate from within the dictates of that tradition. Debates over the appropriateness of such an act are doctrinal debates within any given tradition and therefore fall well outside the realm of public reason.'[17]

This laissez-faire attitude to religious marriage has the appeal of compromise. However, it comes at the expense of equality, and that is a heavy price to pay. If religions remain legally entitled to discriminate in ways that are rightfully outlawed for others, there is a significant recognitional injustice. Thus Elizabeth Brake is right to worry that libertarian versions of privatized marriage 'cede control of this still socially-powerful institution to the churches and other private-sector groups'.[18]

It is true that religious under-inclusiveness is far worse in a marriage regime than in the marriage-free state. The current situation in the UK, where the

---

[14] Richard H. Thaler and Cass R. Sunstein, *Nudge: Improving Decisions about Health, Wealth and Happiness* (New Haven, CT: Yale University Press, 2008) p. 216.

[15] Thaler and Sunstein, *Nudge* pp. 218–19.

[16] Lawrence Torcello, 'Is the State Endorsement of Any Marriage Justifiable? Same-Sex Marriage, Civil Unions, and the Marriage Privatization Model' in *Public Affairs Quarterly* 22(1) (2008) p. 51.

[17] Torcello, 'Is the State Endorsement of Any Marriage Justifiable?' p. 52.

[18] Elizabeth Brake, *Minimizing Marriage* p. 187.

Church of England is not only exempted but actually legally prevented from conducting same-sex marriages, is intolerable, not least because the Church of England is an established church with a constitutional role in government. In 1984 Swedish legislators rejected introducing same-sex marriage precisely for fear of this situation: a Parliamentary Commission recommended that same-sex couples should have the same legal protection as different-sex couples, but argued that same-sex *marriage* should not be introduced since the church was unwilling to conduct them, and it would be discriminatory if same-sex couples did not have access to a church marriage.[19] Shifting that discrimination to the private sphere may lessen the evil but it is an evil nonetheless.

It is perhaps easier to make this case if we turn attention away from sexuality and towards race. We are used to religions refusing to marry same-sex couples— after all, we are used to states discriminating in this way too—and so to many people religious heterosexism seems untroubling, inevitable, or both. However, popular opinion has rightly shifted away from supporting a religion's right to refuse marriages on racial grounds, such as refusing to marry inter-racial couples. So Katherine Franke identifies 'an evolving national consensus that religion can't be used as a justification for discrimination on the basis of race'[20] in the USA, one that is reflected in legal decisions. In the UK, discrimination on grounds of skin colour is generally not permitted, even where discrimination on other grounds such as ethnic origin is acceptable. For example, a club calling itself the 'Black Women's Culture Club' would be legally permitted only if it were 'open to any woman whose origins are in Africa or the Caribbean', regardless of skin colour.[21]

Yet there remain religious and other groups which are both heterosexist and racist, such as the US Council for Conservative Citizens (CCC).[22] Discrimination on racial grounds has a particularly shameful history and continued existence, and it is absolutely right that it should be straightforwardly ruled out. But then why not rule out discrimination on other grounds too, including sex and sexuality?

---

[19] Margareta Brattström, 'Registered Partnerships as a Functional Equivalent to Marriage' presented at *The Future of Registered Partnerships Durham-Cambridge Conference* (University of Cambridge, 10–11 July 2015). Same-sex marriage was introduced in Sweden in 2009.

[20] Katherine Franke, *Wedlocked: The Perils of Marriage Equality—How African Americans and Gays Mistakenly Thought the Right to Marry Would Set Them Free* (New York: New York University Press, 2015) p. 195.

[21] Government Equalities Office, 'Equality Act 2010: What Do I Need To Know? A Quick Start Guide for Private Clubs and Other Associations' at https://www.gov.uk/government/uploads/system/uploads/attachment_data/file/85047/private-clubs.pdf p. 9.

[22] Franke, *Wedlocked* p. 54. Franke notes that Maggie Gallagher, another prominent advocate of heterosexual-only marriage, has given 'unabashedly white supremacist justifications' for her position. (Franke, *Wedlocked* p. 113.)

One question that arises is whether religious membership and religious practices are properly regarded as chosen.[23] On the one hand, if they *are* chosen, then they might seem to be preferences just like any others, and thus not eligible for special consideration for exemptions from general laws such as anti-discrimination legislation.[24] On the other hand, if they are regarded as unchosen and obligatory, there is reason to treat them not as mere preferences. For some theorists this is enough to justify an exemption for religious practices: since they are unchosen, their adherents should be exempted from other laws on equality grounds.[25] The idea here is that it will be very costly for an individual to give up a religious practice that forms part of her unchosen identity. But if the practice is *both* unchosen *and* harmful, either directly or by way of instantiating inequality, then we have even stronger grounds for protecting people from it rather than removing legal protection.[26] The harm provides the cause for state concern; the lack of choice means the harm is not overridden by respect for autonomy.

Some religious exemptions, that is, are straightforwardly beneficial to those they apply to, since they provide more freedom of choice. Exempting Sikhs from laws forbidding the carrying of knives so they can carry a *kirpan* is like this. Other exemptions give more choice but at the expense of harm of a different sort, as when Sikh men are permitted to wear a turban rather than a helmet when riding a motorcycle. They gain the freedom to wear a turban, but at the expense of a greater risk of head injury. These cases raise dilemmas of equality between religious insiders and outsiders. But the cases under consideration in the marriage context are more problematic since they involve a religion discriminating between its own members. We cannot therefore say that the exemption straightforwardly benefits members of the religion, since some members of the religion are those being discriminated *against*. A claim that a religion makes for an exemption from equality legislation is like this. When the Catholic Church seeks to employ only male priests it wishes to enjoy a benefit that other employers

---

[23] For discussion of the difference between choosing a religion and choosing its practices see Clare Chambers, *Sex, Culture, and Justice: The Limits of Choice* (University Park: Penn State University Press, 2008) ch. 7.

[24] For this position see Brian Barry, *Culture and Equality: An Egalitarian Critique of Multiculturalism* (Cambridge: Polity Press, 2001) and Sonu Bedi, 'Debate: What Is So Special About Religion? The Dilemma of the Religious Exemption' in *Journal of Political Philosophy* 15(2) (2007).

[25] For this position see Michael Sandel, *Democracy's Discontent: America in Search of a Public Philosophy* (Cambridge, MA: Harvard University Press, 1998) and David Miller, 'Liberalism, Equal Opportunities, and Cultural Commitments' in Paul Kelly (ed.), *Multiculturalism Reconsidered: Culture and Equality and its Critics* (Cambridge: Polity Press, 2002).

[26] Chambers, *Sex, Culture, and Justice* chs 4–5.

do not have, namely freedom from the constraints of equality legislation, while at the same time imposing a burden on Catholic women that is not imposed on women outside the Church or on men at all, be they insiders or outsiders, namely exclusion from employment on grounds of sex. We cannot therefore speak of religious exemptions from equality legislation as being in the interests of that religion's members unless we clarify that we mean 'the interests of the religion's leadership and dominant group'.

Standard defences of religious exemptions often gloss over this fact and write as if the only interests at stake are those of outsiders, who are potentially harmed by being subject to a non-universal law, and insiders, who are benefited by the exemption. For example, Lawrence Sager writes of 'the right of the Catholic Church to discriminate in its choice of priests'[27] rather than 'the inability of Catholic women to become priests'. Sager's phrasing implies that Catholics are harmed by equality legislation. But equality legislation *benefits* religious insiders who would otherwise be discriminated against, and it is the exemption that harms them. They are harmed because they are not treated equally with respect to whatever matter is at hand: access to a religious marriage or divorce, employment as a priest, and so on. But they are also harmed by the denial of their religious freedom, since the exemption prevents them from practising their religion unless they fit in with the discriminatory practice.[28] When Sager justifies the male-only priesthood by reference to 'concerns of bounded comfort' for members, enabling them to form 'an associative milieu in which they can flourish as individuals' forming 'open and enriching bonds'[29] the existence of Catholic *women* is completely erased—as would be, in the marriage context, the existence of lesbian and gay Catholics. *They* are not considered as part of the 'associative milieu'; *their* 'comfort' and 'bonds' are not considered. They are outsiders by omission, the people who must be excluded for the comfort and bonds of others.

---

[27] Lawrence Sager, 'Why Churches (and, Possibly, the Tarpon Bay Women's Blue Water Fishing Club) Can Discriminate' in Micah Schwartzman, Chad Flanders, and Zoë Robinson (eds), *The Rise of Corporate Religious Liberty* (Oxford: Oxford University Press, 2016). See also Kevin Vallier, 'The Moral Basis of Religious Exemptions' in *Law and Philosophy* (2015); Miller, 'Liberalism, Equal Opportunities and Cultural Commitments' and Bedi, 'What is So Special About Religion?'

[28] An opponent might argue that they are permitted to practise their religion since the religion includes the discriminatory practice. However, that response would be question-begging since it assumes what is at issue: whether that practice is indeed a necessary component of the religion. The discriminated-against religious insider is not able to practise her religion *as she interprets it* without accepting discrimination, and it is quite possible that her interpretation aligns with that of the religious leaders on all other matters, and with a significant number of co-religionists.

[29] Sager, 'Why Churches' p. 88.

The only Catholics whose comfort is considered are those who wish to exclude; the only people who even count as Catholic in this analysis are straight men.

Why, then, have religious exemptions been endorsed so widely in liberal thought and practice? Religious freedom of discrimination is sometimes endorsed by reference to freedom of association.[30] This defence conceptualizes religions as akin to private members' clubs, and argues that if religions-as-clubs wish to perform marriage or other ceremonies for their own members on any grounds whatsoever, that is their own affair. So far as the group acts generally within the law, this argument goes, there is nothing wrong with it discriminating in any marriage ceremonies it conducts in the context of a marriage-free state.

As I argue elsewhere,[31] the problem with this argument is that most religions do not act in any sense like private members' clubs. They do not, that is, seek to recruit members only once they are adult and fully aware of the group's commitments. On the contrary, most religions want children to be brought up according to their religious tenets, often sanctified as members through rites such as Christian baptism and confirmation, Jewish *bar* and *bat mitzvah*, Jewish and Muslim circumcision, and Hindu *akshara abhyasam*. Religious education of children is also commonplace, ranging from the liberal, largely autonomy-promoting, National Curriculum-following education of a Church of England state school to more single-minded approaches.

What this means is that many children grow up finding themselves already members of a religion. This pre-consensual membership affects a great many aspects of their lives. It affects who their friends, family, and community are; it affects their own perception of what is normal and possible; and it affects their beliefs. What it does not do is determine that they will not be gay, or female, or a member of any other group that the religion discriminates against. So someone who is brought up in a particular religion and who endorses many of its tenets may find herself excluded from a religious marriage on discriminatory grounds. Moreover, in many religions marriage is seen as obligatory or at least strongly preferable.[32] This religious discrimination cannot be justified on the basis of

---

[30] See, for example, Sager, 'Why Churches' and Stuart White, 'Freedom of Association and the Right to Exclude' in *Journal of Political Philosophy* 5(4) (1997).

[31] Chambers, *Sex, Culture, and Justice* ch. 4.

[32] This is not the case in some Christian doctrines, which see marriage as the second best alternative to celibacy, or in Buddhism, in which the family is sometimes seen as a distraction or even a 'cosmic error'. (Alan Cole, 'Buddhism' in Browning et al., *Sex, Marriage, and Family* p. 304.) But 'Celibacy is not a Jewish virtue' and a good Jew will not eschew marriage. (Rabbi Ute Steyer, 'Conservative answer' at http://www.jewishvaluesonline.org/515.) In Islam there is disagreement as to whether marriage is a duty, or simply a desirable or even permissible act, but there is no notion that celibacy is preferable. (Azizah Y. Al-Hibri and Raja' M. El Habti, 'Islam' in Browning et al.,

freedom of association, since children brought up in the religion are not members as a result of free association. So it does not make sense to think of religions as they currently are as like private members' clubs, and the arguments that purport to justify religious exemptions from equality legislation on freedom of association grounds are unsuccessful.

In fact, since religions are not formed by free association it is reasonable to think that religions should be subject to *greater* restrictions than private members' clubs. Since religions are trans-national, historical, institutional authorities that set laws and norms for huge numbers of people who are members by birth, they are a lot more like states and other public institutions than they are like private clubs. In liberal terminology, and *contra* Rawls, religions look like part of the basic structure: major social institutions that profoundly affect people's life chances. On a liberal account, that should require them to comply with principles of justice including non-discrimination. But, problematically, the situation in most liberal states is the other way around: religions are allowed to discriminate in ways that are illegal for private clubs and businesses. In the UK, associations such as private members' clubs may restrict membership to those from a certain sex or sexuality or nationality (although they may not discriminate on grounds of race), and they may restrict access to guests on the same grounds. However, once members and guests are admitted they cannot then be discriminated against. For example, a social club may not allow both women and men to be members or guests yet have a men-only bar; and protected characteristics cannot be used to discriminate between members, such as by charging women higher entry fees.[33]

If current UK equality law were applied in the marriage-free state, a club or society that performed private marriages would *not* be able to deny marriage to lesbians and gays, for example, unless they were also not allowed to join the club. And UK law imposes even more stringent requirements where a service is being provided for money. Associations and businesses may advertise in ways that are more likely to appeal to people of a certain protected group. But they cannot provide services only to people with a certain protected characteristic, which is why Asher's bakery in Northern Ireland was prosecuted for refusing to make a

*Sex, Marriage, and Family* p. 166.) In Hinduism, while asceticism is appropriate later in life, marriage is seen as a *dharma* (a duty appropriate to one's stage of life) in early adulthood, one that parents are under a duty to arrange. (Paul B. Courtright, 'Hinduism' in Browning et al., *Sex, Marriage, and Family* pp. 229–30.)

[33] Equality and Human Rights Commission, 'What equality law means for your association, club or society' *Equality Act 2010 Guidance for Service Providers* Vol. 2 at http://www.equal ityhumanrights.com/publication/what-equality-law-means-your-association-club-or-society. Protected characteristics under the Act are disability, gender reassignment, race, religion or belief, sex, sexual orientation, pregnancy, and maternity including breastfeeding.

cake with the slogan 'Support Gay Marriage'.[34] So, if it were applied in the marriage-free state, existing equality law would not allow private associations or businesses to refuse to provide paid-for wedding ceremonies to same-sex couples or others on the basis of protected characteristics.

Religions, however, are subject to fewer restrictions than associations, even though membership is often not the result of choice. In the UK, religions are exempted from many aspects of equality legislation. In employment law, religions may discriminate if doing so is required 'so as to comply with the doctrines of the religion' or 'to avoid conflicting with the strongly held religious convictions of a significant number of the religion's followers'.[35] No consideration is made of the strongly held religious convictions of those being discriminated against. So the Catholic Church, for example, is legally permitted to employ only male priests since women priests violate the doctrines of the religion or the strongly held convictions of a significant number of the religious followers. The fact that a significant number of Catholics have different, anti-discriminatory convictions has no legal weight.[36]

Religious acts of worship and services are not covered by the UK Equality Act 2010 at all, so there is nothing to stop a religion from refusing to allow black people or women into their services. Legally, the content of religious services may also be discriminatory. Even the provision of services other than religious acts of worship may be discriminatory on grounds of religious belief, or sexual orientation, or provided for one sex only or on sex-segregated terms, if doing so is needed 'to comply with the purpose of the religion or belief organisation, or to avoid causing offence to members of the religion or belief that the organisation

[34] '"Gay cake" row in Northern Ireland: Q & A' *BBC News* (19 May 2015) at http://www.bbc.co.uk/news/uk-northern-ireland-32065233.

[35] UK Equality Act 2010 Schedule 9 at http://www.legislation.gov.uk/ukpga/2010/15/schedule/9.

[36] These include Vatican consultant and Catholic priest Fr Pablo D'Ors, The Wjingaards Institute for Catholic Research, Roman Catholic Women Priests, Catholic Women's Ordination, Women's Ordination Worldwide, Women's Ordination Conference, and twelve Irish Catholic priests who signed a statement to that effect. See Paddy Agnew, 'Vatican consultant "absolutely" in favour of women priests' in *The Irish Times* (6 November 2014) at http://www.irishtimes.com/news/world/europe/vatican-consultant-absolutely-in-favour-of-women-priests-1.1989855; http://www.womenpriests.org; http://romancatholicwomenpriests.org; http://www.catholic-womens-ordination.org.uk; http://womensordinationworldwide.org; http://www.womensordination.org; Tony Flannery, 'Statement from Twelve Priests on Women's Equality in Church' at http://www.tonyflannery.com/statement-from-twelve-priests-on-womens-equality-in-church/. According to the Women's Ordination Conference 'The majority of Catholics would like to see women have equal standing in ordained ministry: in France (83%), Spain (78%), Argentina (60%), and Italy (59%) and the USA (63%).' (Women's Ordination Conference, 'Fact sheet on Catholic Women's Ordination' at http://www.womensordination.org/resources/fact-sheet-on-catholic-womens-ordination/.)

represents'.[37] In other words, religions are not subjected to the same restrictions as businesses and associations even when religions provide services for money. A religion which hires out a venue to the general public, such as a church hall or meeting space, could refuse to hire that space to a woman or a gay person or a disabled person or a breastfeeding mother or a trans person or a Syrian, merely on the grounds that hiring to such people might offend some members of the religion. Once again, the law gives no weight to any offence that the *discrimination* may cause—even if the offence is caused to members of the very same religion. The views of the religion's female or gay or disabled or breastfeeding or trans or Syrian members—or even just those who oppose discrimination—have no legal significance. So, if it were applied in the marriage-free state, current UK equality law would permit religions to conduct private marriages on whatever discriminatory basis they chose.

This existing legal structure gives far too much leeway to religions, allowing them to violate equality to an unacceptable degree. Standards that may be justifiable for consenting adults are applied to unconsenting children and then to the adults they become. It is appropriate for the state to leave religions to determine their own doctrines and rites insofar as they respect the equal rights and liberties of their members. But if religions wish to contravene equality then they must, as a minimum, be willing to restrict themselves to adult members. It is wrong to allow religions *more* leeway to discriminate than private clubs, when clubs and not religions contain only fully-consenting adult members.

This is a radical proposal. One way of understanding it is to consider what would happen if religions were subject to the same restrictions that apply to private members' clubs, for example under legislation such as the UK Equality Act 2010. I use this example not because it is the perfect or only possible legislation, but because this Act provides a workable, real-life example. On this approach it would be legal for religions to deny membership on the basis of protected characteristics, such as to allow only men, or only heterosexual people, or only people of a certain nationality, to be members. It would also be legal for religions to deny entry to guests on the same basis as the restrictions on members, so that a male-only church would not have to allow women in at all. In other words, freedom of association would be strongly protected. But if members were allowed in, either as adults or by being brought up within the religion from

---

[37] Equality and Human Rights Commission, 'What equality law means for your voluntary and community sector organisation (including charities and religion or belief organisations)' *Equality Act 2010 Guidance for Service Providers* Vol. 3 at https://www.equalityhumanrights.com/en/publication-download/what-equality-law-means-your-voluntary-and-community-sector-organisation p. 23.

childhood, they would have to be treated equally. Just as a private club may not invite women in but then prevent them from entering the bar, so too a religion would not be able to invite gay people or women in, including from childhood, but then prevent them from entering the ministry or fully participating in religious services such as marriage.

This doctrine does not mean that it would be legitimate for churches to expel gay people or women that have been brought up within the church. Doing so would be an act of cruelty, forcing those expelled to leave their communities and networks, friends and family, as well as the traditions, beliefs, and practices with which they are deeply familiar and to which they most likely are strongly attached. Instead, my proposal means that, if a religion or religious group wants to discriminate, it must restrict membership to adults who explicitly consent to that discrimination and are not its targets. Religions may transmit themselves to children only if they meet certain basic egalitarian requirements.

This proposal is offered more as a philosophical provocation than a policy prescription. Of course, there are significant practical questions about how we might stop a religion including children, since the state cannot stop parents from transmitting their values to their children without seriously violating parental freedom and family life.[38] We can identify some clear policy implications: a discriminatory religion would not be allowed to admit children to religious services or events, or to hold ceremonies of religious membership or sanctification for children, or to provide formal education in its doctrines to children in faith schools or after-school education programmes.[39] Beyond that, the picture is less clear; my intention is not to promote any specific set of policies so much as to insist on the impermissibility of religions admitting or training children while also discriminating against groups such as women, or gay men. Religions must either respect equality or restrict themselves to consenting adults.

The obvious objection here is that there is something special about religions and religious belief. One version of this claim says that the state, particularly the liberal state, should not get involved in complex questions of religious doctrine. According to this argument, requiring a religion to practise gender equality or conduct same-sex weddings would be tantamount to the state proclaiming on matters of theology. The state would be making a judgement about the true meaning of religious texts, or what it means to be a true Catholic, Jew, Muslim,

---

[38] For discussion of this point see Harry Brighouse and Adam Swift, *Family Values: The Ethics of Parent-Child Relationships* (Princeton, NJ: Princeton University Press, 2014).

[39] These restrictions may be justified for all religions on autonomy grounds, although I do not offer any comments on that issue here.

and so on. But this argument gets the issue the wrong way round. In fact, it is in allowing an exemption that the state involves itself in religious doctrine. Universal equality law for all involves the state keeping out of religious argument. It sets civic standards and leaves it to religions to determine how to comply, whether by (re-)interpreting religious texts, introducing new practices, restricting membership to adults or some other means (examples of creativity in Jewish responses to gender issues are discussed next).

In other words, a state which does not grant religious exemptions makes no claims whatsoever about whether some practice is central to a religion. In contrast, a state that does grant a religious exemption thereby wades straight in to the murky waters of religious doctrine. It recognizes, first, that the exempted practice is properly described as a *religious* practice (rather than, say, a mere preference or cultural norm). Second, in granting the exemption, it declares that the religious significance of the practice is sufficient to override the original legislative purpose. Third, if the exemption is from equality legislation, and if the exemption is not universally welcomed by religious members, the state additionally declares both who is in control of religious meaning—who counts as a religious authority—and which members of a religion count for more than others. None of this can accurately be described as the state staying out of religion.

Other versions of the 'religion is special' claim refer to the unique character of religious belief. It is beyond the scope of this book to deal adequately with the issue of the uniqueness of religious belief, not least because the under-inclusivity of marriage in the marriage-free state raises the same issues as other areas of religious discrimination. So the problem of under-inclusivity in the marriage-free state is reducible to the question of religious discrimination in general, an issue on which there is a large literature.[40] My suggestion is simply that religions should have the courage of their convictions. If they wish to discriminate against great swathes of the population then they should set themselves up as private clubs open only to adult members of their preferred demographic.

---

[40] Works not cited elsewhere in this chapter include Tom Bailey and Valentina Gentile (eds), *Rawls and Religion* (New York: Columbia University Press, 2014); Ronald Dworkin, *Religion Without God* (Cambridge, MA: Harvard University Press, 2013); Kent Greenawalt, *Religion and the Constitution* Volumes 1 & 2 (Princeton, NJ: Princeton University Press, 2009); Jeff Spinner-Halev, *Surviving Diversity: Religion and Democratic Citizenship* (Baltimore, MD: Johns Hopkins University Press, 2000); Bikhu Parekh, *Rethinking Multiculturalism: Cultural Diversity and Political Theory* (Cambridge, MA: Harvard University Press, 2002); Charles Taylor, 'The Politics of Recognition' in Amy Gutmann (ed.), *Multiculturalism and 'The Politics of Recognition'* (Princeton, NJ: Princeton University Press, 1992); Kevin Vallier, *Liberal Politics and Public Faith: Beyond Separation* (London: Routledge, 2004).

If they wish to include everyone, including children, it should be illegal for them to discriminate.[41]

## 6.3 Internal Inequality: Sexism

The marriage-free state permits religions and other private groups or persons to set their own standards for what counts as a marriage. But this does not mean that within private marriage anything goes. Certainly behaviour that is illegal in general should be illegal in marriage, however defined. But the marriage-free state also has a legitimate interest in the norms and practices that religions mandate for religiously-married people, including for religious divorce, because those norms may be deeply inegalitarian or oppressive and because they are upheld by powerful institutions.

It would be wrong to suggest that state marriage is always more egalitarian than religious marriage. On the contrary, Browning et al. argue that the state's influence is sometimes malign. For example, '[e]arly Christianity and Islam were more progressive in their treatment of gender issues, women, and children than later expressions of the religion, especially as it became more established by the state, closer to powerful and economic interests, and therefore mirrored some of the hierarchical structures of empires, kings, and caliphs'.[42] Nonetheless, religious rules may be less egalitarian that the rules of the state within which they reside,[43] certainly in the ideal form of the marriage-free state.

Minority religions are more likely to have developed their own internal system of law regulating marriage and divorce, as majority religions tend to align themselves with the state. Judaism, which has been a minority, stateless religion for much of its history, has a rich system of religious family law. Jewish law is thus a useful case study for how the marriage-free state might respond to religious marriage, and this section discusses it in some detail.[44]

---

[41] There are various ways of easing the transition to non-discrimination, such as by permitting individual ministers to opt out of conducting same-sex marriages. Any opt-outs should be temporary, providing a means for existing ministers to continue with their ministry on the terms to which they signed up. As religious policy changes towards equality, so should the attitudes of newly-ordained ministers.

[42] Browning et al., *Sex, Marriage and Family in World Religions* p. xxvii.

[43] For examples see Susan Moller Okin, 'Is Multiculturalism Bad For Women?' in Susan Moller Okin, Joshua Cohen, Matthew Howard, and Martha Nussbaum (eds), *Is Multiculturalism Bad For Women?* (Princeton, NJ: Princeton University Press, 1999).

[44] My most recent thinking on this issue has been greatly enhanced by discussions with Daniel First.

In the nineteenth century, pressures to assimilate led to the development of three main Jewish denominations (each of which has further subdivisions). Reform Judaism is largely liberal, and integrated with the prevailing civil laws of marriage. For example, Reform Jews generally accept a civil divorce as sufficient to establish a religious divorce.[45] But Conservative and Orthodox Judaism kept their adherence to religious law. According to Michael Berger, for Conservative Jews religious law retains significance as part of a general under-standing of Jews as a 'people' with 'distinctive beliefs and practices'; Orthodox Jews adhere to religious teachings, particularly those of the Talmud, as 'a divinely revealed set of laws that could not be altered'.[46]

Orthodox and Conservative Jews in liberal states thus find themselves subject to two sets of laws, religious and civil, which often conflict. Divorce is a significant area of conflict, since a civil divorce and remarriage can be obtained without a religious divorce, yet a Jewish woman who remarries without having obtained a religious divorce is viewed as committing adultery. This means that she cannot remarry within her religious community. Moreover, any children of her second marriage, together with their descendants for all time, are regarded as *mamzer* (illegitimate) within the Orthodox community and within Israel, a designation that has devastating exclusionary effects.[47] This situation is particularly prob-lematic for women, since Jewish law states that divorce requires the consent of the husband in a document called the *get*, regardless of the wife's reason for seeking a divorce.[48] It therefore follows that a woman may be able to obtain a civil but not a religious divorce, if her husband refuses to provide the *get*. She will thus be considered still married by her religious community, even if the state regards her as divorced. The Hebrew term for a separated or civilly-divorced woman whose husband refuses to give her the *get* is an *agunah*, or chained wife.

---

[45] 'The Get: Jewish Divorce—Reform Perspective' in *Living a Jewish Life* at http://mazorguide. com/Living/Divorce/Reform/divorceReform.htm.

[46] Michael S. Berger, 'Judaism' in Browning et al. *Sex, Marriage and Family in World Religions* p. 11.

[47] Rabbi Jeffrey Wolfson Goldwasser, 'Is a Get Needed Before Second Marriage?' in *Living a Jewish Life* at http://www.mazorguide.com/Living/Divorce/Reform/IsGetNeeded.htm.

[48] Since the tenth-century *herem* of Rabbenu Gershom many branches of Judaism have regarded the act of divorce as requiring the consent of both parties, so that a man must also receive a *get* from his wife if he is to be divorced. However, women are still at a significant disadvantage since the 'severe outcomes do not apply to a husband whose wife is unable or unwilling to accept the get, neither in terms of the status of his children, nor in terms of his potential marriage to another woman. Indeed, permission may be granted for him to remarry, should his wife refuse, unlawfully, to accept the *get*.' (Aviad Hacohen, *The Tears of the Oppressed: An Examination of The Agunah Problem: Background and Halakhic Sources* (Jersey City, NJ: Ktav Publishing House, 2004) p. viii.)

In earlier work I criticized the view that a liberal state should take no interest in norms such as this.[49] It is not right, I argued, to say that the state exhausts its duties by failing to recognize religious divorce and providing a secular egalitarian divorce law of its own. I drew an analogy between religious divorce and discrimination in employment: just as we would not say that sex discrimination in employment is legitimate because women who do not like it can leave and look for a job elsewhere, so too we should not say that discrimination in religious divorce is legitimate because women who do not like it should leave the religion and seek a divorce elsewhere, such as from the state.

In the marriage-free state this problem is even more pertinent, because there is no state recognition of marriage and thus no state divorce that a religiously-married person can seek, yet in religious communities the salience of marriage may endure. The issue of religious divorce in the context of a marriage-free state is this: can a religiously-married person come to be regarded as divorced, and thus eligible for re-marriage, within her own community? If a religious marriage has no legal standing (or if, in a marriage regime, a religious person has access to secular divorce), and if there is no abusive behaviour on the part of the spouse or other religious members that prevent a woman from physically leaving a marriage, then what is at stake for a woman seeking a religious divorce is precisely that she wishes to be seen as divorced *by her own religious community*. She does not need help in physically leaving her religion or her husband, for she can do that with the support of her existing legal rights. She does need help in separating her marital status from her good standing as a member of her religious community. But a person's religious standing is not in the purview of the state.

It follows that it is very difficult for the state to help an *agunah*. The state cannot force other members of her religious community to consider her as divorced, and thus to consider her as eligible for religious remarriage. The state can free her from any obligations to live with, or care for, or provide for, or have sex with her husband, by granting her the legal rights to reject all of these purported obligations. But it cannot forcibly change the consciences of her co-religionists, and it cannot provide a new marriage for her within her religious community.

Yet this is a serious issue that profoundly affects women and leaves them vulnerable to oppression and abuse from their husbands, as Mark Oppenheimer

---

[49] Chambers, *Sex, Culture, and Justice* ch. 4.

explores in an episode of *This American Life* discussing the case of American chained wife Gital Dodelson:

Gital, of course, could just walk away. She's already got her civil divorce. The finances are all settled. So is the child custody. But she can't get remarried. She's a 25-year-old woman. She'd like to have more kids. And, I should point out, most Jews won't care. Plenty of less religious Jews would be happy to marry Gital. But in the Orthodox world—where she was raised, where her whole family is, where she wants to stay—she can't make a new life for herself. Her ex-husband can cast about for a new wife, and then give Gital a *get* if he finds somebody. But for Gital it's different.

[Mark Oppenheimer:] What would it be like? Could you, could you date?

[Gital Dodelson:] Well, I mean, in my community you don't date unless you're actively looking to get married and, since I'm already married, that would pose a little bit of a problem. I don't think I could find anyone who would be willing to date me under these circumstances, where I say 'I'm looking to get married but you might have to wait 2, or 3, or 4, or 10, or 20 years because, you know, there's this man who's refusing to give me the *get*.' And he doesn't feel any urgency, because he can get out of it whenever he wants. He can give me the *get* and be done with the whole thing within a day, as soon as he decides he wants to. So for him it's just a waiting game where, why not wait longer? If his demands were something that I could give, I would have given them a long time ago because this, this life is *agony*. I mean, to wait and wait and never know, and to be tied together like this...I would give anything I could to be finished with it.[50]

As Oppenheimer writes elsewhere, withholding the *get* is a means for husbands to exercise all sorts of control over their wives: 'Some of these husbands are bitter men who just want to torture their wives. More often, the *get* is used for extortion. A husband may say he'll give the *get* after his wife pays him huge sums of money. Or agrees to lower alimony. Or agrees to a different child custody arrangement [from the one agreed in court].'[51] Dodelson's husband's demands change daily, and include sums of money of up to $1million and child custody arrangements that violate those agreed in the civil courts and would require their child to attend a different school each week. Other women become *agunot* as the result of abandonment, as with the case of Raya Dinenberg who was forced to live as an *agunah* in Israel for 28 years. Her husband abandoned her and her two children

---

[50] Mark Oppenheimer, 'Sunrise, Sun-Get' in *This American Life 516: Stuck in the Middle* (17 January 2014) at http://www.thisamericanlife.org/radio-archives/episode/516/stuck-in-the-middle?act=2#play.

[51] Mark Oppenheimer, 'To Give and To *Get*: Why a Congressman can't order his aide to give his wife a Jewish divorce' in *Slate* at http://www.slate.com/articles/news_and_politics/jurisprudence/2012/03/rep_dave_camp_can_t_order_aide_aharon_friedman_to_give_his_wife_a_jewish_divorce_.html.

immediately after receiving his share of the marital property but before giving her the *get*.[52]

Inequalities such as these will arise in the marriage-free state just as they arise now, in a marriage regime. Regardless of the state's view of whether or not a marriage exists, religious marriage is extremely significant and can be used to exert considerable power over women.

At this point some might be tempted to object in the name of those women who accept being discriminated against by their religion. Many Catholic women do not wish to become priests, many Jewish women do not wish to divorce without their husbands' consent. This category includes women who wholeheartedly embrace their status, perhaps thinking of it as different rather than inferior. It also includes women who wish that the relevant discrimination did not exist but nevertheless accept the authority of their religion and its leaders, such as a Catholic woman who wishes that the Pope would ordain women priests but wholeheartedly accepts Papal authority, or an Orthodox Jewish woman who fully endorses Talmudic doctrine even while she would love to divorce her husband.

The first response to this objection is to notice that legal prohibition of religious discrimination is not equivalent to forcing women to take up their equal rights. If a Jewish woman does not feel that she should be divorced without her husband's consent then she can choose not to pursue a unilateral divorce. If a Catholic woman does not feel women should be priests then she need not seek holy orders. My position does not prevent religious women from continuing to live in ways that are unequal or even inferior to men; it simply prevents such lives from being mandated by religious authorities. This fact lessens the force of the objection, from a liberal point of view. For it shows that my proposals are entirely compatible with individual freedom of religion, understood as an individual's choice to follow a particular religious teaching or doctrine.

However, another aspect of the objection remains. My proposals *do* restrict the freedom *to follow a religious authority*. That is to say, they do not allow women to live under a religious authority that discriminates against them *without their consent*. But why should that be a valuable freedom?

An instructive example here might be John Stuart Mill's prohibition on voluntary slavery. Mill famously opposes paternalistic law, arguing that people's actions may only be restricted so as to prevent harm to others. However, he argues that this fundamental principle of freedom does not extend to voluntary

---

[52] Jeremy Sharon, 'Agunah of 28 years granted divorce two days before Passover' in *Israel News* (4th January 2015) at http://www.jpost.com/Israel-News/Agunah-of-28-years-granted-divorce-two-days-before-Passover-395881.

slavery. 'The principle of freedom,' he writes, 'cannot require that [someone] should be free not to be free. It is not freedom to be allowed to alienate his freedom.'[53] The central problem with voluntary slavery, on Mill's account, is that it permanent: its restrictions last even after they are no longer consented to. One might wholeheartedly want to be a slave at some initial point in time, but if a contract to that effect is permitted and upheld then liberty is lost forever. To agree to slavery is to forgo 'any future use of [one's freedom] beyond that single act.... [The slave] is no longer free; but is thenceforth in a position which has no longer the presumption in its favour that would be afforded by his voluntarily remaining in it.'[54]

Mill's account would distinguish between a person who wants to live *as if* a slave, perhaps in some sort of BDSM arrangement, and a real slave. The person living as if a slave is, to outward appearances, under the control of her master. However, the mantra of BDSM is 'safe, sane, and consensual', so that the as-if slave must always be consenting deep down, underneath the role-play. If you were to take her out of character she would affirm her consent to the arrangement, and if she were no longer consenting to it then it would be a grave injustice and deep wrong to continue the game even from the perspective of the players.[55] A Millian account would presumably permit the as-if slave.

But the as-if slave strongly contrasts with the real slave: someone whose enslavement is no longer consensual. The real slave is someone who cannot leave the enslavement, whose deep-down consent or lack thereof is irrelevant. The real slave is not playing a role: the character she plays is the character she is. The real slave is voluntary only in the historical sense: she consented once. For the real slave there are no safe words and no curtain-call.

Mill permits the as-if slave but not the real slave. My proposals concerning religious discrimination are similar. They permit (without endorsement) arrangements whereby women actively embrace their inequality, such as choosing not to divorce without their husbands' consent or choosing not to seek the priesthood. But they rule out mechanisms for forcing women to submit to unequal treatment against their will. A woman cannot be forced to remain married, or forcibly

---

[53] John Stuart Mill, *On Liberty and the Subjection of Women* (Ware: Wordsworth, 1996 [1859 and 1869]) p. 172.

[54] Mill, *On Liberty* p. 172.

[55] For an ethnographic account of BDSM practices see Margot Weiss, *Techniques of Pleasure: BDSM and the Circuits of Sexuality* (Durham, NC: Duke University Press, 2012). Weiss discusses what I call the 'as-if' slave on p. 165. There is much more to be said about BDSM practices including master/slave relationships. I recount those practices from within their own self-understanding, without endorsing either that understanding or the practices themselves. As Weiss points out, BDSM practices are deeply intertwined with social meanings and hierarchies, including hierarchies of gender and race.

prevented from becoming a priest. That is to say, she cannot choose to live under a regime that alienates her choice permanently, as Mill would conceptualize it. This commitment to genuine consent, and the prohibition of unwilling inequality, is basic to all forms of liberalism and feminism.

What can be done? In some religions there is a doctrinal impossibility to changing unequal norms of marriage and divorce. Orthodox Judaism is defined by adherence to Talmudic law, and Talmudic law is regarded as divinely-revealed. So Orthodox Jews cannot reject the unequal divorce law set out in the Talmud without thereby ceasing to be Orthodox. A demand that Orthodox Jews violate the Talmud would be a demand for the end of Orthodox Judaism.

The fact that changing a religious tenet would mean the end of a religion is not a decisive reason against requiring such change; after all, religions must comply with basic laws and human rights, and religions that refuse to do so may legitimately be prosecuted. We have no qualms about anti-terrorism legislation ruling out the most extreme forms of Islamic fundamentalism, for example. But we should have qualms about legislation that would rule out a religious tradition such as Orthodox Judaism which is not based on the destruction of non-believers. It is vital to avoid religious persecution in general and anti-Semitism in particular.

Nonetheless, the fact that a religious group regards its laws as divinely-revealed does not mean that they are not open to interpretation. In Judaism, the written law or *halakha* is interpreted by rabbis, with different Jews following different rabbis. Some rabbis become extremely influential, with their teachings leading to revisions in the interpretation of *halakha*. Perhaps the most significant is the tenth-century *herem* of Rabbenu Gershom, which forbade polygamy and was followed by most branches of Judaism (with the Yemenite Jews a notable exception).[56] Later in this chapter I discuss some contemporary rabbinical responses to the *agunah* problem.

In any case, it is not necessary for civil law to accord precisely with religious law. For example, the *Mishnah* that requires the *get* by stating 'A woman is divorced with her consent or against her will, while the man divorces only wilfully'[57] also states 'A man may offer his daughter in marriage while she is still a maiden (younger than 12.5 years).'[58] But child marriages are illegal not only in the diaspora but also in Israel, and this illegality does not entail an unjust restriction of religious freedom or the end of Orthodox Judaism.

---

[56] I am grateful to Avia Pasternak for observations on this issue.
[57] *The Mishnah* Tractate Yevamot cited in Berger, 'Judaism' p. 31.
[58] *The Mishnah* Tractate Kiddushin cited in Berger, 'Judaism' p. 29.

One way of thinking about this point is that, in general, there is no restriction of religious freedom if the state *prohibits* something that a religion merely *permits*—as opposed to a state prohibiting something that a religion *requires*. There is nothing in orthodox Jewish religious teachings forbidding the use of heroin, for example, but this does not mean that Jews must use heroin, or that there is any religious requirement that a Jew should live in a state that permits heroin use.[59] Since heroin use is religiously permitted (by omission) rather than mandated, a religious person can abide by legal restrictions on its use without violating her religion.

Brian Barry uses this sort of reasoning to justify legal prohibitions on *halal* and *kosher* meat on grounds of animal cruelty. The fact that Islamic and Jewish doctrine *permits* the eating of meat only if it has been killed in a *halal* or *kosher* way does not mean, Barry argues, that it is a denial of religious freedom to outlaw such slaughter as inhumane, since 'nobody is bound to eat meat'.[60] If meat-eating were a requirement of Islam or Judaism then the case for prohibiting *halal* and *kosher* slaughter would be more problematic.

It would also be problematic if the state were to *force* a person to do something that her religion *forbids*. So it would be a profound violation of religious freedom, and liberalism in general, if the state were to force a Jewish person to eat non-kosher meat, or if it were to force a Sikh man to ride a motorcycle while wearing a helmet and thus to remove his turban. In cases like these, where the law prohibits something that a religion requires, we must weigh up the justification behind the law and the content of the religious requirement.

Sometimes the fact that the prohibited practice is religious is not relevant. It would not be justified for a liberal state to force anyone to eat meat or ride a motorcycle, regardless of their religious views, because such force would be an illegitimate use of state power. It would violate individual liberty without good cause, and the liberal state avoids coercion unless necessary for some very weighty interest such as preventing harm to others, ensuring justice, or providing public goods.

In other cases, the fact that a practice is religious may seem relevant. Consider the case of the male-only priesthood again. Anti-discrimination employment legislation is a legitimate use of state power since its aim is to secure equality, a vital part of justice. We could frame that legislation as the state *forcing* Catholics to do something that their religion *forbids*, namely ordaining women priests. This framing makes the legislation look suspect, and suggests that we need to assess it

---

[59]  I am grateful to Daniel First for this example.
[60]  Barry, *Culture and Equality* p. 45.

by weighing up the values of equality and freedom of religion. On the other hand, we could frame anti-discrimination legislation as the state *preventing* something that Catholicism *permits*, namely discrimination against women. We might justify this framing by pointing out that the only person who can ordain priests is the Pope, and Catholicism gives him the power to interpret and change the religion's catechism. So the Pope currently permits discrimination against women, but it is not necessary for him to do so: it would be within his power to permit or even require non-discrimination. On this interpretation the clash looks less serious: it is now between the demands of justice and the wishes of one particular religious leader, and equality should win.

However, some Catholics might push back against this interpretation and describe anti-discrimination legislation as the state preventing something (the all-male priesthood) that the religion *requires*. On this framing, it is more accurate to describe anti-discrimination employment legislation as forcing the Pope to do something that he does not believe he *should* do, even something that he does not believe he *can* do while acting as Pope in good faith, because he believes that he is implementing the will of God. This framing returns us to the clash between religious freedom and equality, and to the questions discussed so far.

First, there is considerable disagreement within the Catholic church (and all religions) about theological matters: whether Catholicism permits or requires discrimination is a matter of internal theological debate, and by offering an exemption from generally-applicable legislation the state effectively takes a stance on matters of theological interpretation. Second, we must proceed on the basis that anti-discrimination legislation is legitimate and even required by justice: that it is sufficiently weighty, in other words, to form the basis of coercive legislation. And if the law does have this presumptive normative force, if its legislative purpose is sufficiently weighty, then the fact that it lies in tension with religious teachings is not a sufficient reason to abandon it. As Barry argues, either a law is sufficiently weighty to justify the coercion it entails for everyone, or it is not and should be abandoned for everyone.[61] So, if a law prevents someone from doing something that her religion requires, the relevant question is whether the law has or lacks sufficient justification; and whether the requirement of the religion is itself discriminatory and disputed.

How should we apply this reasoning to the *agunah* problem, and other similar cases of inegalitarian religious marriage? On the one hand interference might look like an example of illegitimate state action, if we interpret it as the state

[61] Barry, *Culture and Equality* p. 38.

*allowing* or, more problematically, *forcing* something which the religion *forbids*. So we might say that a state law that interferes with unequal orthodox Jewish divorce allows a woman to divorce unilaterally, something her religion forbids, or that it forces other Jews to do something their religion forbids, namely recognize a woman as divorced even if she does not have the *get*.

On the other hand, we could just as easily describe the proposed legislation as an example of the state *preventing* something which the religion merely *permits*, a situation which was acceptable in the heroin case. Orthodox Jewish law *permits* a man to deny a *get* to his wife, even if their relationship meets other standards for divorce. It does not *require* a man to deny the *get*. Divorce is perfectly permissible and, in some cases, it is regarded as a *mitzvah* (obligation).[62] So Jewish law does not demand that a man refuse a divorce. It simply *allows* him to exercise a unilateral veto.

On this interpretation, the state need not interfere in the Orthodox principle that a *get* is required for a religious divorce. Instead, it could make it a criminal or civil offence for a man to refuse to provide a *get*. On this approach, a *get* would still be required for religious divorce, but the state would deny a Jewish husband the act of withholding the *get*, an act that his religion permits but does not mandate.

What this example shows is that it may be possible to implement egalitarian measures and restrictions on religious practices in ways that do not fundamentally conflict with religious freedom. It is important to exercise caution in condemning or preventing central aspects of major and ancient religions, for reasons of religious freedom and multiculturalism. But options can be found that avoid both religious oppression of women and state oppression of religions. The egalitarian case against religious exemptions relies on the idea that there is a way for religious people to obey both the law and their religious principles. The state need not set out the precise method or doctrine by which a religion should comply with equality legislation, but it can and should set the requirement that they do comply.

Jewish communities are deeply aware of the *agunah* problem. Various internal solutions have been implemented, any of which might meet an egalitarian requirement. Some branches of Judaism follow the Babylonian *takanta de-metivta*, which allows a *de-metivta* court to force a husband to provide a *get* to his wife even if he does not want to.[63] Other branches of Judaism look to contract as the solution. As Michael Berger explains, 'the Conservative movement composed a *ketubah*, the

---

[62] Michael J. Broyde, 'The 1992 New York Get Law' in *Tradition* 29(4) (1995).
[63] Berger, 'Judaism' p. 8.

religious marriage contract, that could demand a husband and wife submit to a Jewish court, and many Orthodox organizations endorsed a prenuptial agreement, which contractually binds a husband to pay his wife's maintenance until he divorces her religiously'.[64] In the USA, Conservative Jews typically sign a premarital contract agreeing to have any marital dispute referred to the Beth Din of America. The contract authorizes the Beth Din of America 'to decide all matters related to a get' and to determine child custody and financial support arrangements 'based on principles... customarily found in the United States as found in the Uniform Marriage and Divorce Act'.[65] An egalitarian state could require a *beth din* (Jewish court) to rule in non-discriminatory ways, such that judgments should not differ in their implications for men and women.[66]

These methods are ingenious but not always successful. In the case of Gita Dodelson described above, her husband Avrohom Meir Weiss refused to attend a *beth din*, resulting in the court issuing a judgment against him. Orthodox Jewish practice dictates that the judgment should have led to his ostracism from the Orthodox Jewish community, usually sufficient to convince a man to give the *get*. However, Weiss no longer lived in the area of the issuing *beth din*, and his local Orthodox community did not follow the court's judgment.[67] Similarly, many couples do not get a prenuptial agreement for the reasons explored in Chapter 4: it can seem like a bad omen, or a problematic break from tradition.[68] As a measure of desperation some women turn to rabbis who will work with hired hit men to use violence to force husbands to give the *get*, following the teaching of Maimonides who advocated beating a recalcitrant husband until he complies.[69]

These tortuous or even torturous arrangements to secure 'consent' may seem nonsensical from a philosophical point of view. Why adhere to a consent requirement that is deemed satisfied when extorted by violence or financial pressure? They reveal the enduring and imprisoning nature of religious teachings, teachings that may be followed by rabbis even as they condemn the situation they bring about. But these efforts from within Conservative and Orthodox Judaism also reveal the ability of religions to find workarounds for unequal religious law. They show, that is, that the state should not claim impotence or disinterest regarding religious marriage. Religious law can be followed in

---

[64] Berger, 'Judaism' p. 11; see also p. 66.
[65] Beth Din of American Binding Arbitration Agreement as cited in Berger, 'Judaism' p. 69.
[66] As I argue in Chambers, *Sex, Culture, and Justice* ch. 4.
[67] Oppenheimer, 'To Give and To Get'.
[68] Mark Oppenheimer, 'Where Divorce Can Be Denied, Orthodox Jews Look to Prenuptial Contracts' in *The New York Times* (16 March 2012) at http://www.nytimes.com/2012/03/17/us/orthodox-jews-look-to-prenuptial-contracts-to-address-divorce-refusals.html.
[69] Oppenheimer, 'To Give and To Get'.

different ways, and it can interact with new laws and norms that change its effects in the community. Religious law, as all law, is open to interpretation, and even divinely-revealed law does not tell the whole story about the practices that are acceptable in any given community.

The state must do whatever it can to ensure that women and other vulnerable people are not trapped in oppressive religious marriages. But, where possible, it should do so without requiring religions to abandon their basic tenets, perhaps by providing workarounds such as compulsory prenuptial contracts or by offering incentives for religions to develop their own workarounds. The state can play a role in many of the potential solutions just outlined. In Israel, for example, the law requires all divorcing parties to go before a *beth din*, regardless of any contract. An Israeli *beth din* can order a husband to provide the *get* and divorce his wife in certain circumstances, and can even imprison men who fail to provide the *get* after being commanded to do so.[70] This is not a complete solution, since the *beth din* may not rule in a way that secures equality (certainly Israeli *batai dinim* reach conclusions that would not align with secular liberal practice).[71] Still, this system offers a method of reform that does not require interfering with Talmudic law.

Alternative state-provided solutions include the one offered in New York and Montreal, where 'withholding a get is considered a compensable injury under tort law, which addresses private or civil injury. Initiating action in civil court under tort law often causes a recalcitrant husband to have a "change of heart."'[72] New York law also allows a judge in a civil divorce court to take into account whether a husband has issued a *get* when determining financial settlements, so that recalcitrant husbands can be punished financially.[73] Here, then, the state can provide penalties that discourage or prevent a man from doing that which his religion permits but does not require, namely withholding the *get*.

Other options come from within the Jewish community. Jewish practices and religious laws of marriage and divorce have varied historically, and have included complete discretion of the husband, court-granted divorces, court-ordered *gets*, and various mechanisms of property-distribution and sanction.[74] Various options

---

[70] Hillel Fendel, 'Bill: Jailed get-refusers to be banned from studying Torah' in *Arutz Sheva* (14 June 2016) at http://www.israelnationalnews.com/News/News.aspx/213633.

[71] Soriya Daniels, 'Potential Solutions to the Agunah Problem' on My Jewish Learning at http://www.myjewishlearning.com/article/potential-solutions-to-the-agunah-problem/ p. 1.

[72] Daniels, 'Potential Solutions to the Agunah Problem' p. 2.

[73] For critical discussion of this law see Broyde, 'The 1992 New York Get Law'.

[74] Berger, 'Judaism' p. 39.

are used today. For example, Soriya Daniels describes an approach used by New York Rabbi Moshe Morgenstern, whose words are quoted first:

'When all other methods have failed, we do not extort a woman, or cause her to live in celibacy or childlessness because her vindictive spouse has decided to withhold divorce. We simply say: At the time of the marriage, she didn't know what a sadist this man has proven himself to be. Therefore, her agreeing to marry him is a mistake.' His solution comes from the notion that marriage is a contract and when one side falsifies the terms (by being a secret sadist), then the marriage was invalid to begin with and may be annulled by a rabbi.... According to Morgenstern, the *heter* (permission) key unlocks her, simply by doing what other great rabbis of our past have done: using rabbinical power to change even a divine command if it will prevent suffering and cure injustice.[75]

Of course, solutions like this (and many others have been suggested and used) work only if they are generally accepted in the relevant communities, and so progressive rabbis such as Morgenstern need to convince others. While many support him, others vehemently do not: his methods 'have incurred the wrath of Orthodox rabbis from Jamaica Estates to Jerusalem'.[76] The state cannot force this process but may be able to promote it, by requiring religions to refrain from discrimination along the lines set out in Section 6.2. If a religion is legally required to restrict its membership to people it is willing to treat equally, it will likely be motivated to find solutions to ensure equal treatment.

## Conclusion

The marriage-free state is not justified on libertarian grounds. While it does allow significant freedom for individuals and groups to define marriage as they see fit, this freedom is constrained by the demands of equality.

The problem of over-inclusivity is not significant in the marriage-free state. The marriage-free state should not set limits on use of the term 'marriage' beyond what is required to prevent harm. Most fundamentally this will mean that a group should not perform a marriage ceremony, or apply the label and norms of marriage, unless the persons involved are consenting adults. Additional limitations, for example a limitation on incestuous marriage, may be justified so as to prevent harm to vulnerable people such as children, but any restrictions must be evidence-based, with harm prevention and equality rather than moral propriety at heart. Beyond these restrictions people should be free to marry as they wish.

---

[75] Daniels, 'Potential Solutions to the Agunah Problem' p. 4.
[76] Eric J. Greenberg, 'Breaking The Chains' in *The New York Jewish Week* at http://www.thejewishweek.com/features/breaking_chains.

The problems of under-inclusivity and internal inequality are more significant, and I propose a similar approach to both. If religions are to remain major, non-voluntary social institutions, containing children and others who are members by birth and upbringing, and playing a significant role in determining people's life chances, rights, and duties, then they should be subject to the same laws and principles of justice that apply to other such institutions, including the state. In other words, religions that act in those ways should not be permitted to discriminate.

On the other hand, if religions are committed to continuing their discrimination, their position can be justified only by appealing to freedom of association and the other liberties of consenting adults. This justification requires religions to be treated in the same way as other private members' clubs and associations. One model for doing so is UK equality law, according to which discrimination on the basis of protected characteristics is permitted only at the membership stage. It should therefore be possible for religions to welcome only fellow religious believers, or heterosexuals, or men. But if a religion opens its doors to all, including by bringing up children within the faith, then it must not discriminate between them by offering unequal access to marriage or unequal marriage and divorce law. Responses to the *agunah* problem within Orthodox and Conservative Judaism demonstrate the creative possibilities for accommodating equality that exist within even divinely-revealed systems of law. The marriage-free state ought to assist in this endeavour by providing a regulatory framework requiring equality.

# Conclusion

I ... feel it my duty to put on record a formal protest against the existing law of marriage.... And in the event of marriage between Mrs Taylor and me I declare it to be my will and intention, and the condition of the engagement between us, that she retains in all respects whatever the same absolute freedom of action and freedom of disposal of herself and of all that does or may at any time belong to her, as if no such marriage had taken place; and I absolutely disclaim and repudiate all pretension to have acquired any rights whatever by virtue of such marriage.[1]

The declaration above was made by John Stuart Mill in 1851, before his marriage to Harriet Taylor. Mill's objection was to the English law of marriage at the time, which gave husbands vast control over their wives' activities, property, and bodies. The most egregious aspects of legal inequality in marriage no longer apply in liberal democratic states. But marriage remains an institution that instantiates inequality.

*Against Marriage* is bookended by chapters discussing the inequalities of marriage. Marriage is fundamentally a gendered institution. It has been the main mechanism for maintaining the gendered division of labour, for regulating men's access to women's bodies, and for giving men ownership and control of children. Marriage provides a structure within which men and women are represented as opposites: complementary but stratified, roles separate and ranked. He works, she cooks and cleans; his work is paid, hers is not; his work is borne of power and entitlement, hers of love and duty. The state recognition of marriage has been the state recognition of this gendered arrangement: a celebration of separation simultaneous to unification. Two become one: one household, one legal entity, husband and wife separable only by the public/private divide. Or death.

---

[1] John Stuart Mill, Statement of 6 March 1851, quoted in Alice S. Rossi (ed.), *Essays on Sex Equality* (Chicago: The University of Chicago Press, 1970) pp. 45–6.

As women have increasingly resisted their confinement to the private sphere, awareness of the gendered nature of marriage has recently been replaced with a focus on its assumption of heterosexuality. Marriage is heterosexual in the same way that it is gendered: it functions as a mechanism for the reproduction of gender precisely by mandating heterosexual coupledom for all. The move to same-sex marriage disrupts but does not destroy the gendered and hierarchical nature of marriage. Same-sex marriage succeeds rhetorically by painting same-sex relationships as 'just like' different-sex ones; since the model of relationships upheld by marriage is gendered and socially conservative this may not be such a good thing.

The movement for equal marriage gains political and philosophical traction by its emphasis on equivalence. But equal rights to what? The inequalities of marriage cannot be justified without reference to controversial statements about meaning and value. State recognition of marriage makes sense only against an assumption that some ways of life are more valuable than others, that some family forms are more worthy than others, and that some religious or secular understandings of virtue are the correct ones. These assumptions are not only gendered; they are partial in other ways too. They hold up as universally preferable a way of life that is typical for some racial and social groups but not others. And so state-recognized marriage is part of a system of inequality distinguishing us and them, stable and feckless, reliable and flaky, deserving and undeserving, celebrated and abjected.

Moreover, state-recognized marriage relies on the assumption that these value judgements justify imposing burdens on those who disagree, and on the children of unmarried parents. This imposition of burden undermines both the liberty and equality of dissenters and their children—children who, according to the defenders of marriage, are *already* disadvantaged.

The fact that state-recognized marriage undermines both liberty and equality is why I have argued against it. But I have also put forward a positive programme for change: the marriage-free state.

The marriage-free state is based on the principle that Mill invokes: the idea that his future wife's rights should be 'as if no such marriage had taken place'. The marriage-free state starts by identifying the rights and duties that are appropriate for the unmarried. It then applies those rights and duties to everyone. So the marriage-free state has to answer difficult questions, such as what sort of relationship functions should bring duties and rights, who counts as a parent, whether domestic work within a family should bring financial entitlements, whether immigration should be limited or expanded. But it does not have to answer any questions that are not also faced by a marriage regime. A marriage regime also has to determine how to deal with those people who are unmarried but nevertheless in relationships of caring and sharing, positions of vulnerability or interdependence. At its most basic the marriage-free state simply demands that the rights and duties that apply to the unmarried should apply to everyone.

When Mill was writing marriage was not only profoundly gender-unequal. It was also strongly normative, for women at least. As Mill put it, 'A single woman is . . . felt by herself and others as a kind of excrescence on the surface of society, having no use or function or office there.'[2] So women were strongly pressured into marriage, a condition that rendered them utterly vulnerable and dependent. In twenty-first-century liberal democracies marriage is neither so essential nor so unequal. In one sense, of course, this is an improvement. But in another sense the current state recognition of marriage in liberal societies is anachronistic. Family life, property-ownership, parenting, immigration, and so on are regulated on the assumption of marriage, but this assumption is no longer statistically sensible. As we saw in Chapters 1 and 5, only about half of children are born to parents who are married or in civil partnerships in countries such as Britain, the USA, Denmark, Sweden, and New Zealand. For African American children it is twice as common to live with unmarried parents rather than married ones. So it is no longer true to say that marriage is the default position for raising children or forming a family. Marriage is neither a requirement nor a guarantee of familial stability.

Instead of basing regulation on the ideal-type of a married couple, an ideal-type that is neither ideal nor typical, an egalitarian state should be marriage-free. Relationships should be regulated according to their practices, with no assumption that practices coincide. These default regulations should be based on ensuring equality, both internal to a relationship and between those who are and are not partnered. Deviations may be allowed, where they are compatible with justice, and the conditions for deviation should be clear and accessible. Avoiding default regulation should be a conscious and unanimous choice.

The marriage-free state takes no interest in the definitions of private marriage beyond what is necessary to prevent harm. It does not stipulate that marriage should be monogamous, or sexual, or permanent. However, it does take an interest in the actions of private groups, including businesses, associations, and religions. The final chapter returned to equality, and noted that religious teachings and traditions can be deeply discriminatory. It also noted that religious people and leaders can and do resist that discrimination. I suggested a model

---

[2] Mill, 'Early Essay on Marriage and Divorce (1832)' in Rossi (ed.), *Essays on Sex Equality* p. 72.

whereby general anti-discrimination legislation, such as UK equality law, would be applied to religions in the same way that it is applied to associations. On a general application of the UK model discrimination would be permitted at the membership stage but not beyond. Once people are admitted as members of a religion, including by being brought up in that religion as children, it should be illegal to discriminate between them. This would mean that religions would not be able to discriminate against lesbians and gays unless only adult heterosexuals were admitted as members or guests, and no religion would be allowed to discriminate against women and girls if girls were brought up within it. Religions affected by this position would have a choice: restrict membership to adults of the preferred demographic, or reform practices of inequality.

The marriage-free state does not rule out weddings, or ceremonies, or celebrations. It does not rule out stability, or family, or commitment, or devotion. It does not rule out love. It *does* rule out the idea that those values are the preserve of one very particular relationship format. It *does* rule out the state proceeding in such a way as to disadvantage, discriminate against, or stigmatize those whose families are not structured according to that format. It aims to secure equality for all, regardless of relationship or family type. In the marriage-free state no one, whether adult or child, needs marriage—or suffers unduly from it. Marriage must be neither prerequisite nor hindrance.

# Bibliography

Adams, Laura S., 'Privileging the Privileged: Child Well-Being as a Justification for State Support of Marriage' in *San Diego Law Review* 42 (2005).

Advocate http://www.advocate.com/marriage-equality.

Agnew, Paddy, 'Vatican consultant "absolutely" in favour of women priests' in *The Irish Times* (6 November 2014) at http://www.irishtimes.com/news/world/europe/vatican-consultant-absolutely-in-favour-of-women-priests-1.1989855.

Al-Hibri, Azizah Y. and Raja' M. El Habti, 'Islam' in Don S. Browning, M. Christian Green, and John Witte Jr, *Sex, Marriage and Family in World Religions* (New York: Columbia University Press, 2006).

Altman, Dennis, 'Sexual Freedom and the End of Romance' in Andrew Sullivan (ed.), *Same-Sex Marriage Pro and Con: A Reader* (New York: Vintage, 2004 [1982]).

Appleton, Susan Frelich, 'Illegitimacy and Sex, Old and New' in *Journal of Gender, Social Policy, and the Law* 20(3) (2012).

Arber, Sara and Jay Ginn, 'The Mirage of Gender Equality: Occupational Success in the Labour Market and within Marriage' in *The British Journal of Sociology* 46(1) (1995).

Arkes, Hadley, 'The Role of Nature' in Andrew Sullivan (ed.), *Same-Sex Marriage Pro and Con: A Reader* (New York: Vintage, 2004 [1993]).

Atkins-Sayre, Wendy, 'The Emergence of "Ms." As a Liberatory Title' in *Women and Language* 28(1) (2005).

Australian Marriage Equality http://www.australianmarriageequality.org.

Bailey, Tom and Valentina Gentile (eds), *Rawls and Religion* (New York: Columbia University Press, 2014).

Baker, Paul, 'Will Ms ever be as Frequent as Mr? A Corpus-based Comparison of Gendered Terms across Four Diachronic Corpora of British English' in *Gender and Language* 4(1) (2010).

Bala, Nicholas and Christine Ashbourne, 'The Widening Concept of "Parent" in Canada: Step-Parents, Same-Sex Partners, and Parents by Art' in *Journal of Gender, Social Policy, and the Law* 20(3) (2012).

Ball, Carlos A., 'Moral Foundations for a Discourse on Same-Sex Marriage: Looking Beyond Political Liberalism' in *The Georgetown Law Journal* 85 (1996–7).

Barry, Brian, *Culture and Equality: An Egalitarian Critique of Multiculturalism* (Cambridge: Polity Press, 2001).

BBC News, 'Britney's short marriage annulled' (6 January 2004).

BBC News, '"Gay cake" row in Northern Ireland: Q & A' (19 May 2015) at http://www.bbc.co.uk/news/uk-northern-ireland-32065233.

Bedi, Sonu, 'Debate: What Is So Special About Religion? The Dilemma of the Religious Exemption' in *Journal of Political Philosophy* 15(2) (2007).

Bedi, Sonu, *Beyond Race, Sex, and Sexual Orientation: Legal Equality without Identity* (Cambridge: Cambridge University Press, 2013).

Bennett, William, 'Leave Marriage Alone' in Andrew Sullivan (ed.), *Same-Sex Marriage Pro and Con: A Reader* (New York: Vintage, 2004 [1996]).

Berger, Michael S., 'Judaism' in Don S. Browning, M. Christian Green, and John Witte Jr, *Sex, Marriage and Family in World Religions* (New York: Columbia University Press, 2006).

Bevacqua, Maria, 'Feminist Theory and the Question of Lesbian and Gay Marriage' in *Feminism & Psychology* 14(1) (2004).

Björgvinsson, David Thór, 'Registered Partnerships—Marriage: Iceland' presented at The Future of Registered Partnerships Durham-Cambridge Conference (University of Cambridge, 10–11 July 2015).

Bourdieu, Pierre, *Masculine Domination* (Cambridge: Polity Press, 2001).

Bourdieu, Pierre and Loïc Wacquant, *An Invitation to Reflexive Sociology* (Cambridge: Polity Press, 1992).

Bowman, Cynthia Grant, 'The New Illegitimacy: Children of Cohabiting Couples and Stepchildren' in *Journal of Gender, Social Policy, and the Law* 20(3) (2012).

Boynton, Petra, 'Abiding by The Rules: Instructing Women in Relationships' in *Feminism & Psychology* 13(2) (2003).

Bradley, Gerard V., 'What's in a Name? A Philosophical Critique of "Civil Unions" Predicated Upon a Sexual Relationship' in *The Monist* 91(3/4) (2008).

Brake, Elizabeth, 'Minimal Marriage: What Political Liberalism Implies for Marriage Law' in *Ethics* 120(1) (January 2010).

Brake, Elizabeth, *Minimizing Marriage: Marriage, Morality, and the Law* (Oxford: Oxford University Press, 2012).

Brattström, Margareta, 'Registered Partnerships as a Functional Equivalent to Marriage' presented at The Future of Registered Partnerships Durham-Cambridge Conference (University of Cambridge, 10–11 July 2015).

Braun, Virginia, 'Thanks to my Mother...A Personal Commentary on Heterosexual Marriage' in *Feminism & Psychology* 13(4) (2003).

Briggs, Margaret and Emma Peart, 'The Future of Registered Partnerships: New Zealand' presented at The Future of Registered Partnerships Durham-Cambridge Conference (University of Cambridge, 10–11 July 2015).

Brighouse, Harry and Adam Swift, 'Parents' Rights and the Value of the Family' in *Ethics* 117 (October 2006).

Brighouse, Harry and Adam Swift, *Family Values: The Ethics of Parent-Child Relationships* (Princeton, NJ: Princeton University Press, 2014).

Brinig, Margaret F. and Steven M. Crafton, 'Marriage and Opportunism' in *Journal of Legal Studies* 23(2) (1994).

Brooks, Thom, 'The Problem with Polygamy' in *Philosophical Topics* 37(2) (2009).

Browning, Anna, 'Mrs? Or is that Ms, Miss?' on BBC News (20 March 2009) at http://news.bbc.co.uk/1/hi/7952261.stm.

Browning, Don S., M. Christian Green, and John Witte Jr, *Sex, Marriage and Family in World Religions* (New York: Columbia University Press, 2006).

Broyde, Michael J., 'The 1992 New York Get Law' in *Tradition* 29(4) (1995).

Butler, Judith, 'Is kinship always already heterosexual?' in *differences: A Journal of Feminist Cultural Studies* 13(1) (2002).

Butler, Judith, *Gender Trouble* (London: Routledge, 1999).

Calhoun, Cheshire, *Feminism, the Family, and the Politics of the Closet: Lesbian and Gay Displacement* (Oxford: Oxford University Press, 2000).

Calhoun, Cheshire, 'Who's Afraid of Polygamous Marriage? Lessons for Same-Sex Marriage Advocacy from the History of Polygamy' in *San Diego Law Review* 42 (2005).

Callahan, Joan, 'Same-Sex Marriage: Why It Matters—At Least for Now' in *Hypatia* 24(1) (2009).

Cameron, David, 'David Cameron's welfare speech in full' in *The Telegraph* (25 June 2012) at http://www.telegraph.co.uk/news/politics/david-cameron/9354163/David-Camerons-welfare-speech-in-full.html.

Cameron, David, Speech in Parliament in *Hansard* 6 February 2013: Column 268 Q1 [141634].

Card, Claudia, 'Against Marriage and Motherhood' in *Hypatia* 11(3) (1996).

Catholic Women's Ordination http://www.catholic-womens-ordination.org.uk.

Centers for Disease Control and Prevention, 'Percentage of Births to Unmarried Mothers by State' at https://www.cdc.gov/nchs/pressroom/sosmap/unmarried/unmarried.html.

Chambers, Clare, *Sex, Culture, and Justice: The Limits of Choice* (University Park, PA: Penn State University Press, 2008).

Chambers, Clare, ' "The Family as a Basic Institution:" A Feminist Analysis of the Basic Structure as Subject' in Ruth Abbey (ed.), *Feminist Interpretations of Rawls* (University Park, PA: Penn State University Press, 2013).

Chambers, Clare, 'The Marriage-Free State' in *Proceedings of the Aristotelian Society* 113(2) (2013).

Chambers, Clare, 'The Limitations of Contract: Regulating Personal Relationships in a Marriage-Free State' in *After Marriage: Rethinking Marital Relationships* (Oxford: Oxford University Press, 2016).

Chambers, David, 'Polygamy and Same-Sex Marriage' in *Hofstra Law Review* 26(1) (1997).

Chambers, Samuel A. and Terrell Carver, *Judith Butler and Political Theory: Troubling Politics* (London: Routledge, 2008).

Christensen, Craig W., 'Legal Ordering of Family Values: The Case of Gay and Lesbian Families' in *Cardozo Law Review* 18 (1996–7).

Citizens Advice, 'Living together and marriage: legal differences' at https://www.citizensadvice.org.uk/relationships/living-together-marriage-and-civil-partnership/living-together-and-marriage-legal-differences/.

Cochrane, Kira, 'You're fired' in *The Guardian* (23 April 2008) at http://www.theguardian.com/money/2008/apr/23/worklifebalance.discriminationatwork.

Cole, Alan, 'Buddhism' in Don S. Browning, M. Christian Green, and John Witte Jr, *Sex, Marriage and Family in World Religions* (New York: Columbia University Press, 2006).

Corvino, John, 'Homosexuality and the PIB argument' in *Ethics* 115(3) (2005).

Corvino, John and Maggie Gallagher, *Debating Same-Sex Marriage* (Oxford: Oxford University Press, 2012).

Coupet, Sacha M., 'Beyond "Eros": Relative Caregiving, "Agape" Parentage, and the Best Interests of Children' in *Journal of Gender, Social Policy, and the Law* 20(3) (2012).

Courtright, Paul B., 'Hinduism' in Don S. Browning, M. Christian Green, and John Witte Jr, *Sex, Marriage and Family in World Religions* (New York: Columbia University Press, 2006).

Cronan, Sheila, 'Marriage' in Anne Koedt, Ellen Levine, and Anita Rapone (eds), *Radical Feminism* (New York: Times Books, 1973).

Curry, H. and D. Clifford, *A Legal Guide for Lesbian and Gay Couples: A NOLO Press Self-Help Law Book* §8 (1989).

Daniels, Soriya, 'Potential Solutions to the Agunah Problem' on My Jewish Learning at http://www.myjewishlearning.com/article/potential-solutions-to-the-agunah-problem/.

de Beauvoir, Simone, *The Second Sex* (London: Vintage, 1997 [1949]).

De Schrijver, Lynn, 'Registered Partnerships as an *Alternative* to Marriage: The Netherlands' presented at The Future of Registered Partnerships Durham-Cambridge Conference (University of Cambridge, 10–11 July 2015).

Den Otter, Ronald C., *In Defense of Plural Marriage* (Cambridge: Cambridge University Press, 2015).

Dettmer, Lisa, 'Beyond Gay Marriage: the assimilation of Queers into neoliberal culture' at https://www.academia.edu/11879158/Beyond_Gay_Marriage_the_assimilation_of_Queers_into_neoliberal_culture.

Dnes, Antony W. and Robert Rowthorn (eds), *The Law and Economics of Marriage & Divorce* (Cambridge: Cambridge University Press, 2002).

Dworkin, Ronald, *Religion Without God* (Cambridge, MA: Harvard University Press, 2013).

*The Economist* style guide http://www.economist.com/styleguide/t#node-21532475.

Eichner, Maxine, 'Marriage and the Elephant: The Liberal Democratic State's Regulation of Intimate Relationships Between Adults' in *Harvard Journal of Law and Gender 30* (2007).

Eichner, Maxine, *The Supportive State* (Oxford: Oxford University Press, 2010).

Eisenberg, Melvin A., 'The Limits of Cognition and the Limits of Contract' *Stanford Law Review* 47 (1995).

Eisenberg, Melvin A., 'Why There Is No Law of Relational Contracts' *Northwestern University Law Review* 94 (1999–2000).

Ellman, Ira Mark, '"Contract Thinking" was *Marvin's* fatal flaw' in *Notre Dame Law Review* 76 (2000–1).

Ellman, Ira Mark and Sharon Lohr, 'Marriage as Contract, Opportunistic Violence, and Other Bad Arguments for Fault Divorce' in *University of Illinois Law Review* 71 (1997).

Emens, Elizabeth F., 'Just Monogamy?' in Mary Lyndon Shanley (ed.), *Just Marriage* (Oxford: Oxford University Press, 2004).

Emens, Elizabeth F., 'Monogamy's Law: Compulsory Monogamy and Polyamorous Existence' in *New York University Review of Law and Social Change* 29 (2004).

The Equal Love Campaign http://equallove.org.uk.

Equality and Human Rights Commission, 'What equality law means for your association, club or society' *Equality Act 2010 Guidance for Service Providers* Vol. 2 at http://www.equalityhumanrights.com/publication/what-equality-law-means-your-association-club-or-society.

Equality and Human Rights Commission, 'What equality law means for your voluntary and community sector organisation (including charities and religion or belief organisations)' *Equality Act 2010 Guidance for Service Providers* Vol. 3 at https://www.equalityhumanrights.com/en/publication-download/what-equality-law-means-your-voluntary-and-community-sector-organisation.

Equality and Human Rights Commission, 'Pregnancy and Maternity-Related Discrimination and Disadvantage' BIS Research Paper No. 235 (2015) at http://www.equality humanrights.com/sites/default/files/publication_pdf/Pregnancy-and-maternity-related-discrimination-and-disadvantage_0.pdf.

Eskridge, Jr, William K., *Equality Practice: Civil Unions and the Future of Gay Rights* (New York: Routledge, 2002).

Estlund, David M., 'Commentary on Parts I and II' in David M. Estlund and Martha C. Nussbaum (eds), *Sex, Preference, and Family: Essays on Law and Nature* (Oxford: Oxford University Press, 1997).

Estlund, David, 'Shaping and Sex' in David M. Estlund and Martha C. Nussbaum (eds), *Sex, Preference, and Family: Essays on Law and Nature* (Oxford: Oxford University Press, 1997).

Ettelbrick, Paula L., 'Since When is Marriage a Path to Liberation?' in Mark Blasius and Shane Phelan (eds), *We Are Everywhere: A Historical Sourcebook of Gay and Lesbian Politics* (London: Routledge, 1997 [1989]).

European Convention on Human Rights at http://www.echr.coe.int/Documents/Convention_ENG.pdf.

Farré, Lídia, 'The Role of Men in the Economic and Social Development of Women: Implications for Gender Equality' in *The World Bank Research Observer* 28(1) (2013).

Fein, Ellen and Sherrie Schneider, *The Rules: Time Tested Secrets for Capturing the Heart of Mr Right* (London: Thorlens, 1995).

Fendel, Hillel, 'Bill: Jailed get-refusers to be banned from studying Torah' in *Arutz Sheva* (14 June 2016) at http://www.israelnationalnews.com/News/News.aspx/213633.

Ferguson, Ann, 'Gay Marriage': An American and Feminist Dilemma' in *Hypatia* 22(1) (2007).

Fineman, Martha Albertson, *The Neutered Mother, The Sexual Family, and Other Twentieth Century Tragedies* (London: Routledge, 1995).

Fineman, Martha Albertson, 'Why Marriage?' in *Virginia Journal of Social Policy and the Law* 9(1) (2001).

Fineman, Martha Albertson, *The Autonomy Myth: A Theory of Dependency* (New York: The New Press, 2004).

Fineman, Martha Albertson, 'The Meaning of Marriage' in Anita Bernstein (ed.), *Marriage Proposals: Questioning a Legal Status* (New York: New York University Press, 2006).

Finlay, Sarah-Jane and Victoria Clarke, '"A Marriage of Inconvenience?" Feminist Perspectives on Marriage' in *Feminism & Psychology* 13(4) (2003).

Finnis, John, 'Marriage: A Basic and Exigent Good' in *The Monist* 91(3/4) (2008).

Firestone, Shulamith, *The Dialectic of Sex* (London: The Women's Press, 1979).

Flannery, Tony, 'Statement from Twelve Priests on Women's Equality in Church' at http://www.tonyflannery.com/statement-from-twelve-priests-on-womens-equality-in-church/.

Franke, Katherine, *Wedlocked: The Perils of Marriage Equality—How African Americans and Gays Mistakenly Thought the Right to Marry Would Set Them Free* (New York: New York University Press, 2015).

Fraser, Nancy, 'After the Family Wage: A Postindustrial Thought Experiment' in Nancy Fraser, *Justice Interruptus: Critical Reflections on the Postsocialist Condition* (London: Routledge, 1997).

Friedan, Betty, *The Feminine Mystique* (London: Penguin Books, 1963).

Frug, M. J., 'Re-reading Contracts: A Feminist Analysis of a Contracts Casebook' in *American University Law Review* 34 (1985).

Gallagher, Maggie, 'Re-creating Marriage' in David Popenoe, Jean Bethke Elshtain, and David Blankenhorn (eds), *Promises to Keep: Decline and Renewal of Marriage in America* (London: Rowman & Littlefield, 1996).

Galston, William A., *Liberal Purposes* (Cambridge: Cambridge University Press, 1991).

Galston, William A., 'The Reinstitutionalization of Marriage: Political Theory and Public Policy' in David Popenoe, Jean Bethke Elshtain, and David Blankenhorn (eds), *Promises to Keep: Decline and Renewal of Marriage in America* (London: Rowman & Littlefield, 1996).

Galston, William A., 'Causes of Declining Well-being Among U.S. Children' in David M. Estlund and Martha C. Nussbaum (eds), *Sex, Preference, and Family: Essays on Law and Nature* (Oxford: Oxford University Press, 1997).

'The Get: Jewish Divorce—Reform Perspective' in *Living a Jewish Life* at http://mazor guide.com/Living/Divorce/Reform/divorceReform.htm.

GodWeb, 'A Christian Wedding Ceremony: Traditional Version' at http://www.godweb. org/marriage3.htm.

Goldin, Claudia, 'Marriage Bars: Discrimination Against Married Women Workers, 1920s to 1050s' NBER Working Paper No. 2747 (1988).

Goldman, Emma, 'Marriage and Love' in Goldman, *Anarchism and Other Essays* (Createspace, 2011 [1910]).

Goldwasser, Rabbi Jeffrey Wolfson, 'Is a Get Needed Before Second Marriage?' in *Living a Jewish Life* at http://www.mazorguide.com/Living/Divorce/Reform/IsGetNeeded.htm.

Goodrich, P., 'Gender and Contracts' in A. Bottomley (ed.), *Feminist Perspectives on the Foundational Subjects of Law* (London: Cavendish, 1996).

Gorman, Benjamin A., 'Brief Refutations of Some Common Arguments Against Same-Sex Marriage' in *American Philosophical Association Newsletter on Philosophy and Lesbian, Gay, Bisexual, and Transgender Issues* 4(1) (2004).

Gornick, Janet C., 'Reconcilable Differences in *The American Prospect Online* (25 March 2002) at http://prospect.org/article/reconcilable-differences.

Government Equalities Office, 'Equality Act 2010: What Do I Need To Know? A Quick Start Guide for Private Clubs and Other Associations' at https://www.gov.uk/govern ment/uploads/system/uploads/attachment_data/file/85047/private-clubs.pdf.

Greenawalt, Kent, *Religion and the Constitution* Volumes 1 & 2 (Princeton, NJ: Princeton University Press, 2009).

Greenberg, Eric J., 'Breaking the Chains' in *The New York Jewish Week* at http://www. thejewishweek.com/features/breaking_chains.

Gullette, Margaret Morganroth, 'The New Case for Marriage' in *The American Prospect Online* (5 March 2004) at http://www.prospect.org.

Gupta, Sanjiv, 'The Effects of Marital Status Transitions on Men's Housework Performance' in *Journal of Marriage and the Family* 61 (1999).

Gutman, David, 'Against Gay Marriage' in *The American Spectator* (15 June 2010) at https://spectator.org/39416_against-gay-marriage/.

Hacohen, Aviad, *The Tears of the Oppressed: An Examination of the Agunah Problem: Background and Halakhic Sources* (Jersey City, NJ: Ktav Publishing House, 2004).

Halberstam, J. Jack, *Gaga Feminism: Sex, Gender, and the End of Normal* (Boston, MA: Beacon Press, 2012).

Hartley, Christie and Lori Watson, 'Political Liberalism, Marriage and the Family' in *Law and Philosophy* 31 (2012).

Herbst, Diane, 'First Same-Sex Couple Marries in Dallas County After 50-Year Wait' in *Time* (26 June, 2015).

Herring, Jonathan, 'Why Marriage Needs To Be Less Sexy' in Joanna Miles, Perveez Mody, and Rebecca Probert (eds), *Marriage Rites and Rights* (Oxford: Hart Publishing, 2015).

Hochschild, Arlie Russell and Anne Machung, *The Second Shift: Working Parents and the Revolution at Home* (London: Piatkus, 1990).

Human Rights Campaign at http://www.hrc.org/campaigns/marriage-center.

Irish Marriage Equality at http://www.marriagequality.ie.

Jänterä-Jareborg, Maarit, Margareta Brattström, and LisaMarie Eriksson, 'National Report: Sweden' (Commission on European Family Law, 2015) at http://ceflonline.net/wp-content/uploads/Sweden-IR.pdf.

Jeffreys, Sheila, 'The Need to Abolish Marriage' in *Feminism & Psychology* 14(2) (2004).

Jesus College, 'St Radegund' at https://www.jesus.cam.ac.uk/college/about-us/history/people-note/st-radegund.

Johnson, Michael P. and Kathleen J. Ferraro, 'Research on Domestic Violence in the 1990s: Making Distinctions' in *Journal of Marriage and the Family* 62(4) (2000).

Jordan, Alexander H. and Emily M. Zitek, 'Marital Status Bias in Perceptions of Employees' in *Basic and Applied Social Psychology* 34 (2012).

Kingdom, Elizabeth A., 'Cohabitation Contracts: A Socialist-Feminist Issue' in *Journal of Law and Society* 15(1) (1988).

Kingston, Anne, *The Meaning of Wife* (London: Piatkus, 2004).

Kitzinger, Celia and Sue Wilkinson, 'The Re-branding of Marriage: Why We Got Married Instead of Registering A Civil Partnership' in *Feminism & Psychology* 14(1) (2004).

Krauthammer, Charles, 'When John and Jim Say "I Do"' in Andrew Sullivan (ed.), *Same-Sex Marriage Pro and Con: A Reader* (New York: Vintage, 2004 [1996]).

Kukathas, Chandran, *The Liberal Archipelago: A Theory of Diversity and Freedom* (Oxford: Oxford University Press, 2003).

Labour Manifesto for Women 2015 at http://action.labour.org.uk/page/-/150414%20women%27s%20manifesto%20final.pdf.

Larmore, Charles E., *Patterns of Moral Complexity* (Cambridge: Cambridge University Press, 1987).

Law Commission of Canada, *Beyond Conjugality: Recognizing and supporting close personal adult relationships* (Ottawa: Law Commission of Canada, 2001).

The Law Commission of England and Wales, *Cohabitation: The Financial Consequences of Relationship Breakdown*. LAW COM No 307 (2007).

Lee, Patrick, 'Marriage, Procreation, and Same-Sex Unions' in *The Monist* 91(3/4) (2008).

Lewis, Jane, *The End of Marriage? Individualism and Intimate Relations* (Cheltenham: Edward Elgar, 2001).

LGBTQ Nation http://www.lgbtqnation.com/tag/gay-marriage/.

Lima, Dafni, 'Draft National Report: Greece' presented at The Future of Registered Partnerships Durham-Cambridge Conference (University of Cambridge, 10–11 July 2015).

Lister, Andrew, *Public Reason and Political Community* (London: Bloomsbury, 2013).

Lloyd, S. A., 'Situating a Feminist Criticism of John Rawls's *Political Liberalism*' in *Loyola of Los Angeles Law Review* 28 (1994–5).

Lund-Andersen, Ingrid, 'Registered Partnerships in Denmark' presented at The Future of Registered Partnerships Durham-Cambridge Conference (University of Cambridge, 10–11 July 2015).

McClain, Linda C., *The Place of Families: Fostering Capacity, Equality, and Responsibility* (Cambridge, MA: Harvard University Press, 2006).

McDonough, Richard, 'Is Same Sex Marriage an Equal Rights Issue?' in *Public Affairs Quarterly* 19(1) (2005).

Macedo, Stephen, 'Sexuality and Liberty: Making Room for Nature and Tradition?' in David M. Estlund and Martha C. Nussbaum (eds), *Sex, Preference, and Family: Essays on Law and Nature* (Oxford: Oxford University Press, 1997).

Macedo, Stephen, *Just Married: Same-Sex Couples, Monogamy, and the Future of Marriage* (Princeton, NJ: Princeton University Press, 2015).

McLanahan, Sara, 'The Consequences of Single Motherhood' in David M. Estlund and Martha C. Nussbaum (eds), *Sex, Preference, and Family: Essays on Law and Nature* (Oxford: Oxford University Press, 1997).

McLellan, David, 'Contract Marriage—The Way Forward or Dead End?' in *Journal of Law and Society* 23(2) (June 1996).

Macneil, Ian R., 'Contracts: Adjustment of Long-Term Economic Relations Under Classical, Neoclassical, and Relational Contract Law' in *Northwestern University Law Review* 72 (1978).

March, Andrew F., 'What Lies Beyond Same-Sex Marriage? Marriage, Reproductive Freedom and Future Persons in Liberal Public Justification' in *Journal of Applied Philosophy* 27(1) (2010).

March, Andrew F., 'Is there a Right to Polygamy? Marriage, Equality and Subsidizing Families in Liberal Public Justification' in *Journal of Moral Philosophy* 8(2) (2011).

Marriage Equality USA (http://www.marriageequality.org).

Martin, Steve, 'Australia' presented at The Future of Registered Partnerships Durham-Cambridge Conference (University of Cambridge, 10–11 July 2015).

*Marvin v Marvin* 18 Cal.3d 660 (1976).

Matt Stopera, '60 Awesome Portraits of Gay Couples Just Married in New York State' *Buzzfeed* (25 July 2011) at http://www.buzzfeed.com/mjs538/portraits-of-gay-couples-just-married-in-new-york#.pnZwZWdzz.

Maushart, Susan, *Wifework* (London: Bloomsbury, 2001).

Mercier, Adèle, 'Mercier's reply to Lee' in *The Monist* 91(3/4) (2008).

Mercier, Adèle, 'On the Nature of Marriage: Somerville on Same-Sex Marriage' in *The Monist* 91(3/4) (2008).

Metz, Tamara, 'The Liberal Case for Disestablishing Marriage' in *Contemporary Political Theory* 6 (2007).

Metz, Tamara, *Untying the Knot: Marriage, the State, and the Case for their Divorce* (Princeton, NJ: Princeton University Press, 2010).

Mill, John Stuart, 'On Liberty' in *Utilitarianism, On Liberty, Considerations on Representative Government* ed. Geraint Williams (London: Everyman, 1993).

Mill, John Stuart, *On Liberty and the Subjection of Women* (Ware: Wordsworth, 1996 [1859 and 1869]).

Miller, David, 'Liberalism, Equal Opportunities, and Cultural Commitments' in Paul Kelly (ed.), *Multiculturalism Reconsidered: Culture and Equality and its Critics* (Cambridge: Polity Press, 2002).

Millett, Kate, *Sexual Politics* (London: Abacus, 1972).

Minow, Martha and Mary Lyndon Shanley, 'Relational Rights and Responsibilities: Revisioning the Family in Liberal Political Theory and Law' in *Hypatia* 11(1) (1996).

Mitchell, Juliet, *Woman's Estate* (London: Verso 2015 [1971]).

Morison, Sara J., Elinor W. Ames, and Kim Chisholm, 'The Development of Children Adopted from Romanian Orphanages' in *Merrill-Palmer Quarterly* 41(4) (1995).

Mothers at Home Matter http://www.mothersathomematter.co.uk.

Munoz-Dardé, Véronique, 'Is the Family to be Abolished then?' in *Proceedings of the Aristotelian Society* XCIX (1999).

Murphy, Kate, 'A Marriage Bar of Convenience? The BBC and Married Women's Work 1923–39' in *Twentieth Century British History* 25(4) (2014).

Murray, Melissa, 'What's So New About the New Illegitimacy?' in in *Journal of Gender, Social Policy, and the Law* 20(3) (2012).

Neave, M., 'Private Ordering in Family Law—Will Women Benefit?' in M. Thornton (ed.), *Public and Private: Feminist Legal Debates* (Melbourne: Oxford University Press, 1995).

Nichols, Most Reverend V. and Most Reverend P. Smith, 'A Letter on Marriage from the President and Vice-President of the Bishops' Conference of England and Wales', *The Independent* (6 March 2012).

Norrie, Kenneth McK., 'Scotland' presented at The Future of Registered Partnerships Durham-Cambridge Conference (University of Cambridge, 10–11 July 2015).

Nussbaum, Martha, *Sex and Social Justice* (Oxford: Oxford University Press, 1999).

Nussbaum, Martha, *Hiding From Humanity: Disgust, Shame and the Law* (Princeton, NJ: Princeton University Press, 2004).

Nussbaum, Martha C., *From Disgust to Humanity: Sexual Orientation and Constitutional Law* (Oxford: Oxford University Press, 2010).

*Obergefell v Hodges* (2015) at http://www.supremecourt.gov/opinions/14pdf/14-556_3204.pdf.

O'Donovan, K., *Sexual Divisons in Law* (London: Weidenfeld and Nicolson, 1985).

Office of National Statistics, *Births in England and Wales, 2017* at http://www.ons.gov.uk.

Office of National Statistics, 'Families and Households, 2014' at http://www.ons.gov.uk/ons/rel/family-demography/families-and-households/2014/families-and-households-in-the-uk–2014.html.

Okin, Susan Moller, *Justice, Gender, and the Family* (New York: Basic Books, 1989).

Okin, Susan Moller, 'Sexual Orientation, Gender, and Families: Dichotomizing Differences' in *Hypatia* 11(1) (1996).

Okin, Susan Moller, 'Is Multiculturalism Bad For Women?' in Susan Moller Okin, Joshua Cohen, Matthew Howard, and Martha Nussbaum (eds), *Is Multiculturalism Bad For Women?* (Princeton, NJ: Princeton University Press, 1999).

OnePlusOne, 'Nearly half of UK citizens believe in the common law marriage myth' at http://www.oneplusone.org.uk/2013/02/05/nearly-half-of-uk-citizens-believe-in-the-common-law-marriage-myth/.

Oppenheimer, Mark, 'Where Divorce Can Be Denied, Orthodox Jews Look to Prenuptial Contracts' in *The New York Times* (16 March 2012) at http://www.nytimes.com/2012/03/17/us/orthodox-jews-look-to-prenuptial-contracts-to-address-divorce-refusals.html.

Oppenheimer, Mark, 'Sunrise, Sun-Get' in *This American Life 516: Stuck in the Middle* (17 January 2014) at http://www.thisamericanlife.org/radio-archives/episode/516/stuck-in-the-middle?act=2#play.

Oppenheimer, Mark, 'To Give and To *Get*: Why a Congressman can't order his aide to give his wife a Jewish divorce' in *Slate* at http://www.slate.com/articles/news_and_politics/jurisprudence/2012/03/rep_dave_camp_can_t_order_aide_aharon_friedman_to_give_his_wife_a_jewish_divorce_.html.

Parekh, Bikhu, *Rethinking Multiculturalism: Cultural Diversity and Political Theory* (Cambridge, MA: Harvard University Press, 2002).

Pateman, Carole, *The Sexual Contract* (Cambridge: Polity Press, 1998).

Perelli-Harris, Brienna and Nora Sánchez Gassen, 'How Similar are Cohabitation and Marriage? Legal Approaches to Cohabitation across Western Europe' in *Population and Development Review* 38(3) (2013).

Polikoff, Nancy D., 'We Will Get What We Ask For: Why Legalizing Gay and Lesbian Marriage Will Not 'Dismantle the Legal Structure of Gender in Every Marriage' in *Virginia Law Review* 79(7) (1993).

Polikoff, Nancy D., *Beyond (Straight and Gay) Marriage: Valuing All Families Under the Law* (Boston, MA: Beacon Press, 2008).

Polikoff, Nancy D., 'The New "Illegitimacy": Winning Backward in the Protection of the Children of Lesbian Couples' in *Journal of Gender, Social Policy, and the Law* 20(3) (2012).

Quong, Jonathan, *Liberalism without Perfection* (Oxford: Oxford University Press, 2011).

*R (Steinfeld and Another) v Secretary of State for International Development* UKSC 32 (2018), 3 WLR 415 (2018).

Radicalesbians, 'The Woman-Identified Woman' in Mark Blasius and Shane Phelan (eds), *We Are Everywhere: A Historical Sourcebook of Gay and Lesbian Politics* (London: Routledge, 1997 [1970]).

Rajczi, Alex, 'A Populist Argument for Legalizing Same-Sex Marriage' in *The Monist* 91(3/4) (2008).

Rauch, Jonathan, *Gay Marriage: Why it is Good For Gays, Good For Straights, and Good For America* (New York: Henry Holt, 2004).

Rauch, Jonathan, 'Marrying Somebody' in Andrew Sullivan (ed.), *Same-Sex Marriage Pro and Con: A Reader* (New York: Vintage, 2004).

Rawls, John, *Political Liberalism* (New York: Columbia University Press, 1993).

Rawls, John, 'The Idea of Public Reason Revisited' in his *The Law of Peoples* (Cambridge, MA: Harvard University Press, 1999).

Raz, Joseph, *The Morality of Freedom* (Oxford: Oxford University Press, 1998).

Reynolds, Jill and Margaret Wetherell, 'The Discursive Climate of Singleness: The Consequences for Women's Negotiation of a Single Identity' in *Feminism & Psychology* 13(4) (2003).

Robinson, Elise L. E. et al., 'Fluid Families: The Role of Children in Custody Arrangements' in Hilde Lindemann Nelson, *Feminism and Families* (London: Routledge, 1997).

Robson, Ruthann and S. E. Valentine, 'Lov(h)ers: Lesbians as Intimate Partners and Lesbian Legal Theory' in *Temple Law Review* 63 (1990).

Roman Catholic Women Priests http://romancatholicwomenpriests.org.

Rosenblum, Nancy L., 'Democratic Sex: Reynolds v U.S., Sexual Relations, and Community' in David M. Estlund and Martha C. Nussbaum (eds), *Sex, Preference, and Family* (Oxford: Oxford University Press, 1997).

Rossi, Alice S. (ed.), *Essays on Sex Equality* (Chicago: The University of Chicago Press, 1970).

Sadler, Brook J., 'Re-Thinking Civil Unions and Same-Sex Marriage' in *The Monist* 91(3/4) (2008).

Sadler, Brook J., 'Public or Private Good? The Contested Meaning of Marriage' in *Social Philosophy Today* 26 (2011).

Sager, Lawrence, 'Why Churches (and, Possibly, the Tarpon Bay Women's Blue Water Fishing Club) Can Discriminate' in Micah Schwarzman, Chad Flanders, and Zoë Robinson (eds), *The Rise of Corporate Religious Liberty* (Oxford: Oxford University Press, 2016).

Sandel, Michael, *Democracy's Discontent: America in Search of a Public Philosophy* (Cambridge, MA: Harvard University Press, 1998).

Sandel, Michael, *Justice: What's the Right Thing to Do?* (London: Penguin, 2010).

Sandfield, Anna and Carol Percy, 'Accounting for Single Status: Heterosexism and Ageism in Heterosexual Women's Talk about Marriage' in *Feminism & Psychology* 13(4) (2003).

Sassler, Sharon and Amanda J. Miller, 'Class Differences in Cohabitation Practices' in *Family Relations* 60 (2011).

Scherpe, Jens M., 'The Nordic Countries in the Vanguard of European Family Law' in *Scandinavian Studies in Law* 50 (2007).

Schouten, Gina, 'Citizenship, Reciprocity, and the Gendered Division Of Labor' in *Politics, Philosophy & Economics* (2016).

Schwartz, Pepper, *Love Between Equals: How Peer Marriage Really Works* (New York: The Free Press, 1994).

Schwartzman, Micah, 'The Sincerity of Public Reason' in *The Journal of Political Philosophy* 19(4) (2011).

Scott, Elizabeth S. and Robert J. Scott, 'Marriage as Relational Contract' in *Virginia Law Review* 84(7) (October 1998).

Shanley, Mary Lyndon, *Just Marriage* (Oxford: Oxford University Press, 2004).

Shanley, Mary Lyndon, 'The State of Marriage and the State in Marriage' in Anita Bernstein (ed.), *Marriage Proposals: Questioning a Legal Status* (New York: New York University Press, 2006).

Shapiro, Julie, 'Counting From One: Replacing the Marital Presumption With a Presumption of Sole Parentage' in *Journal of Gender, Social Policy, and the Law* 20(3) (2012).

Sharon, Jeremy, 'Agunah of 28 years granted divorce two days before Passover' in *Israel News* (4 January 2015) at http://www.jpost.com/Israel-News/Agunah-of-28-years-granted-divorce-two-days-before-Passover-395881.

Shell, Susan M., 'The Liberal Case against Gay Marriage' in *The Public Interest* (Summer 2004).

Shultz, Marjorie M., 'Contractual Ordering of Marriage: A New Model for State Policy' in *California Law Review* 70 (1982).

Singer, Jana B., 'The Privatization of Family Law' in *Wisconsin Law Review* (1992).

Social Trends Institute, 'The Sustainable Demographic Dividend' at http://www.sustaindemographicdividend.org.

Somerville, Margaret, *The Ethical Imagination: Journeys of the Human Spirit* (Montreal: McGill–Queen's University Press, 2008).

Song, Sarah, *Justice, Gender, and the Politics of Multiculturalism* (Cambridge: Cambridge University Press, 2007).

South, Scott J. and Glenna Spitze, 'Housework in Marital and Nonmarital Households' in *American Sociological Review* 59(3) (1994).

Spinner-Halev, Jeff, *Surviving Diversity: Religion and Democratic Citizenship* (Baltimore, MD: Johns Hopkins University Press, 2000).

St Andrew's University, 'Women and the Law in Victorian England' at http://www.st-andrews.ac.uk/~bp10/pvm/en3040/women.shtml.

Steyer, Rabbi Ute, 'Conservative answer' at http://www.jewishvaluesonline.org/515.

Stoddard, Thomas B., 'Why Gay People Should Seek the Right to Marry' in Mark Blasius and Shane Phelan (eds), *We Are Everywhere: A Historical Sourcebook of Gay and Lesbian Politics* (London: Routledge, 1997 [1989]).

Storrow, Richard F., '"The Phantom Children of the Republic": International Surrogacy and the New Illegitimacy' in *Journal of Gender, Social Policy, and the Law* 20(3) (2012).

Strauss, Greg, 'Is Polygamy Inherently Unequal?' in *Ethics* 122(3) (2012).

Sullivan, Andrew, 'Three's A Crowd' in Andrew Sullivan (ed.), *Same-Sex Marriage Pro and Con: A Reader* (New York: Vintage, 2004 [1996]).

Swain, Sally, *The Great Housewives of Art* (New York: HarperCollins, 1988).

Taylor, Charles, 'The Politics of Recognition' in Amy Gutmann (ed.), *Multiculturalism and 'The Politics of Recognition'* (Princeton, NJ: Princeton University Press, 1992).

Terminal, Laurence Francoz, 'Registered Partnership as an alternative to Marriage—France' presented at The Future of Registered Partnerships Durham-Cambridge Conference (University of Cambridge, 10–11 July 2015).

Testy, Kellye Y., 'An Unlikely Resurrection' in *Northwestern University Law Review* 90 (1995).

Thaler, Richard H. and Cass R. Sunstein, *Nudge: Improving Decisions about Health, Wealth and Happiness* (New Haven, CT: Yale University Press, 2008).

Tidwell, Patricia A. and Peter Linzer, 'The Flesh-Colored Band Aid: Contracts, Feminism, Dialogue, and Norms' *Houston Law Review* 28 (1991).

Tobin, Brian, 'The Future of Registered Partnerships in the Republic of Ireland' presented at The Future of Registered Partnerships Durham-Cambridge Conference (University of Cambridge, 10–11 July 2015).

Toerien, Merran and Andrew Williams, 'In Knots: Dilemmas of a Feminist Couple Contemplating Marriage' in *Feminism & Psychology* 13(1) (2003).

Torcello, Lawrence, 'Is the State Endorsement of Any Marriage Justifiable? Same-Sex Marriage, Civil Unions, and the Marriage Privatization Model' in *Public Affairs Quarterly* 22(1) (2008).

TUC, *The Motherhood Pay Penalty* at https://www.tuc.org.uk/sites/default/files/MotherhoodPayPenalty.pdf (March 2016).

UK Equality Act 2010 Schedule 9 at http://www.legislation.gov.uk/ukpga/2010/15/schedule/9.

The United States Census Bureau, 'America's Families and Living Arrangements: 2015: Children: Table C3' at http://www.census.gov/hhes/families/data/cps2015C.html.

University of Cambridge, 'Flexible working arrangements—career break scheme' in *Cambridge University Reporter* (15 December 1999).

Vallier, Kevin, *Liberal Politics and Public Faith: Beyond Separation* (London: Routledge, 2004).

Vallier, Kevin, 'The Moral Basis of Religious Exemptions' in *Law and Philosophy* (2015).

Warhurst, Myf, 'Mrs or Miss: Why do forms require women reveal their marital status?' in *The Guardian* (8 April 2015).

Warren, Justice, 'Race and the Right to Marry' in Andrew Sullivan (ed.), *Same-Sex Marriage Pro and Con: A Reader* (New York: Vintage, 2004 [1967]).

Washington, Tanya, 'The new battleground for same-sex couples is equal rights for their kids' in http://www.theconversation.com (7 October 2015).

Wax, Amy, 'Bargaining in the Shadow of Marriage: Is there a Future for Egalitarian Marriage?' in *Virginia Law Review* 84(4) (May 1998).

Wedgwood, Ralph, 'The Fundamental Argument for Same-Sex Marriage' in *The Journal of Political Philosophy* 7(3) (1999).

Wedgwood, Ralph, 'Is Civil Marriage Illiberal?' in Elizabeth Brake (ed.), *After Marriage* (Oxford: Oxford University Press, 2016).

Weiss, Margot, *Techniques of Pleasure: BDSM and the Circuits of Sexuality* (Durham, NC: Duke University Press, 2012).

Weitzman, Lenore J., *The Marriage Contract: Spouses, Lovers and the Law* (London: Free Press, 1983).

White, Stuart, 'Freedom of Association and the Right to Exclude' in *Journal of Political Philosophy* 5(4) (1997).

Wightman, John, 'Intimate Relationships, Relational Contract Theory, and the Reach of Contract' in *Feminist Legal Studies* 8 (2000).

Willems, Geoffrey, 'Belgium—Legal cohabitation' presented at The Future of Registered Partnerships Durham-Cambridge Conference (University of Cambridge, 10–11 July 2015).

Williams, Joan, *Unbending Gender: Why Work and Family Conflict and What To Do About It* (Oxford: Oxford University Press, 2001).

Williams, Reginald, 'Same Sex Marriage and Equality' in *Ethical Theory and Moral Practice* 14(5) (2011).

Wilson, Robin Fretwell, 'Evaluating Marriage: Does Marriage Matter to the Nurturing of Children?' in *San Diego Law Review* 42 (2005).

Wintemute, Robert, 'The Future of Civil Partnerships in England and Wales' presented at The Future of Registered Partnerships Durham-Cambridge Conference (University of Cambridge, 10–11 July 2015).

Wjingaards Institute for Catholic Research http://www.womenpriests.org.

Wollstonecraft, Mary, *A Vindication of the Rights of Woman* (London: Constable and Company Ltd, 1996 [1792]).

Women's Ordination Conference http://www.womensordination.org.

Women's Ordination Worldwide http://womensordinationworldwide.org.

Young, Iris Marion, *Intersecting Voices: Dilemmas of Gender, Political Philosophy, and Policy* (Princeton, NJ: Princeton University Press, 1997).

Yuracko, Kimberley A., 'Does Marriage Make People Good or Do Good People Marry?' in *San Diego Law Review* 42 (2005).

# Index

Printed and bound by CPI Group (UK) Ltd, Croydon, CR0 4YY